# The Tidal Model

*The Tidal Model* represents a significant alternative to mainstream mental health theories, emphasising how those suffering from mental health problems can benefit from taking a more active role in their own treatment.

Based on extensive research, *The Tidal Model* charts the development of this approach, outlining the theoretical basis of the model to illustrate the benefits of a holistic model of care, which promotes self-management and recovery. Clinical examples are employed to show how, by exploring rather than ignoring a client's narrative, practitioners can encourage the individual's greater involvement in the decisions affecting their assessment and treatment. The appendices guide the reader in developing their own assessment and care plans.

*The Tidal Model*'s comprehensive coverage of the theory and practice of this model will be of great use to a range of mental health professionals and those in training in the fields of mental health nursing, social work, psychotherapy, clinical psychology and occupational therapy.

**Phil Barker** is a psychotherapist in private practice and also Visiting Professor at Trinity College, Dublin. He was the UK's first Professor of Psychiatric Nursing at the University of Newcastle (1993–2002).

**Poppy Buchanan-Barker** is a therapist and counsellor and was a social worker for over 25 years. Presently she is Director of Clan Unity, an independent mental health recovery consultancy in Scotland.

# The Tidal Model

A guide for mental health professionals

Phil Barker and
Poppy Buchanan-Barker

Brunner-Routledge
Taylor & Francis Group
HOVE AND NEW YORK

First published 2005 by Brunner-Routledge
27 Church Road, Hove, East Sussex BN3 2FA

Simultaneously published in the USA and Canada
by Brunner-Routledge
270 Madison Avenue, New York, NY 10016

*Brunner-Routledge is an imprint of The Taylor & Francis Group*

Typeset in Times by RefineCatch Ltd, Bungay, Suffolk
Printed and bound in Great Britain by
TJ International Ltd, Padstow, Cornwall
Paperback cover design by Sandra Heath

This publication has been produced with paper manufactured to
strict environmental standards and with pulp derived from
sustainable forests.

*British Library Cataloguing in Publication Data*
A catalogue record for this book is available from the British Library

*Library of Congress Cataloging-in-Publication Data*
Barker, Phil, 1946–
   The tidal model : a guide for mental health professionals / Phil
Barker and Poppy Buchanan-Barker. – 1st ed.
      p.   cm.
   Includes bibliographical references and index.
   ISBN 1-58391-800-0 (hardback : alk. paper) –
ISBN 1-58391-801-9 (pbk. : alk. paper)
   1. Mental health – Philosophy.   2. Mental illness – Philosophy.   3.
Psychology, Pathological – Philosophy.   I. Buchanan-Barker,
Poppy.   II. Title.
   RC437 .5.B365 2004
   616.89′001 – dc22                                    2004011089

ISBN 1-58391-800-0 (Hbk)
ISBN 1-58391-801-9 (Pbk)

This book is dedicated to all those who have been our 'crew' down many years – friends, former clients and colleagues. They provided the wind for our sails, cobbled our boats, patched our sails, and balanced our compass. Even the loneliest journey can never be taken alone. We are grateful for these supports that flow to our human horizon.

# Contents

# Figures

# The poetics of experience

**Mutiny in the body**

My good health slipped away
In a lifeboat;
I didn't see it go,
Only felt the anchor rise,
The sails unfurl
And catch the wind.
Afloat
On the current of torn,
Unruly tides.

I didn't wave goodbye
Or watch the boat escape
I was further the other way,
Complacent
That good health was locked into my shape,
And not a gift
Without replacement.

I know something
Had left me stranded
In the dark without a light
But then it was too late.

I faltered in my abandoned ark,
In search of fuel,
Hoping I could illuminate
The gasping lamps.
In time
I've made them both
A signal
That good health can now return.

© Deborah Carrick 2001[1]

# Values

---

**Twentieth-century values**

First they came for the Communists
and I didn't speak up
because I wasn't a Communist.

Then they came for the Jews
and I didn't speak up
because I wasn't a Jew.

Then they came for the trade unionists
and I didn't speak up
because I wasn't a trade unionist.

Then they came for the Catholics
and I didn't speak up
because I was a Protestant.

Then they came for me
and by that time
No one was left to speak up.
                    Pastor Martin Niemoeller,
                    victim of the Nazis, 1953

### Twenty-first-century values

First they came for the dispossessed
But we didn't speak up
Because we thought that we weren't dispossessed.

Then they came for the marginalised
But we didn't speak up –
Because we thought that we weren't marginalised.

Then they came for dissidents
But we didn't speak up
Because we thought that we weren't dissidents.

Next they came for the asylum seekers
But we didn't speak up –
Because we thought that we would never be asylum seekers.

Then they came for the mentally ill
And there was no one left to speak for anyone.

Poppy Buchanan-Barker and Phil Barker, 2003

# Foreword

## A view from the UK

In February 2004 I reached my half century. The celebrations lasted all month. One of my friends took me to see the film *Chicago*. This reminded me of 1981 when my partner took me to see the stage version of *Chicago* at a theatre in London's West End. I had been getting stressed out writing up my doctoral thesis and he decided that I needed a night out. That night I experienced my first hypomanic episode during which I went missing for two days. I went to the vicarage of my local church and told the vicar that I was the Virgin Mary. He dismissed me as either being drunk or mad.

I was hospitalised for three months during which time no one explained the 'symptoms' I was experiencing or the medication I was receiving. Most importantly, my identification with the Virgin Mary was confined to my notes and never mentioned again. The conversations I had with nurses were very mechanistic, motivated by their desire to keep the ward running smoothly.

After being discharged, I became very active in MIND, a national mental health charity in England. Together with a group of other mental health activists I founded MindLink, the Consumer Network within MIND. In 1988 I left my career as a college lecturer to work in the mental health voluntary sector. For the next five years I set up two projects in advocacy and user involvement and in 1993 I set myself up as a user consultant.

When I first met Professor Phil Barker in Newcastle, England, we were both very new to our positions. He had expected me to bring some material to the meeting which we could discuss. I preferred to spend the hour getting to know him, and in him getting to know me. At the end of the meeting he gave me a signed copy of his latest book, *Severe Depression*. I promised to send him two reports of some work I'd completed on user involvement.

Having dealt with so many professionals who disagreed with my way of thinking, it was extremely refreshing to meet someone – especially at his level – who agreed with much of my viewpoint and who treated me with so much respect. That initial meeting developed into a very longstanding working relationship based upon equality and respect. During the past ten years we have discussed a great many issues in mental health. The three issues that seem to have preoccupied our thinking are: positive images of mental health, self-management, and recovery.

When Phil first showed me a diagrammatic representation of the Tidal Model I'm afraid I was rather dismissive: 'Surely you are reinventing the wheel in that this is already happening?' Then I thought for a minute. This was my ideal of what *should* be happening, but certainly wasn't what was happening at the time. The key features of the Tidal Model that set it aside from other models are:

- It is based on the *personal stories* of service users.
- It is a *holistic* model of care.
- It promotes *self-management* and *recovery*.
- It is based on '*caring with*' rather than '*caring for*'.
- It promotes the concept of '*therapeutic experience*' rather than '*containment*'.

When the Tidal Model is in use, each service user undergoes an assessment with a specifically trained mental health nurse. This is carried out in such a way that service users feel comfortable about expressing their views. All experiences are accepted as '*true*' and not dismissed as '*hallucinations*' (for example) and added to the notes without discussion. The mental health nurse discusses with the service user what the person feels may have caused their admission and what they feel they need to do to address these problems. Every service user receives a copy of their assessment, which is recorded in their own words.

This process helps to build up trust between the service user and the mental health nurse. They form a partnership whereby the nurse supports the service user through the recovery process. The emphasis is on '*caring with*' rather than '*caring for*'. The attitudes, beliefs and expressed needs of the service user are accepted at each stage of the recovery process. The user knows that the advice of the nurse may not necessarily be accepted.

This partnership works to identify what *needs to be done* to promote recovery, thereby easing service users back into their home lives more effectively. There is a right time for everything and the service user must be allowed to dictate the pace of their own recovery. Above all the mental health nurse is always the bearer of *hope* and belief in recovery, no matter what particular path they have had to follow. In that sense, the Tidal Model is truly '*groundbreaking*'.

*Dr Irene Whitehill*
*Northumberland, England*

## A view from the USA

My first experience with mental illness was a breakneck journey that led me into dimensions I had never known before, and a consciousness that would alter my life forever. It was a spiritual experience that was colourful and scary, and it landed me in the mental hospital.

Yet when I tried to talk about this with the psychiatrist at the hospital, he was not in the least bit interested. This was my first experience with the medical model. I realised that my doctor was convinced that whatever I had felt was meaningless and irrelevant, and that my recovery depended not on understanding what I had experienced but rather on taking the medications that were prescribed to me and to quit asking questions. This was a disempowering experience that hobbled my life for years afterwards, and it was the kind of negativity that characterises mental health treatment to this day. Such treatment attitudes disable a person more certainly than does the mental disorder itself.

Several years later I became active in the mental health consumer movement, and began writing essays and poems about my experiences. A lot of my friends did the same, and many of us began talking about what had happened to us, not only to each other, but also to interested audiences such as college classes and church groups. We published our stories far and wide in newsletters and small books of poetry. 'Telling our stories' is now recognised as an essential part of peer support, and indeed it is an essential part of recovery from mental illness.

I first came to know Dr Phil Barker when we were both members of the 'Madness' internet mailing list. 'Madness', along with other online lists, greatly expanded the boundaries of our storytelling and communications. Although most of the members of this list were, like me, mental health users, I was impressed by the respect and interest that Dr Barker brought to the discussion as a psychiatric nurse. Later I was pleased to participate in writing a chapter for one of his earlier books, *From the Ashes of Experience* (Clay 1999).

When Dr Barker introduced the Tidal Model as a system of care in the late 1990s, I believe that he incorporated much of what he had learned on the 'Madness' list. The Tidal Modal makes authentic communication and the telling of our stories the whole focus of therapy. Thus the treatment of mental illness becomes a personal and human endeavour, in contrast to the impersonality and objectivity of treatment within the conventional mental health system. One feels that one is working with friends and colleagues rather than some kind of 'higher up' providers. One becomes connected with oneself and others rather than isolated in a dysfunctional world of one's own. The Tidal Model is a model for effective recovery, and is appropriate for both residential settings and in the community. When I think of the Tidal Model, I hear the sound of the surf in a seashell, and I envision sand and seawater between my toes: very organic and very healing.

*Sally Clay*
*Florida, USA*

# Preface

> At any given moment, life is completely senseless. But viewed over a period, it seems to reveal itself as an organism existing in time, having a purpose, trending in a certain direction.
>
> (Aldous Huxley)

Any book is like a reflection of its authors in a stream. It captures something of the story of who they are, but distorts the image at the same time. Such is the nature of water – such is the nature of reflection. We hope that the reader will find something of us here that is recognisable, in a human sense. There is much of us in the Tidal Model. However, expressing that, as with anything else, is often difficult. Words are great tools, but as we marvel at their beauty, we may fear what we might actually do with them.

This is a storybook. It is a story of the development of Tidal Model and a tale of the importance of story in mental health care, if not also in all our lives. For the main part, it is a simple story; but we hope that does not mean that the complexities and subtleties of the life story are overlooked. Life is simple – we are born, we live and then we die. The story of that simple progression can be made to appear complex, full of dark, impenetrable secrets and mysteries. But the same events can reveal wonders, joy, wisdom and amazement. It all depends on the storyteller – and the listener.

Our story of the Tidal Model mirrors closely our own development as professionals in the field that we would choose to call 'human services'. The Tidal Model probably says more about our interest in people and their problems of living, than it does about patients, clients, users, or consumers. Some of the people we have worked with over the years have become our friends. In every case, they were our teachers. Also, they were people whom we have grown to respect, if only from afar. Indeed, it was our privilege to work with such people, many of whom stretched us in challenging ways. Others shaped us into more effective versions of our original selves. Few of them could be called anything other than 'interesting'. We hope that we seemed half as interesting to them.

We have spent almost 40 years together as a couple, and have spent most of that time talking, often with no particular purpose, other than because it felt good or necessary to talk. From those conversations we came to understand ourselves better as individuals and also as a couple. Maybe we just crafted a different story that seemed to be a 'better' story. As we talked, the original notion of the Tidal Model seemed to flow, effortlessly, into our stream of consciousness. The more we talked about it, the more real it became – as is the case with most things. In time it flowed into a reflection of many of the things we had been doing, or trying to do, or wished we could do, or dreamed of doing, in our professional lives. The more we saw flickers of our reflection in the model, the calmer the waters became. Soon it became inviting; something we wanted to get into and to feel for ourselves. In time, more people wanted to do the same, and so the experience of the Tidal Model broadened and developed new horizons.

We are often asked to summarise the Tidal Model in a few sentences. This is always a challenge as, in keeping with its basis in chaos, its form is continually shifting. However, if pushed we say that it is an approach to value making in the world. For us, value making is the point of life: it is why we are here; it is the sole purpose of our existence – to make something of value that previously did not exist. Value making is the ambition of all human craftspeople. Value making guides us through life. Value making is the compass that we use to steer the course of our lives.

We believe that through value making we can help people to become more aware of their own values, and through such awareness become clearer as to what matters to them and why. We believe that it goes without saying that by endeavouring to assist in this sense-making, value-clarifying process, we too shall become clearer as to what matters to us and why. Values and awareness lie at the base of the pyramid that we might call mental health recovery. This process will involve the discovery of mental health, since many people have told us that they had not previously been aware of their mental health, until they began to experience what is, euphemistically, called mental illness.

The Tidal Model describes various assumptions about people, their inherent value, and the value of relating to people in particular ways. It also describes how people might come to appreciate differently, and perhaps better, their own value, and the unique value of their experience. Roll all this together and the Tidal Model is a paper template for engaging in value making. Does this generate mental health? We are not sure, as there appears to be a multitude of definitions of mental health. However, we believe that value making and the appreciation of value in our lives must be healthy activities for the whole person. So, if that is true, then value making will foster mental health and the Tidal Model may be described, appropriately, as an approach to mental health recovery/discovery.

We hope that this book can be read by anyone with an interest in mental health care, whichever discipline they belong to, or even if they have no special professional affiliation. We hope that the book will be read by people who have a wide range of interests in mental health care and way beyond. We hope that we shall not merely be 'preaching to the converted'. We have tried to keep the use of professional jargon and high-sounding philosophical and technical language to a minimum. If the reader stumbles over any of these boulders in the text, we apologise. We shall try to be even more careful next time.

Clinical and managerial colleagues at what was then called the Newcastle City Health Trust in England deserve a special mention for their original invitation to frame the idea of the Tidal Model as the basis for nursing practice in the mental health programme. If they had not made this request in the first place, and had not helped support its launch into the often difficult waters of ordinary NHS practice, we might not be writing this Preface. So, we thank Tony Byrne, Steven Michael, Anne McKenzie and Robin Farquharson, from the Mental Health Programme for their belief in the possibility of change in mental health professional practice. We also thank Dee Aldridge, Aileen Drummond, Elaine Fletcher, Clare Hepple, Clare Hopkins, Janice O'Hare, Val Tippens and their many clinical colleagues for pushing the boat out into the incoming tide.

Special thanks are also due to Dr Chris Stevenson, who as an old friend and trusted colleague made the perfect original crewmember, and helped develop the first evaluation of the Tidal Model in practice. We also reserve a very special vote of thanks for Mike Davison who in 1993 first inspired Phil Barker to begin to think about what an alternative model of psychiatric and mental health nursing might look like.

We should like to thank the many people with experience of mental illness or psychiatric care and treatment who helped us understand something of the experience of genuine madness, who helped shape our vision of the Tidal Model, or who helped refine the emerging processes for practice. Our heartfelt thanks go to Dr Irene Whitehill, Peter Campbell, Louise Pembroke, Sue Holt, Jan Holloway, Rachel Perkins and Rose Snow from the UK; Paddy McGowan and Kieran Crowe from Ireland; Sally Clay, Dr Patricia Deegan, Julie Chamberlin, Dr Dan Fisher and Ed Manos from the USA; Cathy Conroy, Anne Thomas and Simon Champ from Australia; and Anne Helm and Gary Platz from New Zealand.

Finally, we should like to thank Kay Vaughn and Denny Webster from Denver, Colorado, who helped reinforce our belief that this way of working was possible in the often limiting environment of acute and crisis care.

Now, some years further out to sea, the Tidal Model seems to have a life of its own. Maybe we did not develop it at all. Perhaps we only wrote the story. Certainly, the story of the Tidal Model now seems to be feeling the wind in its sails. As Huxley might have put it, the idea has now gained a life of its own, and is beginning to chart its own course. It is our privilege to be blown along a similar course.

Phil Barker and Poppy Buchanan-Barker
*Newport on Tay, Scotland*

# Chapter 1

# Tales of shipwrecks and castaways

## The problem of being human

### Reflecting on the self

Although people have changed greatly down the ages of recorded history, much of our twenty-first-century thinking, at least in the western world, is still dominated by the philosophical assumptions of the Ancient Greeks. Yet, if we could be transported back to the slopes of Mount Olympus, we would soon find out how much people have changed in the past two and a half thousand years. We no longer think like the Ancient Greeks and probably do not even feel as they did. When Socrates said that the unexamined life was not worth living, he could hardly have imagined how far the notion of 'self-examination' might be taken. Indeed, the changes that occurred during the twentieth century were phenomenal and the pace of change appears to be quickening.

In our lifetime the psychobabble of West Coast USA has become commonplace. Our parents appeared to live what the Greeks might have called 'good lives' without ever reflecting on their 'self-esteem', 'self-image' or 'self-concept'. Their consciousness was not so much simpler as different. The stories of their lives were written in a different language and spoken with a different voice than might be the case today.

The gift of consciousness allows people to 'reflect' on their experience of self. Today, we have a host of linguistic tools, mechanisms and devices that are meant to make this self-examination easier or more productive. At the heart of this process of examination lies – at least in the developed western world – the mercurial notion of the *Self*.[1] However, for most people, who and what they *are* remains something of a mystery. Yet despite this they know that they exist and they know what this is like, even when they find it difficult to express the experience of self.

What does seem clear is that when people experience difficulties in their relationship with the core Self – or in the human relations with others – they are likely to be described as having 'mental health problems'. Traditionally, they would be described as being 'mad'.[2]

The paintings of Hieronymus Bosch, the fourteenth-century Flemish artist, have often been assumed to depict the experience of waking nightmares, such as might be experienced by someone in the most extreme form of madness. His *Garden of Earthly Delights* has often been interpreted as a vivid illustration of psychosis, or by the Freudians as a catalogue of wish fulfilment or sexual anxiety. Paradoxically, there is another way of viewing Bosch, which may be simpler yet more complex. Bosch's work reflected the world view of the Middle Ages (Bosing 2001). The *Garden of Earthly Delights* can be interpreted as a complex warning to all who might stray from the Christian path, framed as a visual catalogue of aversion. Were we able to step into a time machine and to visit Bosch in his studio, we would likely discover that if we pointed to the sexual imagery in his work he would have no idea what we were talking about. Unlike us, Bosch never had a chance to read Freud. Although a highly intelligent man within his own society, Bosch's notions of what it meant to be human, to be a person, were very different from what we understand today. Bosch's story was framed by the context of his age. Today, the context has changed dramatically but the same simple truth remains: who we are is largely a function of the age in which we live. Our individual stories are framed by our reading of the world within which those stories develop. In the western world, which has become so concerned with abstract notions of the Self, it is hardly surprising that so many people frame their human difficulties as self-related problems. Were we to transport ourselves to Malaysia, or to join a so-called 'primitive' people, we would likely find a very different construction of 'selfhood' and human distress.[3]

Indeed, were Sigmund Freud to turn up at our door today, even he might struggle to grasp the complexity of what humans had become in the 60 years since his death. The human *meanings* that Freud conjured with derived from his study of ancient literature, anthropology and various cross-cultural sources, including his interpretation of Bosch's paintings. However, the technological revolution of the latter half of the twentieth century ushered in a whole new catalogue of human being. Not only can we enjoy live dialogue with people on the other side of the globe, but also the stories that we share through our telephones and PCs are no longer framed only by our direct everyday experience, but are highlighted, touched and sometimes tainted by fragments of stories from the lives of other people. The story of our own lives and what it means to be 'ourselves' grows increasingly complex.

### Reflected in a glass, darkly

The human project involves trying to make sense of ourselves, asking 'Who am I?' and 'What on earth am I doing here?' We have been doing this for literally thousands of years. When our ancestors began to daub dirt on the walls of the Lascaux caves, or fashioned crude representations of themselves, or their idealised gods, from the rock, the process of self-reflection that eventually meant so much to Socrates was first born.

Today our emphasis on 'self-reflection' is heavily focused on language. However, we should not forget that much of our reflection is pre-linguistic and, especially in the therapeutic setting, often goes beyond words. In a philosophical sense, what is called the 'lived experience' belongs to this pre-linguistic province: it is what we experience, as we experience it, before we get down to – or are required to – attach words and linguistic meanings to the 'experience'.

Indeed, Rembrandt probably still represents the pinnacle of naive self-reflection on the 'lived experience'. His 90 self-portraits present a fascinating visual story of the decline in his fortunes and also the change in his view of himself. They are essays on 'who' Rembrandt is, without words. The art historian Manuel Gasser (1961) wrote: 'Over the years, Rembrandt's self-portraits increasingly became a means for gaining self-knowledge, and in the end took the form of an interior dialogue: a lonely old man communicating with himself while he painted.'

Whenever we look in a mirror, we have a similar opportunity to reflect on the story that life has written on our faces. Writing in our journal or sharing something of our story with others offers a different kind of reflection on the journey we have taken, out of the past to the here and now. The reflection is rarely clear-cut and steady, but it is always revealing. Indeed, Rembrandt's self-portraits provide us with a useful anchor for our own reflections. We may not always be able to represent exactly what we see and feel, but the story we relate is always true, at least for now. Our reflections are always just that – reflections; a poor image of the complexity of the original. However, they are nonetheless important for all that. They are reflections on what it means to be human.

### Psychiatry and the colonisation of the self

For over one hundred years psychiatry has developed its own story of what it means to be human, promoting the idea that psychological, social and emotional problems are a function of some underlying (but unidentified) biological pathology. Such theories provided a rationale for every kind of psychiatric *treatment* – from insulin coma, through electro-convulsive therapy to neuroleptic medication. However, the contemporary psychiatric story, wherein the professional professes an expert knowledge of what it means to occupy this or that mental state, still stands in Freud's shadow.

Freud's most ambitious and impertinent analysis was of Leonardo da Vinci (Freud 1947). Taking the fragments of biographical information available to him, Freud framed a psychoanalytic story, which his translator believed 'fully explained Leonardo's incomprehensible traits of character' (Brill 1947: 27). Freud himself acknowledged that what he had produced was 'only . . . a psychoanalytic romance' (Freud 1947: 117). However, in addressing the possible weaknesses of his story of Leonardo's sexuality, he was at pains to excuse psychoanalysis from any blame:

> If such an undertaking, as perhaps in the case of Leonardo, does not yield definite results, then the blame for it is not to be laid to the faulty or inadequate psychoanalytic method, but to the vague and fragmentary material left by tradition about this person.
>
> (Freud 1947: 118)

Little has changed in the half-century since this curious romance was published. Our newspapers and magazines show psychiatric professionals following in Freud's footsteps as they craft often fantastic stories about the inner workings of the minds of celebrities and other icons of the popular culture. In the clinic, psychoanalysis may be dead and buried but the legacy of Freudian interpretation still reigns. People may today be described as having 'mental health problems', but the professional reading of those problems has changed little since Freud's day. Now, a range of biological, genetic, cognitive and social factors is employed to *explain* the story that the person brings to the psychiatric setting. Invariably, those professional readings of our human distress overpower, and ultimately submerge, the plain language account that is often spoken or written in powerful metaphorical language (Barker 2000d). The colonising effect of psychiatry, and its various theories, represents the last territorial frontier (Barker and Buchanan-Barker 2001). Some of the people with 'mental health problems' may now call themselves users or consumers, but many of them still refer to 'being bipolar' or 'having dysfunctional beliefs'. The insinuation of 'lunatic language' (Buchanan-Barker and Barker 2002) into the culture reflects the continuing power of psychiatric imperialism. The mental health 'user' or 'consumer' may be freed from the old 'patient' label, but remains chained to the psychiatric discourse.

### Neuroscientific triumphalism

In our youth the psychoanalytic culture reigned supreme and everything from sports cars to bottles of beer on a film commercial was attributed psychosexual significance. Over the years other psychological, biological and genetic theories have emerged, all claiming to offer the final explanation for why we do what we do and what it all means. Arguably, neuroscience has taken up Freud's baton in attempting to explain most, if not all human behaviour. In an elegant piece of intellectual arrogance Francis Crick wrote:

> You, your joys and your sorrows, your memories and your ambitions, your sense of personal identity and free will, are in fact no more than the

behaviour of a vast assembly of nerve cells and their associated molecules.

(Crick 1994: 3)

As Szasz pointed out, this was hardly a new idea. As early as 1819, Sir William Lawrence, President of the Royal College of Surgeons, had declared: 'The mind, the grand prerogative of man, is merely an expression of the function of the brain' (Szasz 1996: 84). Increasingly, people attribute their various problems of living to a specific biochemical imbalance, or to their brain chemistry in general. If the neuroscientific juggernaut continues to colonise our culture, it is only a matter of time before brain chemistry will explain every slip of the tongue, as psychoanalysis did last century.

## Mental illness as metaphor

### Cultural antecedents

The past twenty years have witnessed a dramatic change in the status of psychiatric patients, many of whom are no longer content with the passive role assigned to them by psychiatric medicine, but who wish to play a more active part in the care and treatment of their problems (Read and Reynolds 1996). Indeed, the challenges posed by groups in the UK such as Survivors Speak Out and, more recently, The Hearing Voices Network have shown how many formerly passive patients reclaimed their distress and applied their own labels within a philosophical framework that is personally and culturally meaningful. They have joined ranks with North American psychiatric survivor radicals, Crazy Folks, and their European political partners the Irren Offensive. All such groups aim to reclaim to story of the experience of madness and to challenge the territorialisation and colonisation of madness by the psychiatric establishment. This has led indirectly to the de-emphasis on mental 'illness' and the insinuation of the notion of 'mental health problems' into the popular culture.

However, as with much of the western culture, the idea that we might have 'mental health problems' has North American origins. In his seminal treatise on suicide, the poet and critic Al Alvarez reflected on his own attempts to kill himself, while a visiting scholar at a New England university:

A week later I returned to the States to finish the term. While I was packing I found, in the ticket pocket of my favourite jacket, a large, bright-yellow, torpedo-shaped pill. I stared at the thing, turning it over and over on my palm, wondering how I'd missed it on the night. It looked lethal. I had survived forty-five pills. Would forty-six have done it? I flushed the thing down the lavatory.

(Alvarez 1970: 279)

Alvarez's suicide attempt had not been the singular actions of a man alone. On reflection, he became all too aware that his story of despair did not stand alone. Indeed, nothing stood apart from the life he shared with others:

> The truth is, in some way I *had* died. The overintensity, the tiresome excess of sensitivity and self-consciousness, of arrogance and idealism, which came in adolescence and stayed on and beyond their due time, like some visiting bore, had not survived the coma. It was as though I had finally, and sadly late in the day, lost my innocence. Like all young people, I had been high-minded and apologetic, full of enthusiasms I didn't quite mean and guilts I didn't quite understand. Because of them, I had forced my poor wife, who was far too young to know what was happening, into a spoiling, destructive role she never sought. We had spent five years thrashing around in confusion, as drowning men pull each other under.
>
> (Alvarez 1970: 279)

Much later, Alvarez found himself moving, imperceptibly, into a more optimistic, less vulnerable frame of mind and, like so many other 'failed suicides', he began to reflect on the *meaning* of his suicide attempt:

> Months later I began to understand that I had had my answer, after all. The despair that had led me to try to kill myself had been pure and unadulterated, like the final, unanswerable despair a child feels, with no before and after. And childishly, I had expected death not merely to end it but also to explain it. Then when death let me down, I gradually saw that I had been using the wrong language; I had translated the thing into Americanese. Too many movies, too many novels, too many trips to the States had switched my understanding into a hopeful, alien tongue. I no longer thought of myself as unhappy; instead I had 'problems'. Which is an optimistic way of putting it, since problems imply solutions, whereas unhappiness is merely a condition of life, which you must live with, like the weather. Once I had accepted that there weren't going to be any answers, even in death, I found to my surprise that I didn't much care whether I was happy or unhappy; 'problems' and 'the problem of problems' no longer existed. And that in itself is already the beginning of happiness.
>
> (Alvarez 1970: 282)

It is reassuring that a once-suicidal poet should emerge, like a Greek hero, to rescue us from the banal, theoretical abstractions of psychiatric mythology. In a few short paragraphs, Alvarez's painful reflection on the foolish wisdom of his own lived experience reminded us that life is always the great teacher; but also that we all need a degree of luck to be spared to learn the lessons that life offers. After more than a century of psychiatric pontificating on the meaning (or meaninglessness) of 'mental illness', finally the voice of the distressed person is beginning to be heard. The wisdom that people like Alvarez gained from their close encounter with death is mirrored in the stories related by others who also journeyed to the farthest reaches of their own human natures, in search of a way to live with or recover from their madness (Barker *et al.* 1999a).

## Problems of living

Suicide is one of the most dramatic themes in the problematic theatre of life. Alvarez drew our attention to the potential corrupting influence of language as a colonising force, which takes over the meaning of our lives. However, the idea that people might 'suffer' from 'problems of living' had a longer and more formal history than even Alvarez appreciated.

Almost seventy years ago, in an attempt to describe the complex phenomena of psychosis, Harry Stack Sullivan coined the term 'problems of living' (Evans 1996). Thomas Szasz (1961) later popularised the expression, by describing how a wide range of people experienced great problems in *living with others* and (invariably) in *living with themselves*. These facts of human living become obvious when we spend time with people who are 'mentally suffering' (Lynch 2001). The nature of the distress associated with such suffering, and its effects on their private and public life, are gradually revealed as we are granted privileged access to their story. Indeed, aside from the often fanciful interpretations and observations which professionals make about 'patients' (Kirk and Kutchins 1997), all we have to work with is the story. This embraces everything of any significance for the person. However, the obvious nature of this truth risks challenging the whole empire of psychiatry, which has spent generations submerging the personal narrative in a sea of specious professional theorising

## Metaphorical disorders

Forty years ago Szasz began his radical critique of the medicalisation of what he asserted were 'problems of living' (Szasz 1961). Although medicine strenuously resisted his criticisms, the American Psychiatric Association has now abandoned the notion of an underlying 'disease' process, reframing the various mental 'illnesses' as forms of 'mental disorder' (Kirk and Kutchins 1997), essentially of unknown or unknowable origin. This may represent the subtlest, but most significant, illustration of its capitulation to Szasz's critique.

Szasz emphasised that what psychiatry defined as 'mental illnesses' were 'problems of living', invariably expressed through complex metaphors. People who experience problems of living with themselves or others are no more 'sick' than the office with 'sick building syndrome', or the 'lame economy' that, mixing our metaphors, is often said to be 'sick'. In the absence of any formal way of identifying the 'pathology' assumed to underpin 'mental illness', it seems more appropriate to define these as metaphorical disorders.

Szasz's original critique (Szasz 1961) triggered many imitators, especially focused on the social construction of mental illness, particularly through the diagnostic process, which has long been the subject of debate (e.g. Conrad 1992; Daniels 1970; Farber 1987). However, Kirk and Kutchins (1992, 1997) made the original observation that the repeated revisions and additions to the *Diagnostic and Statistical Manual of Mental Disorders* (DSM) were not initiated by working psychiatrists or therapists, but rather stemmed from the influence of the census, medical groups, the army or psychiatric researchers. Arguably, the 'good practitioner' knows that however many diagnostic categories are available, the resolution of the person's problems (of living) begins with someone who seeks to understand rather than simply classifying the 'patient'.

Aside from concerns about the reliability and validity of psychiatric diagnosis (Kirk and Kutchins 1992), its sheer narrowness is problematic. As Laing (1967) noted: 'It is an approach that fails to view persons *qua* persons, and degrades them to the status of "objects".' Over thirty years later, psychiatry's failure to try to *understand* people and the critical role of the creation of *meanings* within the therapeutic relationship remain enduring concerns (Kismayer 1994; Modrow 1995). Such concerns led Grob (1983) to describe psychiatry as a political and professional 'movement' rather than a scientific enterprise concerned with caring for people who were definably 'ill'. Beverly Hall, the distinguished North American nurse, recognised how psychiatric diagnosis and the medical model served only to disempower people, rather than help them. Their combined adverse effects upon nursing practice led Hall (1996) to argue for the recognition of human values over 'objectivity' in mental health care. In a related vein, Dumont (1984) exposed the fallacious distinction between illness and wellness in western thought, suggesting the urgent need for a paradigm shift in the conceptualisation of 'mental illness'.

### Colonisation and power

The complexity of the human experience of mental distress, framed by its various interpersonal, social and cultural contexts, has been stripped, ransacked and colonised by psychiatry, and its associated psychotherapeutic and psychological theorising. Over the past 30 years, Szasz has highlighted the effects of psychiatric colonisation metaphor, using slavery as the choice psychiatric icon (Szasz 2002).

> The psychiatric profession has, of course, a huge stake, both existential and economic, in being socially authorised to rule over mental patients, just as the slave-owning classes did in ruling over slaves. In contemporary

psychiatry, indeed, the expert gains superiority not only over members of a specific class of victims, but over the whole of the population, whom he may 'psychiatrically evaluate'.

(Szasz 1974: 135)

In Szasz's view, any form of involuntary hospitalisation is a 'crime against humanity', and the practice of psychiatry echoes the fundamental human rights violation perpetrated by slave owners, who also justified their practices as being, somehow, in the 'best interests' of the childlike, primitive, or otherwise enfeebled 'negro'. In this sense, Szasz was the first writer to explore psychiatry's *colonisation of the self*.

The coercive dimensions of contemporary psychiatric practice maintain a link, however disguised, to the colonising power of nineteenth-century psychiatry (Scull 1979), which generated a subtler but no less powerful paradigm of social control (Leifer 1990; Robitscher 1980; Schrag 1978). The psychiatric colonisation literature remains limited, focusing mainly on the after-effects of colonisation – as a socio-cultural phenomenon – on the 'mental health' of indigenous peoples (Deiter and Otway 2001; Samuels 2000). However, the concept of the 'colonisation of the self' finds an echo in the literature on oppression (Bulham 1985), or more specifically in feminism (Hawthorne and Klein 1999). Szasz challenged psychiatry to confront its failure to address the persecution and exploitation inherent in its supposedly humanitarian 'care and treatment' programmes (Szasz 1994). In that sense, he relocated the 'mentally ill' alongside other 'dispossessed' persons whose core identity had been demeaned or misappropriated: notably women and all non-white/non-Christian peoples. For such people, self-determination lies at the core of their struggle to recover their full human status (Alves and Cleveland 1999).

Even psychotherapy, which is commonly assumed to focus on the person and her/his immediate emotional and spiritual needs, has often lapsed into a control and influence agenda. In a recent interview, Szasz pointed out the necessity for psychotherapists to recognise the 'contractual' nature of psychotherapy:

I see psychoanalysis as a contractual conversation about a person's problems and how to resolve them. I tried to avoid the idea, which seemed particularly pernicious, that the therapist knows more about the patient than the patient himself. That seems to me so offensive. How can you know more about a person after seeing him for a few hours, a few days, or even a few months, than he knows about himself? He has known himself a lot longer! . . . My role was as a catalyst. You are making suggestions and exploring alternatives – helping the person change himself. The idea that the person remains entirely in charge of himself is a fundamental premise.

(Szasz 2000: 29)

## The Tidal Model and the voice of experience

### Chaotic change

The perspective offered by traditional psychiatry and much psychology and psychotherapy appears to assume that the person is 'thing', which is static – albeit shaped and moulded by different abstract 'forces', like the personality, or 'illness'. Indeed, the *image* of the person offered by the traditional psychiatric lens is akin to a snapshot: the person is frozen in time, their presentation and appearance captured through an assessment, report or other form of professional examination. The assumption commonly follows that this image is the person. Nothing could be further from the truth.

People are in a constant state of flux, as they negotiate their relationship with an infinite number of influences, some of which appear to come from the world outside and others that appear to spring from 'within'. Most of this activity is imperceptible, in the way, for example, that we mature or simply grow older. Only when we compare snapshots taken at wide intervals do we detect the changes that have been ongoing. These snapshots confirm that change is the only constant; one that is largely silent and unnoticeable, but definitely present, as change flows invisibly through our human experience.

Borrowing from chaos theory (Barker 1996), the Tidal Model recognises that change, growth or development occur through small, often barely visible changes, following patterns, which are paradoxically consistent in their unpredictability. The focus of the professional helper is upon helping people develop their awareness of what has happened to them, what is happening for them now, and how they can use this knowledge to help steer their lives in a positive direction. The fluid and ever-changing nature of human experience provides the basis for the core metaphor of the Tidal Model – *water*.

### The ocean of experience

Life is a journey undertaken on an ocean of experience. All human development, including the experience of illness and health, involves discoveries made on a journey across that ocean of experience. At critical points in the life journey the person may experience storms or even piracy (*crisis*). At other times the ship may begin to take in water and the person may face the prospect of drowning or shipwreck (*breakdown*). The person may need to be guided to a safe haven to undertake repairs, or to recover from the trauma (*rehabilitation*). Only once the ship is made intact, or the person has regained the necessary sea legs, can it set sail again, aiming to put the person back on the life course (*recovery*).

Unlike normative psychiatric models, the Tidal Model holds few assumptions about the proper course of a person's life. Instead, it focuses on the kind of support that people believe they need to live their own 'good life'. People who experience life crises are (metaphorically) in deep water and risk drowning, or feel as if they have been thrown onto the rocks. People who have experienced trauma (such as injury or abuse), or those with more enduring life problems (e.g. repeated breakdowns, hospitalisations, loss of freedom through compulsory detention), often report loss of their 'sense of self', akin to the trauma associated with piracy. Such people need a sophisticated form of life-saving (psychiatric rescue) followed, at an appropriate interval, by the kind of developmental work necessary to engender true recovery. This may take the form of crisis intervention in community or the 'safe haven' of a residential setting. Once the rescue is complete (psychiatric care) the emphasis switches to the kind of help needed to get the person 'back on course', returning to a meaningful life in the community (mental health care).

### Storytelling

The person's story lies at the heart of the Tidal Model. People are the stories of their lives. *Who* we *are* is a heady mix of the stories we tell about ourselves, and the stories others tell about us. Many people lay claim to know Phil and Poppy. Some say they know us 'well'; others even that they know us 'intimately'. Many others will develop their knowledge of 'who' we are based on a reading of, or a listening to, such stories. This is frequently the case in psychiatry, where our knowledge of the individual patient is often based on reading the stories written in records, letters and other notes by other professionals.

We like to think that we own our selves – after all we are the Phil and Poppy whom people are talking about. Not surprisingly, we often have been offended, irritated and sometimes amazed by the stories told 'in our name'. In that sense we have some appreciation of what it might be like to be a psychiatric 'patient' – assessed, studied, discussed and 'written up' by a professional team, each member of which claims to possess some knowledge – if not all the important insights – of the person who has become the patient. It would be tidy to suggest that *our* story is the one and only *true* story. After all, only we can legitimise it; only we can corroborate it. However, at least in mental health care practice people often find it difficult to assert their own story, finding themselves instead framed by the stories written by others in their professional records.

The Tidal Model is a philosophical approach to the recovery or discovery of mental health. It is not a 'treatment' model, which implies that something needs to be done to change the person. Instead, the Tidal Model assumes that the person is already changing, albeit in small and subtle ways. The aim of the professional or lay helper is to assist people in making choices that will steer them through their present problems of living, so that they might begin to chart a course for 'home' on their ocean of experience. In that sense the Tidal Model emphasises more the virtues of 'care' – establishing the conditions that will be necessary for the promotion of growth and development.

### History, herstory and the mystery of my-story

In traditional mental health practice, the person's story is taken in the form of a history – usually a medical (or medicalised) account of the events leading up to, and potentially contributing to, the person's current difficulties. The term *history* derives from the Greek, and means simply *an account of one's inquiries*, and is not gendered. However, the feminists recognised that many 'histories' were biased towards a male world view and began to use the ironic term *herstory* to suggest a different kind of perspective on events; one informed more by a feminine perspective. Baron-Cohen (2003) has suggested that the different ways in which women and men relate to the world of their experience might have a biological basis. Men tend to be better at *analysing* systems (better *systemisers*), while women tend to be better at reading people's *emotions* (better *empathisers*). The Tidal Model acknowledges that traditional psychiatric history-taking is very masculine, seeking to reduce people to their component parts or features, which can then be assigned to the various 'pigeon holes' of diagnostic classification. It is unsurprising that the development of psychiatric classification was almost entirely a male dominated enterprise (Sartorius *et al.* 1990).

Although people may value the opportunity to compare their experience with that of others, this should not be allowed to completely submerge the peculiar nature of personal experience. The Tidal Model assumes that there are many ways of reading, interpreting, classifying and relating to the phenomena that flow from our world of experience. During a workshop in Australia in the late 1990s, we were discussing the distinction between our 'history' – which is stripped down to fit some preconceived notion of human functioning – and our 'herstory', which takes a softer, less acutely focused, more exploratory approach to understanding our experience. One participant observed that she was uncertain of what exactly was her experience at that moment. We suggested that, perhaps for everyone, the story of our lives was something of a 'mystery'; something that we might study and try to unravel, but which might ultimately remain a mystery. From this observation developed a discussion which led to the conclusion that, in addition to talking of 'history' and 'herstory', we should acknowledge the 'mystery of my-story'.

### In my own voice

In pursuing this 'mystery', the Tidal Model assumes that people *are* their narratives (MacIntyre 1981). Our sense of self, and world of experience – including our experience of others – is inextricably tied to the life story and the various meanings generated within it, as we unpack our awareness of the past, and what the story means in the present. The Tidal Model constructs a *narrative-based* form of practice (Barker and Kerr 2001), which differs markedly from some contemporary forms of *evidence-based practice*. The former is always about particular human instances, whereas the latter is based on the behaviour of populations, whose elements are merely assumed to be equivalent. More importantly, the narrative focus of the Tidal Model is not concerned to unravel the causative course of the person's present problems of living. Instead it aims to use the experience of the person's journey and its associated meanings to chart the 'next step' that needs to be taken on the person's life journey.

In attempting to *journey with* rather than lead the person through the exploration of their 'world of experience' and its associated problems of living, the core assessment material is written *entirely in the person's own voice*. Typically, professionals interview patients, paraphrase, or more often translate their replies in a professional, often jargon-ridden summary. More often they retire to the office to write up their recollection of what has been said. The Tidal Model acknowledges that the professional helper and the person in care are involved in co-creating a highly specific version of the life narrative. This will include identifying what the person believes is needed, *at that moment*, in terms of support; and holds the promise of what 'needs to happen' to meet that need.

Irrespective of the kind of diagnosis attributed to the person, the Tidal Model gives precedence to the story since this is the location for the enactment of the person's life. Even if it could be demonstrated that the person was suffering from a discrete form of neurological impairment, as Szasz has noted, the person '[would] simply have a disease with which they would have to live, just like Stephen Hawking has to live with amyotrophic lateral sclerosis. In other words, having a disease does not define everything that you do' (Szasz 2000: 32).

Being given a psychiatric diagnosis, or even believing that one has a mental illness, does not define who *is* the person. What does define people are the stories they tell about themselves; the narrative accounts of their lives. The stories told and developed by others also can have a defining effect. On a personal level, the story is the theatre of experience within which reflection and discussion develop into an ongoing form of script editing. The caring process begins and ends here, since all people express a need to develop (create) a coherent account of what *has* happened, and presently *is* happening to them, in the light of their personal experience. This account is most meaningful when framed in the patient's vernacular, illustrated by the metaphorical language drawn from the person's history and the social and cultural setting of their everyday lives.

### The journey towards health

The idea that various psychiatric professionals have the power to resolve, repair or otherwise fix the problems of living, which are called mental illness, is firmly established in the western culture. Increasingly, such western notions of 'fixing' human distress are becoming part of the acculturation process in non-western societies. At least in the west we are as a society even 'sicker' statistically than when Freud began his ambitious project. However, the faith in the psychiatric medications, which appear only to salve rather than cure, endures. Similarly, the expectation that some magic exists in the various 'talking cures' (Barker 1999) appears stronger than ever. However, although 'magic' may exist, it may not lie where we have traditionally been encouraged to believe it lies.

In an important overview of the psychotherapies, Hubble and his colleagues (1999) showed that the actual *methods* or *techniques* of psychotherapy accounted for less than 15 per cent of the change effect. *Placebo effects, hope* and *expectancy of change* accounted for 15 per cent of the change effect; *the person's relationship with the therapist* accounted for 30 per cent and more than 40 per cent of the change effect depended on the *clients themselves*. This led them to describe this as the 'engine' that makes therapy work:

> The client's own generative, self-healing capacities allow them to take what therapies have to offer and use them to self-heal.
>
> (Hubble *et al.* 1999: 14)

Therapists of all kinds certainly set the stage and serve as assistants: 'They do not provide the magic, although they may provide the means for mobilizing, challenging, and focusing clients' magic' (Hubble *et al.* 1999: 95).

The person with a serious and disabling form of mental ill health experiences what the layperson has long called a 'mental breakdown'. In the metaphor of the Tidal Model, such people experience a psychic shipwreck and, if the appropriate form of rescue and recovery does not arrive soon, will begin to feel like a psychiatric castaway. The forms of distress that people experience within the states we glibly call a 'mental breakdown' threaten their very core of being. The kind of care and human treatment that they are offered is often, quite literally, *vital* for their recovery. The combined stories of 'shipwreck' and 'rescue' are obviously key chapters in the autobiography of the person who becomes the patient.

The evaluative stories concerning the Tidal Model that are emerging from the different parts of the world[4] offer an everyday confirmation of the power of the story-teller, alluded to by Hubble and his colleagues. They also suggest how nurses in particular, but also other health and social care professionals, can play a critical role in optimising the power of the story, in the person's journey towards self-healing. They also emphasise the empowering effect of family and friends in enabling people to take charge of their lives, grasping (metaphorically) the rudder of their experience, and beginning to plot the course for home. In this sense, these emerging findings suggest that reverence for the storyteller is the oldest, and most enduring, form of empowerment.

# Chapter 2

# Philosophical assumptions

## A credo

> Rowing harder doesn't help if the boat is headed in the wrong direction.
> (Kenichi Ohmae)

### The virtue of experience

All learning is based on experience. There is much that we can learn from reading and from others, but there remains a great virtue in learning from experience. Indeed, arguably the greatest mind in recorded history – Leonardo – had little formal education, at least by comparison with his peers. He described himself as an 'omo sanza lettere' – a man without letters, and expressed contempt for those who favoured book learning over direct experience (Turner 1995: 12). For Leonardo, experience was to become his mistress.

The mental health field today is dominated by a kind of book learning, called evidence-based practice, which suggests that the accumulated wisdom of scientific studies represents the only valid knowledge base for the development of practice. The value of such 'general knowledge' should not be underestimated but, arguably, we have become infatuated with this limited form of human understanding. We should not forget that there is much we can learn from the individual person who becomes the psychiatric patient, and from our direct experience of working with that person. Indeed, almost all that we need to know is to be found in the shared story of the helping relationship. No one person can ever fully understand the experience of another. We may hear echoes of our own experience, and believe that we know and understand the other, but this is illusory. We remind ourselves of this simple fact of human living – we can only *know* our own experience.

Psychiatry, and to a lesser extent psychology, pretends to understand madness, although all these fields of learning actually address are the apparent similarities between what different people say they experience, or what others make of their experience of such (mad) people. To be fully understood, madness – which we call 'mental illness' – has to be experienced. For those of us who have never really been 'mad' or mentally ill, the best that we can do is to develop empathy. We need to try to fit ourselves as much as we are able – or as much as we dare – inside the experience of the person who really knows.

Sally Clay knows a lot about madness and what it is like to be treated as hopelessly and chronically mentally ill. For Sally, the experience was a human and spiritual problem. Her doctors might have had a different view (or story), but being mad was all about *being* Sally Clay. It was part of who she was (or was becoming). The long and arduous process of recovery, which she described in *Madness and Reality* (Clay 1999), was not so much about getting rid of madness or becoming 'mentally healthy' (whatever that means), but more about recovering her sense of what it meant to be human *and* to be Sally Clay. In a very real sense she re-authored her story of distress, as part of her journey into what could, for convenience sake, be called recovery. Sally wrote:

> Everywhere these days we see people living lives of quiet desperation – lives, as Kierkegaard noted, of 'indifference, so remote from the good that they are almost too spiritless to be called sin, yet almost too spirited to be called despair'. We who have experienced mental illness have all learned the same thing, whether our extreme mental states were inspiring or frightening. We know that we have reached the bare bones of spirit and of what it means to be human. Whatever our suffering, we know that we do not want to become automatons, or to wear the false facade that others adopt.
>
> (Clay 1999: 34–5)

Many people today are afraid of talking about the *human* nature of mental distress, and think that *spiritual* either means religious or some kind of New Age weirdness. Sally Clay knows that the experience of madness frightens us, even when we refuse to admit that we are frightened:

> Whether we have had revelations *or* have hit rock bottom, most of us have also suffered from the ignorance of those who fear to look at what we have seen, who always try to change the subject. Although we have been broken, we have tasted of the marrow of reality. There is something to be learned here about the mystery of living itself, something important both to those who have suffered and those who seek to help us. We must teach each other.
>
> (Clay 1999: 35)

The lessons Sally learned from her experience of swinging wildly and frequently between 'madness and reality' are meaningful for everyone, but will benefit only those with the desire to listen *and* who have the courage to feel something of what Sally felt. As Harry Stack Sullivan said: 'We are all more simply human than otherwise' (Evans 1996: 18).

> There is much that we can learn about ourselves in the process of trying to learn something about the experiences of others.

## Learning from ourselves' and others' experience

The Tidal Model is a philosophical approach to developing genuine mental health *care* (Barker 2000a, 2001a, 2001c). It is less about treating or managing a form of mental illness and more about following a person, in an effort to provide the kind of support that might help them on the way to recovery. As such, it is based on a few simple ideas about 'being human' and 'helping one another'. We believe that these ideas have largely been neglected because they seem so obvious. We have deceived ourselves into thinking that complex problems always need complex solutions. Like the little fish who went looking for the ocean, we are already there. However, just because the knowledge we seek is at hand, this does not mean that we have nothing more to learn. We have never been to the moon, but we have viewed it through a telescope, which brought it much closer. We can also remember watching Neil Armstrong take his 'first step for mankind' on television over thirty years ago. However, studying things from the outside is not quite the same as having *insider knowledge*. If we wanted to know something of what it was like to travel to and walk upon the moon we would need to ask an astronaut, someone who has gone far beyond the boundaries of our experience. There is much that Neil Armstrong, or any of those who followed him, could teach us about moonwalking, even if we have no intention of following in their footsteps.

The analogy holds true for the experience of psychic distress. We can never know what other people really experience, but they can help us appreciate something of that experience. The American philosopher, Thomas Nagel, noted: 'Does it make sense, to ask what my experiences are *really* like, as opposed to how they appear to me?' (Nagel 1974: 438). Even if we think that we shall never follow other people into madness, there is much that we can learn about that *alien* experience. By learning something *of* those experiences, the people in our care will become less like aliens and we may come to understand them better.

> The person who becomes the patient is always the teacher. We must learn how to become the pupil.

## Choice

Many of us spend much of our lives trying to control our circumstances and increasingly we are encouraged to believe that we should control, or at least manage, everything from our emotional state to time itself. However, life, like time, often appears to have other plans and carries on regardless of what we do to try to influence it. Some of us believe that we have succeeded in improving, enhancing, managing or otherwise controlling our 'selves'. With the hindsight of age, we often admit that this was a futile exercise. Time cannot be managed; we can only manage ourselves as time passes. Similarly, many of the aspects of ourselves – such as our looks, our self-esteem, our confidence – cannot be controlled or managed except by deceiving ourselves, or falling for some commercial soft-sell. Life goes on regardless of all our vain efforts. We have wasted precious time that could have been spent 'learning from reality'. As the physicist Hagen comments:

> We see things change, and age, and appear and disappear. Trapped in our three-dimensional world, we do not *see* that the fourth dimension, time, doesn't change or go anywhere. *Now* is a constant. Our 'aging' universe has only local meaning. Non-locality, as a Whole, is ageless, existing always as *Now*. The passage of time is an illusion.
>
> (Hagen 1995: 244)

---

Reality teaches us that, as to what *happens* in life, we may have little choice. As to how we *deal* with it, however, we have total choice.

---

## Learning from reality

We like to think that our lives follow rules within strict boundaries, but reality suggests that our lives are much more. No one knows what is going to happen next. We can be fairly confident that the sun will rise tomorrow, but have only a vague idea of the kind of weather patterns that will accompany it. When it comes to predicting the patterns of the people who share our lives – their behaviour, thoughts and emotions, for example – our ability to predict with any certainty takes a dive. This seems also to be the case for our own patterns of behaviour, thinking and emotion.

What does this have to do with mental health? We only find out *exactly* what happens to people – for example, how they became mentally distressed, what sense they made of it, and how they recovered from it – *after the event*. People look back on their experiences, which are framed within the story of their lives, and from those reflections they have an opportunity to learn something about *what happened*. They have an opportunity to learn from experience. In helping the people in our care towards recovery, we need to be careful that we do not devote all our energies to trying to *control* their experience of mental illness. We need to allow people some time to *learn from reality*, so that they can become wiser about what has happened to them. By sharing something of the experience of mental illness, we might be able to share some of that wisdom too. When we ask people like Sally Clay, who was really helpful, the answer is often: 'someone who didn't try to control me completely . . . someone who let me *own* my experience'.

Reflection is a powerful tool. It may not be the mirror of the soul but is certainly the mirror of experience.

## How people change?

People are in a constant state of flux, like life itself (Gleick 1987). This may be the most unnerving fact of life, and may explain why many of us choose to believe in a life lived in discrete stages or chapters, punctuated with events and circumstances, all of which had a clear beginning, middle and end. If people genuinely believe this – and this belief works for them – then the Tidal Model practitioner will see no value in challenging this belief. However, the Tidal Model is informed by the scientific view of reality – that all is flow, everything is in flux. This view forms the basis for the appreciation of how people change; a view that translates easily into the therapeutic mechanisms of the model in practice.

The Tidal Model emphasises the need to focus on what needs to be done *now*, in response to the person's need for care or support. This focus on *now* acknowledges that this (*now*-ness) is the only aspect of our experience, within which any of us operate. Hagen (1995) pointed out that what we commonly call 'now' is absolute – it is all there is. All that is 'past' is mere memory, and the 'future' is imagination or fantasy. Even when we snap our fingers to denote 'now', the snap itself cannot be grasped: it is already past, as soon as it is executed – just like that. Hagen comments: 'It's not *Here* and *Now*. It's already memory. We can't even get our hands on the immediate *Now*, for it has no duration; even so, *Now* is where we always live' (Hagen 1995: 228). This is a vital scientific fact, one that reveals the illusion of change yet also its reality. Hagen tells the story of Amphibius, thought up by the philosopher James Cargile (1969):

Amphibius, when we meet him, is a tadpole living in a bowl of water. We film him continuously for the next three weeks. At the end of the three weeks Amphibius is a frog. If our movie camera records twenty-four frames per second, at the end of the three-week period we would have approximately 43.5 million consecutive pictures of Amphibius. We then number the frames 1 to 43,500,000 in the very sequence in which they were shot. Frame 1 shows a picture of a tadpole; frame 43,500,000 shows a frog. According to Cargile: 'There will be one moment when Amphibius is a frog, such that, an instant before, he was not . . . It is not being denied that, for the young tadpole Amphibius it will take a long time until he is a frog . . . growing can take lots of time. But acquiring properties does not.'

(Hagen 1995: 229–30)

We commonly think that things, including ourselves, are solid and abiding in the instant we call 'now'. Logically, there should be a frame in the camera sequence that shows a tadpole, followed by one which shows a frog. Reality demonstrates that there is no such sequence. The tadpole/frog just *is*, but at the same time is acquiring properties of something else, which it will in time become. The names we assign to the 'tadpole' and the 'frog' at different points across historical time refer to different things, which are paradoxically, the same thing. This is true of our human 'selves'. We commonly assume that *once* we were like this (happy), and *now* we are like this (sad), and at some point in the *future* we hope we shall be like something else (happy again). This is the way we talk about our world of experience and within the story of our lives all of this is real. In the world of reality, however, there is only *now*, where we play with memory and imagination. There is no specific moment when we *change*, *get better*, or *get worse*. We are always in the process of acquiring properties, which might in time define us as *changed* or *different*.

The Tidal Model acknowledges that people often like to talk about the past and the future as if these were states 'out there' in the world, rather than within themselves. Given that this is how people construe the reality of their experience, the model respects this aspect of the narrative. However, as Powell noted:

The old-style Newtonian universe is an illusion, for there is no such thing as an external world 'out there' that exists apart from our consciousness. Everything is mind. We are not part of the universe, we *are* the universe . . . as conscious observers (we) bring the world of the five senses into being. Along with all creatures of consciousness, we are co-creators of the physical universe.

(Powell 2001: 182)

The Tidal Model accepts the view of reality afforded by contemporary physics, acknowledging that for everyone there is only *now*, and within this moment resides the potential of *action*. This is an important fact of life for the practitioner, and guides the kind of help that might be offered. In the *now* resides the person's response to their memory of the past–now, whether recent or distant. In the *now* resides the person's actions that will influence the future–now. This fact determines that the care offered to the person is focused as much as possible on 'what needs to be done, *now*'.

Unlike many other models of mental health care there, is no emphasis on (for example) short-, medium- or long-term goals, since these are imaginary events in the future, which cannot be addressed *now*. Similarly, there is no need to devote a lot of time to reviewing the past, except to make contact with the person's story of how she or he came to be here and *now*. Instead, the helper focuses on determining what might need to be done *now*, by way of supporting the person.

> The core reality of 'now' focuses attention on what, exactly, is happening *for* and *to* the person *now*; how the person is making sense of all of this, *now*; and what choices the person is making with regard to responding to all of this, *now*.

## The balance of care

The primary need for people in mental distress is support. Ideally, they need someone who can meet their needs without entirely sacrificing themselves in the process. When someone is drowning, life-savers execute swift and efficient rescue, without risking drowning themselves in the process. They 'get involved' with the person; they 'share the experience of drowning'; but by keeping themselves *in balance*, they avoid the risk of going down with the person they seek to rescue. This is a useful analogy for the social construct of *nursing*, which we shall address in the next chapter. We need to get involved with people, sharing something of their experience, showing that we are not afraid to get 'into the swim' with them. However, we need to maintain our *balance*, or else we all risk 'going under'. Learning how to get involved without risking our own emotional or spiritual safety does not come easily. It is not something that can be learned from books or videos, but must be learned from practice. However, *knowing* how difficult it might be to acquire such a human skill may be the first step towards acquiring it. If we can do nothing else, we can remind you how difficult – and possibly lengthy – the process of learning *balance* might be.

As Sally Clay said, we all need to share our experiences and learn from one another. Whether we call this psychotherapy or counselling, clinical supervision or 'just talking', is immaterial. The important thing to remember is that we need to keep on learning from one another's experience – learning from reality.

> In helping people we need to learn how to balance the 'ordinary me' that might risk drowning, and the 'professional me' who might be frightened to get into the water, in the first place.

## Flowing metaphors

The Tidal Model appreciates the fluid nature of human experience, if not life in general. Heraclitus anticipated the world view of quantum mechanics when, two and a half thousand years ago he said 'everything flows and nothing stays'. He also provided a fitting metaphor for the Tidal Model by adding that 'you can't step in the same river twice'. Many models of human functioning try to 'freeze-frame' experience, assuming that human experience can in some way be stable (Barker 2001b). Some models even deceive us into assuming that people are like rocks, when the nearest analogy to the human state is water. Our experience of who we are and of life itself flows through us. When we 'reflect' on our experience we can only ask 'What is the water like *now*?' We cannot ask what is the whole river like, as this is beyond the possibilities of our experience. In the same vein, we can only reflect on ourselves, at this moment in time, as we dip into the experience.

In the Tidal Model water is used as the core metaphor for both the lived experience of the person who becomes the psychiatric patient and the care system that moulds itself to fit the person's need for human support. The water metaphor is apposite for a number of reasons:

- The ebb and flow of our lives is reflected in the way we breathe in and out, like waves lapping at the shore.
- All human life emerged from the ocean.
- We all emerged from the waters of our mother's womb.
- Water is used almost universally as a metaphor for cleansing of the spirit.
- Water evokes the concept of drowning, used frequently by people who are overwhelmed by their experiences.
- The power of water is not easy to contain. We can scoop water from the sea, but we cannot scoop out a whole ocean.
- The only way we can cope with the power of water is to learn how to live with its forces. We learn how to swim in water, or we build boats that float on the waves.
- Ultimately, the power of water is unpredictable.

These metaphors evoke something of the intangibility and power of the experience of mental distress, if not all human experience.

When people are asked 'what helped?' in a time of crisis, in our experience they identify someone who was able to respond sensitively to their often rapidly fluctuating *human* needs (Barker 2000c; Barker *et al.* 1999b, 1999c). Perhaps intuitively, people recognise that they are 'all in flow' and that the most helpful response at a time of crisis involves someone 'getting in the flow' and connecting to the ever-changing scenario of their human needs. Although care has been professionalised, irrespective of who does it, this kind of caring might be called *nursing*. As Florence Nightingale first pointed out, important though the process of care may be, it is not a healing art per se. Rather, good care involves organising or facilitating the necessary conditions for the person to be healed, by nature or by God. Nursing is, therefore, a metaphorical science.

> All significant human experiences are represented in metaphorical language and metaphor plays a key role in the healing process.

## Key principles of the Tidal Model

The Tidal Model is based on four principles:

1   The primary therapeutic focus of mental health care is the natural community. People live on an 'ocean of experience' (their natural lives) and psychiatric crisis is only one thing, among many, that might threaten, metaphorically, to 'drown' them. The aim of mental health care is to return people to that 'ocean of experience', so that they might continue with their 'life journey'.
2   Change is a constant ongoing process. However, although people are constantly changing, this may be beyond their awareness. The Tidal Model aims to help people develop their awareness of the small changes that, ultimately, will have a significant effect on their lives.
3   Empowerment lies at the heart of the caring process. Professional helpers, however they are defined by discipline, help people to identify how they might take greater charge of their lives, and all its related experience.
4   The therapeutic relationship between the professional helper and the person involves a temporary act of unison. They are like dancers united in the dance. Effective nursing involves *caring with people*, rather than simply caring *for* them or caring *about* them. This has implications not only for what goes on within the relationship, but also for the kind of support the professional helper might need to maintain the integrity of the caring process.

## The metaphorical voyage of discovery

The ocean metaphor acknowledges that for everyone life is a spiritual journey. At its most simple level, we all journey from the cradle to the grave. For many people, like Sally Clay, who experience mental illness or madness, the journey provides often painful revelations about themselves and others with whom they share their lives, including family friends and professional helpers. The ocean metaphor also seems apposite since, as people move through the various stages of their lives, they make a journey of exploration and discovery. It yields not only the opportunity to discover new lands, but also carries many risks: metaphorical storms, as well as the risk of running aground, or of the ship sinking. The seaworthiness of the ship may be an apposite metaphor for the person's health status or physical constitution. Clearly, the extent to which we are able to take that journey across our ocean of experience depends on the physical body on which we roll out the narrative of our human lives. In that sense, the 'mind', which becomes metaphorically distressed, is inextricably linked to the body that serves as its vehicle.

English-speaking people frequently use seafaring metaphors, which may be a reflection of the importance of the sea in the development of the English language culture. Dickens acknowledged the tidal nature of life and death through his character Mr Peggotty, who said: 'People can't die along the coast, except when the tides pretty nigh out. They can't be born, unless it's pretty nigh in – not properly born. He's a going out with the tide.' However, a similar understanding is found in much eastern thought, where the breath – the life force or *prana* – heralds life with each inhalation, and death with each exhalation. People are therefore poised constantly on the tidal cusp of life and death. Shakespeare summed up the fundamental assumptions of the Tidal Mode in *Julius Caesar*:

> There is a tide in the affairs of men,
> Which, taken at the flood, leads on to fortune;
> Omitted, all the voyage of their life
> Is bound in shallows and in miseries.
> On such a full sea are we now afloat;
> And we must take the current when it serves,
> Or lose our ventures.
>
> (IV, iii: 217–22)

Ordinary people often express the wisdom of the poets, especially when caught in the grip of serious mental distress. Personal accounts of mental distress and madness are full of powerful metaphors (Barker *et al.* 1999a; Barker and Buchanan-Barker 2003b), since ordinary words often fail to suggest the scale or the detail of their experience (Barker 2001c; Cooper

1986). Some of the most commonly described forms of mental distress evoke powerful seafaring metaphors:

- When people experience a disruption of their sea journey they may, like Coleridge's *Ancient Mariner*, become becalmed at sea. Depression often has just such a becalming effect. As the wind is taken out of their sails, people feel as if they are unable to make any progress. Indeed, the isolated figure of Coleridge's mariner, who finds himself becalmed, through his own fault, provides a powerful poetic representation of guilt-ridden depression.
- Other people may feel as if they have been thrown, violently, onto the rocks. Psychosis often appears like the experience of shipwreck, where people feel that they have run aground in alien or hostile territory.
- The experience of loss is common to many people – who have experienced sexual abuse, or psychosis or bereavement, for example. All feel that they have lost some aspect of themselves, or some vital support in their lives. Both the immediately terrifying nature of the experience of plundering, and the subsequent feeling of the vacuum of loss, evoke powerfully the piracy metaphor.

## Recovery: Drifting or deep-sea diving?

However metaphorical the description, the experience of distress signals that something practical needs to be done. Maintaining the seafaring metaphor, people in acute distress needs a *safe haven*, where they can feel supported sufficiently to begin the necessary repair work on their vessel (the body) and also begin to restore the confidence of the crew (themselves).

Once the immediate crisis is over, the person may feel ready to begin the preparations for returning to their ocean of experience. Some people are content simply to ensure that their ship is seaworthy and will stay afloat. For many, once the immediate crisis is over all they want is to leave the experience behind them and return to everyday life with as little fuss as possible. The Tidal Model acknowledges this by intervening as little as possible, trying to remain focused on the *solutions* that are immediately meaningful to the person.

However, some people signal a need to go beyond simply staying afloat, and want to explore beneath the surface of their predicament. Some people want to understand why they got into these particular difficulties. What did it all mean? What can they learn from the experience that might prevent them getting into similar difficulties in the future? The Tidal Model acknowledges that for some there is a need for 'deep-sea diving', where the submerged causes or threats to the person's physical or emotional security need to be carefully examined. The deep-sea diving metaphor is doubly apposite, since it frequently requires more skill and poses more existential threats to both the helper and the person. For everyone, however, the Tidal Model aims to provide *person-* (or family-) centred care, emphasising:

- the person's fundamental need for *security* – both existential and physical
- the person's capacity for *adaptation* to ever-changing life circumstances
- the person's *existing resources*, both personal *and* interpersonal.

The Tidal Model acknowledges that we should aspire to do as *little* as necessary to help support the person in making personally meaningful and appropriate life choices. In that sense, *intervention* should be our watchword, not *interference*.

# Chapter 3

# Throwing out the lifelines

## The meaning of caring

> An inexhaustible good nature is one of the most precious gifts of heaven,
> spreading itself like oil over the troubled sea of thought, and keeping the
> mind smooth and equable in the roughest weather.
>
> (Washington Irving)

## The facilitative power of caring

### Conversational realities

By returning to the metaphorical roots of human distress, the Tidal Model
offers a radical alternative to traditional psychiatric care. Mental health
services are often so focused on hypothetical constructs of *illness* and *disorder*
that the person who experiences these hypothetical states is lost from view.
The Tidal Model refocuses attention on the *person*, the person's *experience of
distress*, and the person's appreciation of what *needs to be done* to address the
immediate problems of living. The radical focus of the Tidal Model relocates
the person at the heart of the caring process.

The Tidal Model assumes that the person's experience is accessed through
the personal narrative or story. This story is not, however, in any way
'out there' in the world, separate from the person. The Tidal Model assumes
that the person's narrative is developed through collaboration with the professional. The story that becomes the basis of the therapeutic discourse is not
a private monologue, but rather is a story jointly authored through a seamless
series of conversations. These conversations are very different from the interviews that form the basis of traditional psychiatric and psychotherapeutic
practice. In the interview, the power is held and exercised, however gently or
subtly, by the professional who manipulates, guides or otherwise directs the
'patient' towards some perceived therapeutic goal; usually one set by the
professional services. In the *conversation*, the process is defined by reciprocity
and the pursuit of equal status. This kind of dialogue hopefully frees both the

person and the professional to share their experience of the phenomena – the person's immediate problems of living. As Zeldin noted:

> Conversation is a meeting of minds with different memories and habits. When minds meet, they don't just exchange facts: they transform them, reshape them, draw different implications from them, engage in new trains of thought. Conversation doesn't just reshuffle the cards: it creates new cards.
>
> (Zeldin 2000: 14)

Traditional interviewing assumes that a story, belonging uniquely to the individual, lies waiting to be revealed, unearthed or hatched, upon which professionals may impose a layer of meaning. By invoking the concept of the conversational reality, the Tidal Model goes beyond the individual, prizing instead the couple (person/professional) or the communal group. In Zeldin's words, the conversation offers the possibility of 'inventing an art of living together that has not been tried before' (p. 31). In this critical sense the relationship that develops between the person and professional, or within the communal group, is creative. It provides the springboard for a caring response that is specifically crafted, or individually tailored to present circumstances. This differs markedly from conventional practice where professionals bring prepackaged responses – in the form of theories or techniques – designed to manipulate cognitive or emotional states. The Tidal Model emphasises the need to engage with the person, building a genuine human alliance that might begin to address the person's problems of living. The practitioner signals an intention to engage with the person, rather than to manage, treat or otherwise fix the problem, by opening any conversation with the least restrictive question: 'What shall we talk about?' or 'What have you brought with you that you would like to discuss?' Such lines of inquiry are unashamedly focused on opening a conversation that begins 'where' the person feels is appropriate, rather than from serving professional interests.

As noted in Chapter 1, human experience is fluid, flowing and often chaotic in nature (Barker 1996). In practice, care also flows seamlessly and chaotically along a continuum, which extends from addressing critical, short-term needs to more developmental forms of care, focused on the longer term. (This continuum is discussed in detail in Chapter 5.) The practical focus of care is to help develop or nurture understanding. As Frankl (1973) noted, the development of understanding is part of the search for meaning in everyday life, as we make sense of ideas about health or illness. Professionals, like everyone else, must make sense of their own experience. However, they have an added responsibility: to clarify what might need to be done to help the person in the search for everyday meaning.

The process of caring within the Tidal Model is facilitative: it provides the conditions under which something might happen. It does not cause such things to happen. The kind of care offered may be used in whatever way the person thinks appropriate. In that sense, nursing is a gift (Fox 1993; Jackson and Stevenson 1998). Indeed, this concept of caring is like a wrapper: it provides a means of holding together, metaphorically, a complex set of human processes. What the observer might *see* is a caring attitude in action: the wrapping. In this chapter we look beyond the exterior and reveal something of the interior of the caring process. What goes on – or needs to go on – inside the wrapper between the person and the professional?

## The therapeutic culture of care

On one level the experience of madness is a simple phenomenon – it involves a breakdown of understanding or relatedness (Barker *et al.* 1999a). People often retreat from the world of ordinary relationships with others because 'getting on' with other people has become so difficult; or they find it difficult to share their view of themselves or the world with others. People in the grip of madness often find it difficult to communicate and may be viewed as 'speaking another language'. They may become acutely self-aware, experiencing an emotional terrorism, within which abstract forces haunt them, or at least dog their own experiential footsteps. The person who loses control to such an extent needs to recover some semblance of control to continue living – reclaiming the life submerged by madness. Talking about the experience of schizophrenia, Campbell (1972) noted:

> [The doctor] has himself to understand what the fragmentary signs and signals signify that his patient, totally out of touch with rationally oriented manners of thought and communication, is trying to bring forth in order to establish some kind of contact. Interpreted from this point of view, a schizophrenic breakdown is an inward and backward journey to recover something missed or lost, and to restore, thereby, a vital balance. So let the voyager go. He has tipped over and is sinking, perhaps drowning; yet, as in the old legend of Gilgamesh and his long, deep dive to the bottom of the cosmic sea to pluck the watercress of immortality, there is the one green value of his life down there. Don't cut him off from it: help him through.
>
> (Campbell 1972: 203)

Arguably, the first step in the recovery process is to reclaim possession of the story of madness. This might be the most practical way of helping the person through the experience. In acknowledging this, the Tidal Model encourages the person to set both the *agenda* and the *pace* for the conversation that develops with the professional.

### Caring as systematic nurture

*Caring* is everywhere today, at least in name. Everyone from plumbers to cosmetic surgeons claim to 'care' for their clients. Caring was the buzzword of the late twentieth century and the expression has probably suffered from commercial overkill. It was not always the case. Caring was once a lowly process, involving nurses' simple human contact with people called patients and their families. The lowly nature of this practice was reinforced by Virginia Henderson's theoretical definition of caring as something that was merely supportive and not therapeutic in its own right. In her highly influential pamphlet on the *Basic Principles of Nursing Care* (Henderson 1969) she emphasised that 'the physician is regarded as pre-eminent in diagnosis, prognosis and therapy'. This confirmed that nurses, through their caring, merely set the scene for the really important stuff.

However, by the early 1970s others had challenged this view, suggesting that caring might have a therapeutic function. Most of these had strong bases in humanism and holism – especially Travelbee's therapeutic use of self, Watson's science of human caring, and Leininger's transcultural nursing (see Barker 2000b). These theorists located caring at the heart of nursing, defining it as the *essence* of nursing (Barker *et al.* 1995; Peck 1992; Sourial 1997).

Caring has never been confined to the practice of professional nursing and, over the past two decades, various health and social care disciplines have shown how they provide *care for* the person, alongside other services. Various physicians (Dossey 1991), social workers (Brandon 2000b) and psychologists (Smail 1988) have shown that caring can be more complex than simply caring *about* or even caring *for* the person. The recent emphasis on emancipatory systems has revealed a third dimension, which we originally called *caring with* the patient (Barker and Whitehill 1997). It is this specific caring emphasis that is emphasised within the Tidal Model. All these developments remind us that nursing is a social as well as a professional construct. Down the ages all sorts of people, especially parents, but mothers in particular, have expressed and enacted the various attitudes that result in nurturing conditions, which aid the growth and development of the person. When people are in states of mental distress, nursing *care* helps them grow through the crisis.

Some contemporary caring theorists have suggested that the wrapping may be more important than the contents. Bradshaw (1994, 1996) saw caring as largely an ethical pursuit, heavily influenced by the Judaeo-Christian tradition (see Travelbee 1971; Paterson and Zderad 1976). The importance of the philosophical basis of caring cannot be understated, but caring is more than just a professional emotional response to distress. Caring generates power within relationships and, when used appropriately, can help the person in care (and those providing the care) to evolve as persons. Where caring is used differently, it risks engendering dependency. The fact that caring can (and often does) generate negative outcomes, suggests the need for a reflexive definition.

Caring occurs when growth, healing or recovery occurs. When dependency or harm develops, some other (non-caring) human process is at work.

### Transcultural caring

Much of the caring literature is North American or British. However, some theories, such as Watson's science of human caring, appear to cross social and cultural borders and appear to be compatible with multiculturalism (Eddins and Riley-Eddins 1997). Studies of perceptions of important caring qualities in other cultures – e.g. Muslim societies – bear a remarkable similarity to those in the western literature (e.g. Nahas 1997). However, there remains a need to clarify and analyse further the concept (Dyson 1997; Gaut 1993; Greenhalgh *et al.* 1998). Some important steps in this direction have been taken in distinguishing the functions of compassion, empathy, nurture and altruism, as dimensions of caring (Fogel *et al.* 1986), and others have tried to study empirically the effects of formal education on knowledge of, and attitudes towards caring, as well as discrete patterns of caring behaviour (Yang and Lu 1998).

## Unwrapping the caring construct

### Nurture – the caring ambition

Providing care to people at times of need is fundamental to all human societies. Nurture is the cornerstone of human culture. However, the act of caring for another human being, however simple it may appear, is emotionally complex, for both carer and cared for person. The idea of nurture illustrates how caring can be a productive, interactive process, unlike the kind of care we lavish on things that we consider precious or important to our livelihood. When we care for our cars, computers or other sensitive pieces of equipment, we try to ensure that they are kept under the conditions necessary to ensure their optimum functioning. Similarly, with a painting or a piece of jewellry, we try to maintain it under conditions that will safeguard its inherent value. However these 'things' always remain separate from us, the carer. More importantly, those 'things' do not change. They may 'appreciate' in value, but this is perceptual rather than actual. The effects of caring on people is quite different.

When we care for another person, or even an animal, like a racehorse or a pet, the relationship is focused on change. As Fogel *et al.* (1986: 55) suggested, we provide 'guidance, protection and care for the purpose of fostering developmental change congruent with the expected potential of change of the object of nurturance'. However, it is also clear that we can nurture our own 'selves', fostering the development of ourselves as spiritual identities. Many believe that the process of *caring with* another person engenders both technical skill development and spiritual growth in the carer. The mutuality inherent in the nurturing process, especially in mental health, is often greatly overlooked. Indeed, it may often be the case that the professional reaps rewards from the nurturing relationship that far outweigh any benefits accrued by the cared for person.

### Sympathy and empathy and personal distress

Although caregiving involves specific physical interactions, it is primarily an emotional undertaking. In ordinary social interactions, love, joy and compassion are central to the act of caring. The care of an infant typically evokes love and joy and the care of a frail elder evokes love and compassion. Although these emotions are often found within professional caring, two other emotions – sympathy and empathy – tend to feature most.

When we are *sympathetic* to the plight of others, we often have only a loose understanding of what they are experiencing. Typically, sympathy:

- involves heightened awareness of the person's *suffering* or need for support
- is focused on the *well-being* of the person
- is automatic and *effortless* – we just 'feel' it rising up within us
- is a 'moving' experience – we *feel* 'for' the person
- leads to direct attempts to *alleviate the person's distress*.

*Empathy* is quite different. We try to reproduce accurately within ourselves the experiences or world view of the other person. We try to imagine stepping inside the person's skin with a view to feeling, sensing and perceiving the world as they do. Typically, empathy:

- involves a heightened awareness of the other person's *experiences*
- is focused on understanding, conceptualising and 'knowing' what it is like to '*be*' that person
- is *effortful* and requires considerable powers of imagination
- involves *reaching out* to the person.

As Eisenberg (1986) pointed out, different emotions are evoked within caring relationships:

- We may find it relatively easy to 'feel' the same emotion that is being felt by the person. This is *true empathy* or 'emotional contagion'.
- Our emotional reactions to the distress of the other person may not

accurately match their feelings, but are focused on their welfare. This is a form of sympathy that is closely linked to *altruism*.

- Often, the emotional state of the other person evokes feelings within ourselves, related to anxiety, guilt or worry. This is a form of *personal distress* rather than sympathy.

Within the Tidal Model both sympathy (altruism) and empathy are important. Our feelings *for* people serve as the motivation to work towards meeting their needs. Our understanding of the nature of their emotional and psychological experience serves as the basis for determining what exactly needs to be done to meet their needs.

We also recognise that people who are extremely distressed can evoke personal distress within the professional. This indicates the need for adequate support systems (such as individual or group supervision) within which the professionals may explore the impact of the caring process on their emotional state, and also the emotional hurts, defences and vulnerabilities, which are part of their professional personhood.

### Basic attendance – being of service

Viewed from the philosophical perspective of the Tidal Model, the professional's primary therapeutic ambition is to be of service – not to change the person. Consequently, the Tidal Model practitioner tries to shed the therapeutic vanity that encumbers many therapeutic models: the idea that the professional might know what is 'best' for the person. Rather, it is assumed that people always know what is 'best' for them, even when this appears to conflict with the views of those around them, especially those who might be charged with a responsibility for their 'care' and safety.

Although the idea of service is fundamental, this is not a naive laissez-faire position. Practitioners have specific professional responsibilities, not least to ensure the physical safety of the person and others. However, when people are highly distressed, their vulnerabilities are often pre-verbal. The key challenge for the professional is to be able to read the subtle cues that suggest the kind of care needed at this particular moment. Needless to say, this is not an easy task.

Podvoll (1990) borrowed an expression from meditation to describe the ideal emotional state for the development of this service mentality – 'beginner's mind'. Whether the practitioner is highly experienced or a relative novice, each should adopt a 'student' viewpoint, expressing an openness to learn from the person, and a willingness to discover what 'really' needs to be done 'for the person', as opposed to merely fulfilling professional obligations. As Podvoll noted: 'This is not a feigned naiveté; rather, it is an openness to learn from the person one is attending, and a willingness to discover the wellsprings of sanity' (1990: 267). The challenges inherent within this approach are belied by the apparent simplicity of what the professional 'does'. Podvoll described this approach as 'basic attendance', emphasising the professional's need to focus on the person across a wide range of caring scenarios:

> The work of basic attendance requires more than just what one knows, it requires that one use everything of who one *is* and how one relates to the world. A deeper set of clinical skills needs to be cultivated to do basic attendance properly. It is not merely a disciplined 'hanging out' (though at times that is just what is called for – and actually may not be so easy to do). Simply said, basic attendance is 'getting down' to what is immediately relevant to being with someone during the process of recovery – whatever may be required, from taking walks to something approaching more traditional psychotherapy.
>
> (Podvoll 1990: 265)

### Noticing – staying wide awake

The idea that we might be able to promote someone's experience of health and well-being is a challenging one. Often we talk about being mental health practitioners, but fail to clarify what exactly we do to enable or facilitate this fragile experience. To do so requires considerable attention to duty. We need to be able to put ourselves in the right position within which we can notice what is happening for the person and also what is happening to and within us. This requires calmness, alertness and vitality. Needless to say, this can be demanding work.

When working with acutely distressed people – and especially those who might be distressing to others, perhaps even ourselves – we need to *wonder* what is going on within them, and also to *notice* slight changes in mood, appearance, behaviour and general presentation, that suggest how they are taking discrete steps, in one direction or another. The Tidal Model assumes that change is the only constant. The professional must therefore be sensitive to signs that change is occurring, so that these subtle changes can be drawn to the person's attention, discussed and explored further as part of the recovery process. We also need to be able to notice what is happening within our own minds:

- Are we focused and attentive or is our mind wandering?
- Are we thinking of what we might do to *control* the situation or are we letting ourselves *follow* the person in search of a shared understanding of what needs to be done?

This is a skill that can only be learned through the practice of *careful* attention.

## The challenge of ordinary caring

Ironically, it was Edward Podvoll, a psychiatrist, who described this kind of caring as a 'genuine nursing of the mind' (1990: 264). Too often the therapeutic importance of such intimacy is overlooked and dismissed as nothing special – an activity that anyone might be able to fulfil. Podvoll commented:

> So imbued is our culture with the notion of psychological treatment being a white-collar, professional job where the psychotherapist does not have to reveal how he or she walks; eats; handles money; celebrates; does physical labor; relates to friends, children and animals; and so on – or does anything but talk about the past, present and future – that we think that anything else is 'merely nursing' or case management, something inferior to offering psychological 'insight' or the supposed science of prescribing medications.
>
> (Podvoll 1990: 264–5)

Mental health professionals have increasingly focused their attention on developing sophisticated therapeutic 'skills' with which to effect change in the person's behavioural, emotional or cognitive state. However, against this backdrop has re-emerged an interest in the power of 'ordinary' relationships, which might – in actuality – be *extra*-ordinary (Barker *et al.* 1999b). This is not to say that there is no value in sophisticated psychological technologies, or no virtue in learning how to operate them. However, we should not forget that some of the most powerful things we can do *with* people on their recovery journey are imbued with the perfume of ordinariness. Brandon (2000b: 148) illustrated this with a Chinese story about a man's journey in search of a famous teacher:

> After nearly a year, he arrived exhausted but content at the remote place where this great teacher was living and teaching. At the first meeting he prostrated himself three times in the dust, as was the custom, and begged to be taught. 'Please teach me, Oh Great One. I have come from afar.' The great One responded brusquely – 'Do good and avoid evil', and then silence.
>
> After a long wait the deeply disappointed student replied: 'Is that it? Is that all? Is this teaching the reason why I sold everything, crossed all those rivers, nearly died in the mountains, walked a thousand miles, was robbed of all my possessions – to hear what every five-year-old child knows already?' 'Ah,' said the Great One, 'a five year old child may know it but an eighty-year-old man can't practice it.'

Often we search, at great emotional and financial cost, for some new method to heal the human hurts we call madness. Perhaps at least part of what is needed is already known to us, but may not be all that easy to enact in the practice of our professional lives. We may know the value of caring in our hearts, but to what extent can we put caring at the forefront of practice?

### The craft of caring

Much has been written about the 'art' of nursing and the 'science' that informs psychiatric medicine and various psychological therapies. When we talk about the art of nursing, this suggests a sense of self-importance, righteousness or correctness, as if we are being 'artful' like Charles Dickens's 'Artful Dodger'. Although some artists produce their work for sale or on commission, they work mainly to satisfy themselves and their own standards. Only once the artist is satisfied, even if others disagree, will the work be exhibited. At least in high art the artist is the final arbiter of the work's quality and worth.

Science is an occupation with a different kind of correctness; one owned by a universal intelligence, which used to be called nature. The scientist does not *make* things, like the artist, but *discovers* the gods' handiwork. Like the artist, the scientist does not modify or adapt the work to satisfy patrons. Scientists, or at least ethical scientists, are above this on principle; their allegiance is to 'the truth'.

The notion of *craft* suggests a wholly different experience of work, since craft objects are made to satisfy the demands or expectations of a patron or customer. However, the craftsperson needs to be able to combine skill (art), knowledge (science) and the discrete needs or expectations of the patron to produce a workable craft object. The craftsperson needs to know how to weave, dye or cut cloth; how much pressure silver will take, without breaking; how high a temperature is needed to fire a piece of clay. The science of craft is augmented by the imposition of some aesthetic – marrying shapes and colours to suggest an unspoken, and usually culturally based, message. However, the success or value of any crafted object is defined by the unknown gift of appreciation that the owner bestows on the object. The meaning attached to a wedding dress, a talismanic piece of jewellery or pot, emanates from the owner (customer or patron), not from the maker. This meaning is invisible but transformative. With the attribution of meaning the crafted object becomes unique; like no other, despite possible surface similarities.

Within the Tidal Model the professional aims to develop the *craft of caring* – using professional skills and knowledge together to meet the discrete needs of the person, so that a unique experience of being *cared with* can develop.

## Core assumptions of the Tidal Model

The Tidal Model operates from four core assumptions about the kind of care that people need when experiencing mental distress, which reflect the attitudinal set of the practitioner (Barker 1997a).

### I Therapeutic nursing is an interactive, developmental, human activity, more concerned with the future development of the person than with the origins or causes of their present distress

The person's present circumstances are a function of various influences: historical, physical and social. The possible significance of such factors needs to be considered if anything approximating complete (whole) care is to be provided. These factors are the metaphorical milestones for the person's story to date. Traditional psychiatric practice focuses on *excavating* the person's past, in search of an explanation for the person's present circumstances. It is a kind of human archaeology: looking for factors in the person's past which might explain the person's present. This does not provide pointers to the future and is not naturally developmental in nature. Despite its importance, it does not meet the criteria for *nursing*.

The primary focus of nursing is, instead, on the person's *relationship* with health and illness, *not* with the assumed illness, disorder or state of well-being. In terms of its potential for healing, nursing is focused on identifying what *needs to be done* to help the person *now*, to address, resolve, overcome or adapt to the problems of living associated with what might be called their 'mental illness' or 'psychiatric disorder'.

### 2 The experience of mental distress associated with mental illness or psychiatric disorder is represented through public behavioural disturbance, or reports of private events known only to the individual concerned

Although the distress of mental illness may be manifest in the person's behaviour, and therefore observable to others, the experience of distress is always invisible. Much traditional nursing care has focused on managing people's behaviour, trying to help them fit prescribed social roles. Indeed, within such 'rehabilitation' the person may change, but their unique human needs may not be addressed.

Nursing aims to help people access and review their private experiences, in an effort to re-author the story of their lives, and to begin the healing of past and present distress, as a way of opening ways to further human development.

### 3 The professional and the person-in-care are engaged in a relationship based on mutual influence

Nursing care is not a one-way process but always involves some kind of relationship. The Tidal Model assumes that the caring process is better characterised as 'caring with', which incorporates both the need to 'care about' and 'care for' the person. The collaborative nature of *caring with* produces changes for the professional as well as the person.

### 4 The experience of psychiatric disorder is translated into a variety of disturbances of everyday living; the practice of therapeutic nursing is located uniquely within the context of everyday life

Although professionals spend time with the person reviewing and anticipating life events, the primary focus is on engaging with the real world of experience. This approach is characteristic of nursing's focus on the *experience of* and *relationship with* health and illness, rather than health and illness per se.

## The tidal metaphor

The Tidal Model assumes that all people are defined primarily by their experience. Consequently, the central focus of the Tidal Model involves developing the conditions that are necessary to identify and examine in depth the person's experience. Through this process, we gain an appreciation of the person's human needs and what needs to be done to meet them. The fluid, constantly changing, nature of the person's experience of self and others is represented by the core metaphor of the Tidal Model: *water*. People exist on a metaphorical ocean of experience. Everyday experience appears to have boundaries or limits. However, these are illusory and no more real than the concept of the horizon. As we journey, the horizon appears to move with us, always remaining the same original distance away. The metaphor of the horizon suggests the limitless nature of personal experience, and also the illusory boundaries of the self.

The tidal metaphor also suggests the journey that people make during their lives. This journey is akin to a sea voyage. When people talk about their personal development or the stages through which they have passed in their lives, this is similar to sailing from one port to another, or from one continent to another. The nature of the life journey – great or small – determines the changes which occur in human experience.

The guiding metaphor of water also reminds us of the constantly shifting nature of the experience of health and illness. One can drown as easily in a pool of water as in the ocean. If professionals focus on the person's experience, they may gain an appreciation of the seriousness of the situation, rather than be distracted by the context within which the distress occurs.

## The guiding principles

> I never teach my pupils; I only attempt to provide the conditions in which they can learn.
>
> (Einstein)

The Tidal Model is based on six interrelated principles concerning the nature and function of the therapeutic relationship.

1    *The virtue of curiosity*. The professional knows little of any consequence about the person, or the person's ocean of experience. By contrast, people are the world's leading authorities on their own lives. The person is a mystery, which needs to be explored, if their needs are to be identified and met. Given that what the person brings is 'the mystery of my-story', the professional's approach is characterised by curiosity. The professional seeks to find out *what* exactly the person *thinks* and *feels* and *knows* about themselves, and whatever is the problem which brought them into the health care setting in the first place.

2    *The power of resourcefulness*. Traditionally, people who become 'patients' are defined in terms of their problems, deficits, diagnoses or various other symptoms of their illness or disorder. The Tidal Model acknowledges the reality of these problems, but is primarily concerned to focus on and work with the person's *resourcefulness*. How exactly does the person manage to live with, or co-exist with, these aspects of their daily experience? The professional aims to identify the person's invisible resources, and also to identify other resources within the person's interpersonal and social network, which might help the person.

3    *The value of respecting the person's wishes*. Traditional nursing care is often paternalistic, using 'objective' forms of assessment to determine what might be in the person's best interests. The Tidal Model emphasises the importance of active collaboration, to identify what people see as *their* needs at this moment. The model also emphasises the need to respect the person's wishes, by trying to meet whatever need is identified as important. This does not, however, release the team from the responsibility of offering other supplementary forms of care. However, the wishes of the person remain at the human heart of the caring process.

4    *Paradox: Viewing crisis as opportunity*. Traditionally, crises are seen as problems, which need to be managed, controlled or otherwise 'coped with'. Within the Tidal Model, the life events that bring the person into contact with the services are viewed as opportunities. These events are natural signals that 'something needs to be done'. If responded to

appropriately, this might be seen as opportunity for change, a chance to take a new direction in life. These critical events are akin to checking the map or resetting the compass: necessary responses to the ups and downs of life's journey.

5   *Everyday wisdom: Own the goals.* Professionals set goals, which represent the end point of the care process. Within the Tidal Model, small steps are emphasised; the steps that the person needs to take to move away from the circumstances that brought them into the care setting. Any 'goals' set are small and highly specific, representing the steps which the person will take on the road to 'who knows where' for the rest of their life's journey.

6   *The pursuit of elegance.* Traditionally, many nursing care plans are highly complex with various levels of differing interventions. Within the Tidal Model, emphasis is given to identifying the simplest possible action that might bring about the changes necessary for the person to experience a change (however small) in their present circumstances.

The initial aim is to identify 'what needs to be done' and all care that follows focuses on ways of involving the person (and where appropriate, others) in meeting this need. By focusing on what is absolutely necessary, the care plan becomes simpler and more elegant.

## The practical therapeutic philosophy

There is always an easy solution to every human problem neat, plausible and wrong.

(H.L. Mencken)

Given its person-centred emphasis, the Tidal Model involves asking four questions:

1   *Why this – why now?* The professional's first priority is to consider why the person might be experiencing this particular life difficulty now. What makes this particular experience significant at this particular point in the person's life? This is seen as the major presenting problem. The focus of care is very much on what the person is experiencing now, and what needs to be done now to address, and hopefully resolve, this problem.

2   *What works?* Professionals need also to ask 'what works' for the person in the present circumstances? This represents the person-centred focus of care. Instead of using standardised techniques or therapeutic methods that might have general value, the practitioner identifies either what has worked for the person in the past or what the person thinks might work *now* or in the immediate future. This part of the philosophy allows for a possible wider range of therapeutic approaches than often prevails.

3   *What is the person's personal theory?* We need to consider how people
    understand their problems, and what explanations or theories they use
    from their own experience in framing these understandings. In effect, the
    professional wants to know what 'sense' people 'make' of their problems.
    This is a vital part of the overall model. Rather than offering a profes-
    sional explanation or opinion – in the form of some theory or a diagnosis
    – the professional displays a willingness to appreciate how the person
    understands their experience. What is the person's 'personal theory'?

4   *How to limit restrictions?* Often the interventions used in psychiatric care
    and treatment are restrictive and limiting. Professionals should aim also
    to use the least restrictive means of helping the person to address and
    resolve their difficulties. Although this is often taken as read, much
    emphasis is placed within the model on identifying how *little* the profes-
    sional might do to help the person, and also *how much* people might do
    to help bring about therapeutic change for themselves. Together, these
    represent the least restrictive intervention.

# Chapter 4

# Manning the lifeboats

## The Tidal Model in practice

> Make the best use of what is in your power, and take the rest as it happens.
> (Epictetus c. AD 55–c. AD 135)

### Origins of the Tidal Model

The Tidal Model flows from a variety of sources, not least our own experience of ourselves, both as persons and as professional people. However, the Tidal Model would likely not have developed had we not been interested in the nature of caring in a professional and wider social context. Our experiences as psychiatric nurse (PB) and social worker (PBB) had helped us appreciate that people in distress need to feel cared *about*, and cared *for*. Our related experiences as psychotherapists and counsellors helped us appreciate how this caring relationship could be a conjoint, reciprocal effort, and so we came to emphasise the notion of *caring with*.

However, aside from these practice-focused influences, the Tidal Model drew most directly from research conducted originally at the Department of Psychiatry at the University of Newcastle in England, and from clinical projects and pilot studies with colleagues locally at Newcastle City Health Trust, and internationally through various consultations and research studies. Notably, as the Foreword shows, we were fortunate to be supported by many people, most of whom we can count as friends, who had direct experience of madness or psychiatric services. They provided the critical 'consumer's' perspective on the original philosophy and development of the model in practice. Four specific projects served as the springboard for the development of the Tidal Model:

1   A group, comprising researchers, academics, clinicians and managers, met monthly over a one-year period (1974–5) to generate a consensual understanding of the nature and function of psychiatric nursing practice, which was tentatively referred to as a 'meta-theory' (Barker 1997a).
2   A two-day workshop, involving nurse researchers, clinicians and national

representatives of various user/consumer advocacy perspectives, explored the nature of the support which people 'needed' when experiencing mental distress.

3   An international study – focused on six rural and urban settings in England, Northern Ireland and the Republic of Ireland – developed a substantive theory of the 'need for psychiatric nursing', as perceived by users of psychiatric services, family members, psychiatric nurses and other members of the multidisciplinary team (Barker *et al.* 1999b). An English study developed a related model of the 'need' for community psychiatric nursing practice (Walker and Barker 1998).

4   A study of the power relationships between psychiatric nurses and people in receipt of mental health services generated a model of 'empowering relationships'.

A common issue that emerged in all these studies was what made a 'difference' for people – either in terms of helping or hindering their human progress. This was most often perceived to be remarkably ordinary forms of interaction. The psychiatrist, the psychologist and psychotherapist are (usually) held in awe and high esteem by 'patients' and the general public, who attribute to them remarkable powers of influence and sagacity. However, when we asked people whose lives had been blighted by the experience of madness 'who' made a difference, no one rushed to identify any of these august professionals as the key influence in their recovery. When we asked 'what' made a difference in the person's recovery, again no one rushed to identify a specific course of medication, therapy or counselling. This is not to say that these professionals and processes were not helpful; only that they were not identified as such. This should not surprise us. For more than twenty years various studies have suggested that people are more likely to confide in bartenders and hairdressers than in formal mental health professionals (e.g. Cowen 1982; Browning 2003). Perhaps the ears afforded by such 'lay' listeners offer the near-ideal, non-judgemental support that the distressed person so desires.

Contemporaneously, PB was invited by the multidisciplinary management team responsible for the Adult Mental Health Programme in Newcastle to develop an alternative model for psychiatric nursing practice. Preliminary work was begun in 1996 on the development of specific caring processes, and these ultimately formed the basis of the first pilot Tidal Model project (Barker 1998a). Following a formal evaluation of the effects of implementing the Tidal Model, albeit in a limited form, within an acute psychiatric admission ward, the model was formally launched across the whole Adult Mental Health Programme in the spring of 2000. Since then, the model has been adopted and developed in a range of other settings, both within the UK and abroad (these developments are discussed in more detail in Chapter 14).

## Learning from life

Despite the popular expectation, people with mental health problems never actually 'get better', or at least not in any absolute or lasting sense. Hopefully, however, people can become aware of how different they feel, which they might interpret as a state of 'betterness' or even 'wellness'. This feeling may last a short or relatively long time, but ultimately it will pass, to be replaced by some other feelings. The critical fact of life is that 'all things must pass'. Given that change is constant, nothing lasts. This is one of the vital facts of life. It may be one that we all find difficult to accept, and so we struggle to try to keep things the same – and are disappointed.

In our view the awareness of the inevitability of change is part of the mature appreciation of life and its various difficulties. Our lives are landscapes, at one moment in shade but soon to be lit by sunshine, before clouding over again. A Chinese saying reframes our foolish western optimism: *the light at the end of the tunnel is a sign that another tunnel will soon be coming up*. This is as funny as it is so obviously true. Little wonder that oriental wisdom is imbued with so much laughter at adversity.

Life is the great teacher. As we live from moment to moment we experience the flow of change, which is the key lesson that life teaches. In this ever-changing climate our main challenge is to identify what needs to be done *now*, to address our *actual* needs, difficulties or problems of living. When we cast ourselves in the role of helper, the primary task of our *care* is to help the person live with the uncertainties of life, which generate differing needs, by *doing what needs to be done*.

A secondary but no less important aim is to identify what needs to be done *now* to reduce the likelihood that *potential* problems or difficulties will develop in the future. In addition to dealing with the specific problems that life presents *now*, we need also to anticipate possible problems that might emerge later on the person's life journey.

Taken together, these constructive reactions to life's difficulties help us to recover the ground we have lost to mental distress and to begin to reclaim the life that appears to have been lost in the deep and dangerous waters of mental distress.

## The care continuum

Traditionally mental health services have distinguished between the kinds of care offered to people in their own homes or in clinics, and care provided in hospital settings. This split-level thinking derives largely from the history of psychiatry, where institutional care models dominated the asylum era and were gradually replaced with models of 'community care'. Although much mental health care today is focused on community-based services, when people are considered to be seriously distressed or in need of more intensive care and attention they are usually admitted to some kind of hospital or residential care.

The traditional relationship between 'hospital' and 'community' care is shown in Figure 4.1. Typically, people receive two kinds of community care: 'primary care' from their family doctor or counsellor and 'tertiary care' following discharge from hospital, either as an outpatient or supported by other community-based services. When people experience crises in their lives, and require admission to some kind of residential (secondary) care, it is assumed that they have left the natural community; hence the subsequent emphasis on discharging people from hospital 'back into' the community.

However, even when people become 'patients' – taking up temporary residence in a hospital or clinic – in one very important sense they have not moved at all; they remain within the world of their experience. When we consider all the forms of care and treatment that people might need, and frame these *within* their world of experience, the links between 'primary', 'critical' and 'tertiary' care become clearer. Figure 4.2 provides an illustration of a more holistic appreciation of care, using the person's *world of experience* as the overarching emphasis for the 'need for care', rather than traditional institution-led or professional-led systems.

Viewed from yet another different perspective, the kind of care that anyone might need ranges across a continuum: from helping the person to *resolve current, actual problems*, through to helping the person *develop a deeper understanding* of how specific problems of living have developed; and how they might better be resolved, or lived with. Such understandings might also help the person to deal more effectively with potential problems that might emerge in the future. This continuum, illustrating the three key forms of care that the person might need, is illustrated in Figure 4.3.

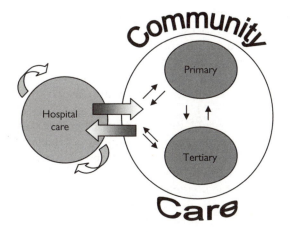

*Figure 4.1* Traditional hospital–community relations

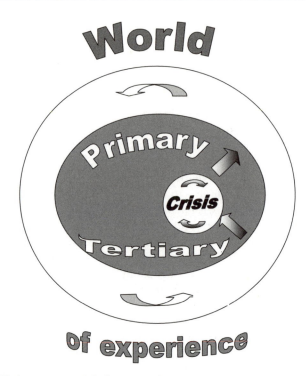

*Figure 4.2* Whole system model of integrated care

### Immediate care

At the 'sharp end' of the care continuum, people need practical help to deal with immediate life problems. *Immediate care* aims to do exactly what it says – focusing on helping people discover or create solutions to their immediate problems. When people experience the crises that require 'immediate care' they are often admitted to hospital, or to some other intensive therapeutic setting. The Tidal focus in such settings is to identify what 'needs to be done' to help people to return home, and to pick up their lives as best as they can. In that sense, immediate care is focused on solving the person's problems in the short term.

However, such crises can also be addressed and resolved as part of 'community care' without requiring admission to a residential facility. Much community care involves *anticipating*, *or* trying to *prevent* or *resolve* such crises. Immediate care might be required, therefore, as a response to an *initial* mental health crisis in the community (primary), when someone enters the mental health system for the first time (secondary), *or* when a crisis occurs in the life of someone who already is an established user of mental health services (tertiary).

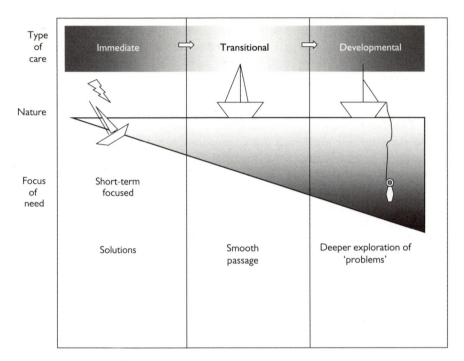

*Figure 4.3* The Tidal Model care continuum

In all three contexts, immediate care aims to develop solutions to the person's immediate problems, using the personal and interpersonal resources identified in the Holistic Assessment. This highly solution-oriented, short-term approach is supported, where appropriate, with a specific care plan – the *Security Plan*. This identifies what needs to happen to ensure the person's physical and emotional security, and to offset any risk of harm coming to the person or others.

### Developmental care

At the other end of the continuum, people may need to develop further their understanding of the nature and function of their problems. Alternatively, they might need to develop their ability to address, resolve or simply live with such problems. Here the person needs *developmental care*. People at this end of the continuum may be receiving follow-up care at home after a stay in hospital, or they may be receiving longer term support, either at home or in residential care, as part of an ongoing programme of rehabilitation. Developmental care focuses, therefore, on more intensive and long-term support or therapeutic intervention.

Where people require developmental care, emphasis is given to helping them develop ways of dealing with *potential* life problems, which may emerge in the medium to longer term. Developmental care may also involve the offer of a sustained period of support, either by an identified professional or team, or by a team working with community-based support groups.

### Transitional care

Where preparations are being made to admit someone to hospital, or to discharge a person home from hospital, or into another form of care, *transitional care* is indicated. Being admitted to hospital or moving from working with one therapeutic team or therapist to another can be traumatic. Transitional care aims to ensure that the person experiences the smoothest possible passage (or transition) from one setting to the other.

It is important also to ensure that all the necessary information about the nature of the care being offered *and* the kind of care expected is passed from one care setting to another. In managing transitional care it is important to ensure that appropriate liaison between all the relevant members of the inter-disciplinary team takes place, and that the person is involved, as much as is possible, in making the *arrangements* for this transfer of care. Although teamwork is vital to all three levels of care, when the person is making the journey from one care setting to another the need for liaison and communication between all parties – including the person and the family members – is essential.

## The content of care

The kind of care that the person needs is determined largely by the person's location on the care continuum. When people first enter the mental health system, usually they will be assessed for *immediate care*: focused on offering the simplest form of support necessary to help 'turn the person around', so that the person might return to the wider 'ocean of experience' of everyday life.

Immediate care is focused on identifying solutions to the person's immediate problems, using the personal and interpersonal resources identified in the Holistic Assessment. This is supported – where appropriate – by the development of the Security Plan, which identifies what needs to happen to ensure the person's physical and emotional security, and to offset any risk of harm coming to the person or any others.

When the person requires *developmental care*, emphasis is given to helping the person develop ways of dealing with problems of living in the medium to longer term. This help may come in various forms – a rehabilitation programme, discrete counselling or psychotherapy. Developmental care invariably involves the provision of more sustained support. This will likely involve an identified professional (keyworker) or team, alongside various family or community supports necessary to generalise the programme of developmental care to the wider sphere of 'everyday life'.

When the person needs *transitional care*, effective and efficient teamwork is essential to ensure that people are supported appropriately as they move between the 'active' components of the care programme. Figure 4.4 illustrates the process of care for people passing through, or re-entering the service.

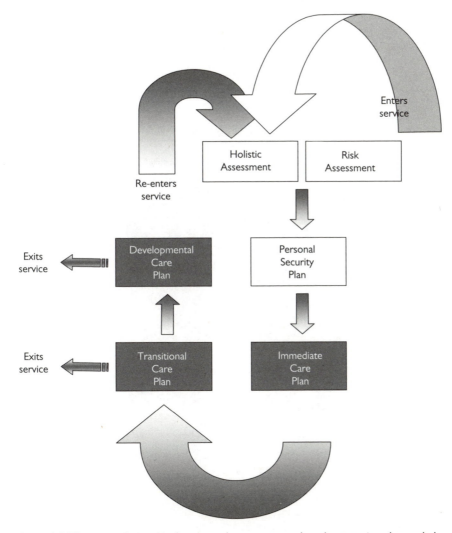

*Figure 4.4* The interrelationship between the core care plan, the security plan and the multidisciplinary team

### The structure of care

Figure 4.5 illustrates the interrelationship between the core care plan, the Security Plan and the multidisciplinary team.

The person lies at the heart of the care structure. The Core Care Plan is based on the Holistic Assessment in the World Domain. This focuses on trying to meet the needs of the person, as seen by the person. The Security Plan is developed from the various Risk Assessments conducted in the Self Domain. This focuses on what the person (supported by the team) needs to do to nurture a degree of emotional and physical security. Both these care plans lie *within* the Others Domain, and are coordinated within the work of the *interdisciplinary team*, where the contributions of different team help support the Core Care and Security Plans.

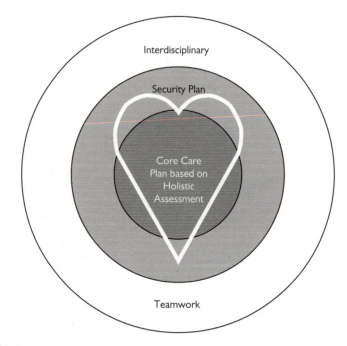

*Figure 4.5* The structure of care

# Chapter 5

# A map of the territory

An actual journey is one thing; a map is something else. A map is a metaphor that can point to but not capture the journey itself. A map is *seen through*; the journey is *lived through*.

(Ron DiSanto)

## Seamless care

### The story, the cast and the locations

The experience of mental distress is a drama. Indeed, one cannot imagine any more dramatic turn of events than the prospect or experience of losing one's mind. No wonder that Shakespeare included so many illustrations of madness in his plays. Similarly, the organisation and delivery of mental health services are part of that drama. Although there is considerable investment in the idea that mental health care can, in some way, be scientific, it is far more like drama and literature. The experience of madness and our attempts to respond to the distress of madness, whether as professionals, family or friends, are invariably full of 'high drama'.

The person's whole lived experience – the story – lies at the heart of this unfolding drama and is channelled through three distinct but interrelated domains – *Self*, *World* and *Others*. These represent dimensions of the person's overall relationship to the theatre of experience. These are the metaphorical settings for the action of the person's story:

- Through the *Self Domain* we relate to our innermost 'selves', processing all the intangible feelings contained in or generated from the evolving story of our lives. This is where we *feel* the story of our lives.
- Through the *World Domain* we relate to the evolving story itself as authors – editing and amending the script of the play as it develops. This is where we *think* and *reflect on* the story of our lives.
- Through the *Others Domain* we relate to all those who make up the cast

of our life story, whether key actors or 'bit players' on the wider stage of our lives. This is where we *enact* the story of our lives.

A *domain* is a metaphorical place, which is 'under the rule' of the person and which doubles as the location for the working relationship with the helper.[1] At this living location both the person and the professional helper use the domain as a 'sphere of control or influence'. Both bring their respective powers of control and influence to bear by collaborating in the examination of the problems of living; determining 'what needs to be done' and following this through with the discrete, negotiated, plan of care.

These three domains are representations of the *separate* yet *interconnected* dimensions of the person's life, all of which represent the key influences on the person's presentation (see Figure 5.1). The vital element that a person brings to the therapeutic arena is, of course, the whole lived experience. This embraces all the dynamic exchanges, both past and present, between the *Self*, *World* and *Others* domains. In terms of the unfolding drama of the person's mental distress, and the professional responses to that distress, the person's story is the core of the therapeutic script.

The helper seeks to understand better the influences that are being exerted on the person from within each of these domains; how these relate to the person's specific problems of living; and how interventions from within each domain might be beneficial for the person.

The needs of the person may change dramatically from moment to moment across the three domains. Consequently, the Tidal Model emphasises the need to identify what requires doing to address the person's needs *immediately* at each of the domains, *and* to continue *monitoring* carefully the extent to which

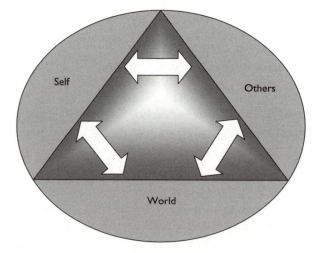

*Figure 5.1* The three domains of the Tidal Model

these needs are being met *or* are changing. Given the assumption that they are inextricably interlinked, the Tidal Model emphasises that all offers of professional help should *flow* smoothly across the three domains, attempting to ensure the development of truly *seamless* form of *care* for the person.

## The Self Domain

The Self Domain represents the most private aspect of the person. This is the emotional hinterland, from which people view the action of their stories as they develop within the World Domain. The Self Domain is the place where people feel their lives in progress. Much of this experience is beyond words (or perhaps pre-linguistic) but can be expressed through metaphors, similes or 'feeling talk'. The crisis, which brought the person into contact with the mental health services in the first place, makes its mark in the Self Domain. Here, people feel the effects of the problem of living, and become aware of the threat that it poses to their identity, self-worth or well-being in general. In practical terms the Self Domain is the place where the person needs the most sensitive support. The helper aims to facilitate the conditions that might represent the safe haven that the person needs to begin the necessary repair work on the story of her or his life.

The practical work of the professional team within the Self Domain is focused on facilitating a sense of *security* – both physical and emotional – through the development of a *Security Plan*. This focuses on nurturing the person's sense of security in very practical terms; defining the role of the person *and* others in facilitating this state.

## The World Domain

In the World Domain we explore the functional nature of the problems of living, which have brought the person to the attention of the mental health services. The Holistic Assessment provides a basis for charting the person's appreciation of what is happening *now* within the 'world of experience', and how this relates to memories of past events. The Holistic Assessment is used to generate a précis of the person's story, or narrative. This will chart the dimensions of the problem(s) that have, metaphorically, been 'washed ashore' with the person. The story generated through the Holistic Assessment includes:

- historical origins and related emotional context
- emotional and functional changes over time
- effects on relationships and current feelings
- personal meanings related to the problem
- expectations of the care that might be needed in the short term.

The Holistic Assessment also includes an evaluation of the person's level of distress and disturbance experienced, and the degree to which the person believes that (s)he can control the problem. In the final phase of the assessment, the person charts the resources – social, physical and spiritual – that may help to form part of the resolution of the problem.

Although much has been written about the perceived need for *holistic* mental health care, there are few examples of how this might be achieved in practice. The Holistic Assessment offers a theoretically supported, flexible template for setting the person's problems into a genuine 'real-life' context.

## The Others Domain

The Others Domain deals with the person's relationship with the social world, especially through the members of the interdisciplinary team, but also giving consideration to the wider sphere of social influence – family and friends among others. The professional team is responsible for synthesising the social, psychological and medical issues, which might comprise an effective care programme. This aims to support the person's recovery from their present crisis and to begin the reclamation process necessary for genuine mental health. Although the person plays an important part in this process, there are discrete responsibilities for coordinating areas of support such as housing, finances, medical services and after-care. All aspects of these actual or potential services and supports are negotiated with the person.

The Tidal Model assumes that the person's mental distress has emerged as a *function* of life experience in the world of the natural community. Consequently, the process of care aims to address the problems that have brought the person into contact with the services, and to craft the seamless connection, through *transitional care*, to ongoing *developmental care*, or full discharge from the service. The Tidal Model emphasises the fluid, ever-changing nature of *human* experience. More specifically, the model emphasises the deeply personal, if not actually spiritual meanings, which people attach to serious mental distress (Barker *et al.* 1999a; Barker and Buchanan-Barker 2003c) and which are invariably part and parcel of the everyday lived experience of the person.

The Tidal Model locates the person at the core of these interconnected processes, which play different roles in the assessment and care planning process. The Tidal Model assumes that professional staff will care *about* people in mental distress, acknowledging their core humanity and, when appropriate, will care *for* people; helping them to fulfil personal and interpersonal activities that they are unable to fulfil unaided. However, the Tidal Model gives special emphasis to the need for professional staff to care *with* the person, developing a constructive, collaborative dialogue of care (Barker and Whitehill 1997).

# Chapter 6

# The Self Domain

## The need for emotional security

People often say that this or that person has not yet found himself. But the self is not something one finds; it is something one creates.

(Thomas S. Szasz)

## The Self System

### Me, myself and I

Most people talk comfortably about 'the self', at least within western society. Usually this is framed in various vernacular forms of personal address: 'I would have done it *myself*', but I felt so *self-conscious*'. English dictionaries list around two hundred forms of *self*-function, from self-*abandonment* to self-*worth*. These all relate in differing ways to the use of relationship to or with, or assumptions about, the assumed *essence* or fundamental individuality of a person. Increasingly, such self-references are used throughout the world, as western society exerts even more influence.

As a simple colloquialism, the identification of *my* self serves to distinguish me from *your* self or *her* or *his* self. It helps draw a defining line between 'me' and everything else that relates to 'me'. However, whether or not this casual use of the concept of 'self' is the same as the idea of 'me' or 'I' or 'The Self' – which becomes the focus of mental distress – is rarely clear. Although we may understand what we mean when we use the expression, usually only the professional philosopher attempts to separate out 'me' from 'myself' and 'I'.

The idea of the singular Self is, as previously noted, a predominantly western and Eurocentric perspective on being human. Our direct experience of Japan and the indigenous peoples of Aotearoa (New Zealand) reveal very different appreciations of the person (Spiro 1993). Within such cultures the notion of individuality is no different from that of the west. Of course everyone *is* an individual, how could they be otherwise? However, in the west people have become, increasingly wrapped up in them*selves*, imprisoned by the cult of individualism that so prizes the unique individuality of experience.

By contrast, in more traditional cultures the individual self is often power-fully linked with the extended family and community. For example, if some-one within a Maori community is insulted, the insult is experienced, through a ripple effect, by the extended family (Ames 1994; Smith 1981). The *individual* is not quite as interpersonally isolated here as in the west.

In effect, the *personal* and the *communal* self are on a human continuum, where one inevitably impacts on the other. In Japan if someone behaves badly this brings great shame on the family and community to which the person belongs. This explains, in some way, how suicide is still viewed as a dignified way of dealing with shame in Japanese society. It is the supreme act of atonement. Although Japanese society has become increasingly westernised since the end of the Second World War, the differences in the construction of personal identity remind us that a great gulf still exists between Japan and its new social mentor (Doi 1986). This reminds us also that ideas about 'selfhood' are not only culture bound, but are also subject to change over time.

In the western world ideas about the self and its psychological offspring – personality – are clearly linked strongly to culture. However, the fickle and changing nature of western society means that notions of 'who' and 'what' we are are also subject to change. As children, we recognise that we have private thoughts and can hold private conversations 'inside our heads', con-versations with our 'selves'. This gives rise to the idea that 'the self' inhabits this private space; what Gilbert Ryle (1949) famously called 'the ghost in the machine'. As we grow into adulthood, the nature of these private conversa-tions is increasingly influenced by the social world, leading many philo-sophers to argue that the Self does not stand alone, but is a function of our social context (Hanson 1986; Richards 1989). Indeed, the idea that we 'possess' a secret inner core may be pure fantasy. However, imagination does play an important part in 'making up' (or constructing) the self and the power of imagination is vital to the world of mental distress and mental health recovery. People can and do *imagine* themselves as weak, defective, broken or beleaguered by various problems of living. The effect of such imaginings is to generate (or construct) a damaged or defective Self, or, as Goffman usefully described it, a 'spoiled identity' (Goffman 1986). The pro-cess of recovery and reclamation within the Tidal Model involves using the power of imagination to reconstruct this notion of the Self, or to build a quite different appreciation of 'who' and 'what' we are, as persons.

### The centre of narrative gravity

Who and what we are is a story and the Self lies at the heart of that story. However, the Self is an abstract idea. It has no form or mass, but has con-siderable effect in our lives. The Self is the centre of gravity of the story of our lives. If the Self is 'centred' or 'in balance' at the focal point of our personal existence, then we perceive ourselves to be 'balanced' and 'focused'.

This view of the Self finds support in contemporary neuroscience (Dennet 1992) but is merely an echo of a much older folk wisdom about the state of being human. In everyday parlance, people talk about being 'unbalanced', 'out of kilter', or needing to 'get focused', suggesting the power of influence stemming from this invisible self-centre. Such expressions suggest that people do know 'what' is the Self and 'how' it functions in their lives, even if they find it hard to express this other than through metaphor.

Although generalisations can be unhelpful, people who find themselves in need of any kind of mental health service often experience what might be called a 'crisis of the self'. Their inner core is very much 'out of kilter', generating various expressions of this unsettled state of affairs. They experience a literal *dis-ease*. The notion of 'mental distress' has become an increasingly popular euphemism for mental *illness* or *disorder* and locates the disturbance and its effects within the person's mental state, which is yet another abstraction. Arguably, everyone who becomes mentally distressed experiences some kind of threat to their 'selfhood'. This may range from experiences that are assumed to lie 'within' the person, such as feelings of worthlessness or hopelessness, or persecutory voices, to the experienced effects of the person's encounter with the world 'outside', interpersonal discord, stigma, discrimination or abuse.

The focus of any assessment and subsequent caring intervention within the *Self Domain* is to identify all possible threats to the person's emotional and physical security and to take the caring action necessary to minimise them. All such actions need to involve a collaborative endeavour between the person and people from the *Others Domain* – family, friends and members of the therapeutic team. Assessment – in the very broadest of senses – is necessary to help identify the form, function and influencing factors related to these threats to the person's sense of emotional and physical security. In contemporary practice these are often referred to as forms of 'Risk Assessment'. However, all too often the importance of the narrative and its invisible yet critical centre of gravity are ignored.

### The need for emotional security

It is taken as read that the physical safety of the person is of paramount importance. Nurses, in particular, often focus much of their efforts on safeguarding the person and making the environment safe for everyone concerned, not just the clientele. Nursing care plans invariably feature nursing actions aimed at reducing (for example) the risk of falling in frail people; or the risk of physical ill-health in the case of people who appear unable or unwilling to address their physical needs. In mental health care much emphasis is given to people who may present a risk to themselves through some act of self-harm or suicide; or to others through some act of violence or aggression. In addition to these *intentional* acts, people may also represent a risk to themselves through failing to take adequate care of themselves physically (self-neglect) and may also represent an unintentional hazard to others. Consequently, the care needed within the Self Domain must be based on a careful consideration of the person's needs, within the context of the person's present environment.

Regrettably, much 'Risk Assessment' is driven by a fear of litigation, or a professional or institutional obligation to abide by specific legislative requirements; what the behaviourists called negative reinforcement (Beck 1992). All too often the person gets lost in the paperwork, which is aimed at people in general but may fail to address this person in particular. The vogue for using standardised 'suicide risk assessments' or 'violence and aggression checklists' are but two examples of this unfortunate, although given the political climate, understandable shift in organisational priorities (see Ryan 1999).

Within the Self Domain emphasis is given to assessing the need for security across all possible areas of risk, and to identifying the part which the person (and significant others) might play in reducing the risk, as well as the role of the professional team members in attempting to offset any such risks to the person's emotional and physical security. Here, we profile briefly the four main forms of risk that are associated with the Self Domain:

- suicide
- self-harm
- self-neglect
- risk to others.

We shall consider briefly the key psychosocial factors associated with each of these in an effort to set them in some kind of context. We conclude this chapter with a consideration of how we approach the assessment of such risks to the Self, and how we might begin to establish the process of engagement, which will lead to the development of the Personal Security Plan.

---

In the next chapter suicide is examined in depth. However, in general the approach to the process of assessment, engagement and care planning is similar for all four forms of risk.

---

## Addressing risks to self

### The risk of suicide

Traditionally, suicide has been associated with mental illness, in particular diagnoses of depression and schizophrenia. However, more recent evidence suggests that many people who commit suicide have no formal diagnosis of any form of mental illness. Instead, there is much evidence to suggest that a wide range of factors may be involved in the precipitation of suicide. Specific forms of mental distress – such as diagnoses of schizophrenia or clinical depression – may only be part of a more complex picture (Hall *et al.* 1999; Harkavy-Friedman and Nelson 1997; O'Connor and Sheehy 2000).

However, five key factors have been associated with high risk of suicide in people who carry a diagnosis of *depression*:

- men
- under 35 or over 65 years of age
- single
- separated, divorced or socially isolated
- history of serious self-harm with insomnia, self-neglect or agitation.

Among the factors more *generally* associated with the risk of suicide are:

- a history of serious self-harm
- current serious drug or alcohol misuse
- recent experience of a major life event, e.g. divorce, separation
- member of a 'high risk' occupational group, e.g. farmer, doctor, unemployed
- current evidence of unwillingness to accept care or treatment
- presence of a life-threatening illness
- poor relationship with carers
- the period following *admission* to a psychiatric care setting, especially in first week
- the period following *discharge* from a psychiatric setting, especially during first month.

It seems likely that suicide or fatal self-harm occurs when several of these factors combine to produce life circumstances that seriously challenge the available resources of the person. Any assessment of suicide risk should aim to understand the possible role played by these and other psychosocial factors in the creation of the kind of life circumstances that make suicide *possible*, if not actually probable (Barker 1997b; O'Connor and Sheehy 2000).

---

In Chapter 7 we describe in detail the use of the *Nurse's Global Assessment of Suicide Risk* (NGASR). This provides a template for identifying the possible influence of 15 psychosocial factors that hold specific significance for the assessment of suicide risk.

---

### The risk of self-harm

Although a wide range of actions might result in self-harm, from excessive drinking and smoking to self-poisoning, self-harm is generally considered to be an action, performed intentionally, in an attempt to reduce or manage the experience of mental distress. (Perhaps this is why it has traditionally been referred to as 'Deliberate Self Harm', although the use of the expression 'deliberate' suggests some moral censure.) By contrast, suicidal acts (such as drug overdose) represent an attempt to bring such distress to a final conclusion. Usually self-harm involves cutting, burning, scratching or scraping the skin or deeper tissue; tying ligatures around parts of the body; or inserting objects into the body or body orifices, with the result that varying degrees of injury are incurred but, at an experiential level, some release from psychic pain is experienced. The extensive publications and self-reports by people who engage in self-harm suggest that, despite its appearance, paradoxically much self-harm acts as a means of coping with distress. However, it should be remembered that a sizeable proportion of people who engage in repeated self-harm will eventually commit suicide by other means. Several key factors are associated with self-harm, which occurs predominantly but not exclusively in:

- women
- younger people (under 30).

Self-harm *may* be a function of:

- past trauma (especially childhood emotional, sexual and physical abuse)
- current stress
- social isolation.

It may also be associated with people who have been attributed a diagnosis of:

- depression
- personality disorder
- psychosis.

Two issues concerning self-harm are worthy of particular emphasis:

1   The distinction between the 'self-mutilation', which may be performed by some people as a function of 'voices' in psychosis, and the 'self-harm' performed by people with a diagnosis of 'personality disorder' who may also hear 'voices' can be very subtle. However, careful assessment may show that the person who self-mutilates as a function of psychosis may be 'following orders' from one or more 'voices', whereas the self-harming person may engage in this behaviour as a way of managing

psychic distress. However, such clear-cut distinctions do not always apply in everyday clinical practice.

2    People who engage in repeated self-harm are likely to experience great private anguish, usually expressed as self-loathing. The assessment and care of such people need to be extremely sensitive and supportive. Regrettably there is much evidence of callous management of such people, due largely to the social taboo surrounding self-harm and professionals' inability to deal with the strong emotions that can arise when working with people with such a serious problem with the self. It is not enough simply to assert that staff *should* be non-judgemental. Rather, staff experiencing emotional problems related to working with a self-harming person need sophisticated individual or group supervision to help them examine and begin to understand their feelings towards such individuals.

### The risk of self-neglect

A wide range of people may be at risk of self-neglect. This may be associated with the influence of some other psychiatric problem, such as impaired cognitive functioning associated with dementia, but may also be a function of social deterioration due to various factors from social isolation to the long-term consequences of institutional care (Alberg *et al.* 1996).

> Although people with eating disorders – either anorexia or bulimia – might be viewed as at risk of neglect, they are not considered here, given that the eating disorder is the primary focus of the care programme.

Self-neglect occurs mainly, but not exclusively in:

- older people (especially men)
- people with intellectual or cognitive impairment.

It may also be associated with people who have been attributed a diagnosis of:

- schizophrenia
- depression
- mania
- alcohol or drug misuse
- dementia
- confusional states.

It may be a delayed function of:

- poor adjustment to, or management of mental ill-health
- response to trauma.

Self-neglect is a broad concept and would include the following:

- failure to maintain an adequate diet, risking malnutrition if not starvation
- failure to maintain an adequate fluid intake, risking dehydration
- failure to maintain personal hygiene, risking (e.g.) infection and tooth decay
- failure to take adequate exercise and/or rest
- inability to discriminate environmental hazards, e.g. risk of poisoning, combustion, drowning.

Most people take for granted the amount of preparation, effort and concentration required to organise and deliver even basic 'self-care'. When a person is experiencing severe mental distress or has even a minor cognitive impairment (or experiences both), the demands of self-care either may be beyond the person's present capacity or may no longer be an everyday priority. If we can begin to appreciate the debilitating effect of mental distress, we might begin to appreciate the person's need for genuine care.

### The risk to others

Although the presentation of a 'risk to others' may not present a direct threat to the welfare or well-being of the person in care, the indirect effect on the person will soon become apparent through loss of liberty, enforced psychiatric treatment or both. However, in our view the risks that individuals pose to other people are invariably a function of the person's relationship with Self. People who are hostile, belligerent or violent are, quite rightly, identified as presenting a threat to others. However, this threat may be a displacement of the threat, which the person feels, rightly or wrongly, is directed at her or his own Self.

As with other forms of risk assessment, the key aim is to establish to what extent the person poses a risk at present and in the immediate future. As with other forms of risk, evidence of past behaviour (violent or aggressive acts) represents a key factor in identifying the likelihood that the person might behave similarly in the future. However, to be able to make such an educated guess it is necessary to understand the context within which the violence or aggression occurred. This includes not only environmental factors but also what was 'going on' within the person at the time. The main factors associated with the risk of *violence* to others are as follows. It occurs mainly, but not exclusively, in:

- younger men
- people from socially deprived backgrounds
- people with unstable living arrangements
- people with unstable employment or who are unemployed.

It is associated with *diagnoses* of:

- alcohol or drug misuse
- paranoid psychosis
- manic depression
- schizophrenia
- psychotic depression.

Other factors that may be important are:

- evidence of an acute psychosis
- angry temperament
- past history of violence
- refusal to accept offers of care and/or treatment
- loss of family support
- breakdown of personal relationships
- clear declarations of violent intent
- expressions of violent attitudes (aggression and hostility).

> The scale of the risk of violence and aggression within mental health settings has been greatly exaggerated by political concerns about public safety. However, there is evidence of a growing trend in violence, which may reflect the levels of violence in society at large. Consequently there is a need to assess the risk of violence and aggression relating not only to the potential harm that might befall other people in care or the general public, but also their own safety.

## Minimising threats to the self

### The nature of the caring for the self

Caring for people who are experiencing any form of mental distress is an interpersonal process (Barker 1998c). The key therapeutic tool at our disposal is our *selves* (Travelbee 1971). However, we live in an increasingly materialistic age where not only the putative *causes* of mental distress but also the form of its resolution are assumed to be physical in nature. All too often emotional distress is assumed to arise from some biological basis and, as such, requires to be treated with drugs. However, the evidence of both research and routine clinical experience tells another story. Although human distress is clearly processed biologically, people – their actions, presence and personality – have a powerful invisible effect on how other people think, feel and ultimately behave. Over a half century ago, Hilda Peplau reminded nurses that their key responsibility was not to treat, cure or otherwise 'fix' people, but to help the people in their care get an 'education'. Among other things, Peplau believed that nursing was: 'a maturing force and an educative instrument. By means of effective nursing, individuals and communities can be aided to use their capacities to bring about changes that influence living in desirable ways' (Peplau 1952: 16).

In effect, *nursing*, whether delivered by professional nurses or by lay people, is focused on helping the person in care to grow (or mature) through the experience of distress, and all the associated problems of living which it might entail. The process of caring is focused not so much on eradicating distress as on helping people find out how they might overcome their distress themselves; or how they might enlist the support of others in attempting to address this psychic intrusion into their lives.

When people are experiencing any of the 'risks to self' noted above, they need the kind of *care* that puts emotional and physical security at the centre stage of the caring process. The Self is the centre of gravity of the person's emerging life story or narrative. When the person begins to experience any of the 'crises of the Self' associated with mental distress, they experience a disturbance of that 'centre of gravity'. They begin to go 'out of kilter' or start to 'lose focus' and rapidly experience the limits of their capacity for living, or at least for tolerating the stresses and strains associated with living. In such circumstances, nursing is involved in helping people to draw out from within themselves an appreciation of deeper layers of human capacity, which they might use to address the problems that brought them to the brink of suicide in the first place. This is what Peplau meant by nursing being an 'educative instrument'. Nursing helps people to 'draw out from within' (*educere*) themselves an appreciation of their human resources.

This process helps people continue their human development. By helping the person to appreciate further the nature of their life problems, and how these affect them emotionally and spiritually, we can help people to understand better the meaning of their human distress. As Frankl noted, the awareness of such meanings lies at the heart of all genuine human development (Frankl 1959). We believe that this is at least one aspect of what Peplau meant when she said that nursing was a 'maturing force'.

The proper focus of all of our responses to people who are 'at risk' is to establish what needs to be done to address this risk. Often, what needs to be done will be fairly simple: providing emotional support, listening, helping the person to express and clarify what they need to do to address these life problems. At other times, what might need doing will be more complex. However, this is always an ongoing, developmental process. What needs doing now is only one step towards identifying what needs doing next.

# Chapter 7

# The assessment of suicide risk

A pessimist sees the difficulty in every opportunity; an optimist sees the opportunity in every difficulty.

(Churchill)

## Why should people want to kill themselves?

A huge suicide research literature has developed over the past one hundred years, drawing on psychology, philosophy, medicine, sociology and literature (Alvarez 1970; Masaryk 1970; Morgan 1993). Despite our increased awareness of the factors that appear to influence suicide, deciding whether or not people intend to kill themselves remains extremely difficult. Knowing *why* they might wish to commit suicide is often beyond our comprehension.

Generalisations never help us understand the specific context of the individual, but by providing us with the 'bigger picture' they help us to locate the individual within a global context. There appear to be five main reasons why people *decide* to kill themselves. (We exclude people who have not obviously chosen death, i.e. those who appear to kill themselves without obviously intending to do so. We shall comment later on such 'accidental deaths'.) These general groupings are:

1   *People who wish to escape from despair*. Some such people might be described as 'suffering' from depression. However, others might experience the classic 'existential despair', which differs markedly from the state that psychiatry defines as depression.
2   *People who wish to escape from pain or the further deterioration of the body*. Chronic insomnia, chronic physical pain, multiple sclerosis or the early stages of dementia are all 'painful' in differing ways. Clearly, some people choose not to continue to experience such suffering, or wish to avoid its worsening.
3   *People who wish to transcend life*. This ranges from people who believe that they will be reunited with dead loved ones in the 'next world', or will

be transported, through self-sacrifice, to some heaven or starship waiting to take them to another planet.

4    *People who are 'following orders'.* Classically, such people are defined as 'delusional' because they say that God, the devil or some deceased relative or friend has 'instructed' them to kill themselves.

5    *People who wish to save others by sacrificing themselves.* History is replete with examples of such 'altruistic' suicides – from Captain Oates who walked into the snow saying 'I am just going outside, and may be some time', to the contemporary 'suicide bomber'. Both believe that some greater good might emerge from their self-sacrifice.

Although the rationales differ, the common feature is that the person *acts* in such a way as to bring about his or her own death. Szasz (1999) reminded us that the term suicide is a relatively recent expression, little more than three hundred years old. From the ancient world up to the Enlightenment, it was self-evident that the taking of life, whether one's own or others', was a deliberate voluntary act and was referred to as such – self-killing or self-murder.

### The need for understanding

Today, the conflation of 'mental illness' with 'suicide' – representing a *happening* (noun) rather than an *act* (verb) – encourages the view that people are not responsible for their own death. We take the view that suicide is fundamentally self-killing, unless it is accidental, which by implication is not suicide at all. The all too common rush to judge the suicidal person is clearly unhelpful. Although grieving friends and relatives might be consoled by the thought that the 'illness was to blame' and the person did not 'mean' to take her or his own life, this appears to offer little by way of a real explanation. In July 2003, David Kelly, a senior official at the Ministry of Defence, committed suicide following an interview by the Commons Select Committee over 'leaking' information to the BBC concerning the war on Iraq. The dead man's family joined many in the media in arguing that his treatment 'in a bullying way by the Select Committee completely took away David's self-esteem and he was left with nothing. He was shattered, traumatised and devastated'. Aaronovitch (2003) observed that others might have experienced very little problem, far less committed suicide over such a difficult interview: 'Kelly was a complex and unpredictable human being who may well have had no idea of his own capacity for self slaughter' (p. 5). Indeed, we would suggest that this applies to us all. The 'inexplicable' nature of many suicides may simply illustrate how little we know of the private world of any suicidal person. Hence the importance of asking people directly about their experience.

However, when we are confronted by the apparent threat of suicide, it is vital to try to understand the *conditions* of the person's life that might have a bearing on such a decision. For whatever reason, the suicidal person believes that suicide offers something. What that might be may be beyond our immediate comprehension; hence the need to explore the person's context, in search of some understanding of her or his motives.

> That suicide may often be consistent with interest and with our duty to ourselves, no one can question ... I believe that no man ever threw away life, while it was worth keeping. (Hume 1992)

In effect, some single 'thing' – an experience, whether actual or imagined, or perhaps a catalogue of things, or an extensive experience of one particularly obnoxious thing – might result in the person forming the opinion that suicide is a 'good idea'; that something might be gained through the loss of one's own life, even if that is a negative gain, as in the release from distress. Those who are left behind, whether family, friends or even members of a professional team, frequently express bewilderment at the suicidal act: '(S)he had everything to live for!' Writing of Cesar Pavese, the Italian novelist and poet, Alvarez noted:

> One month before the end he received the Strega Prize, the supreme accolade for an Italian writer. 'I have never been so much alive as now,' he wrote, 'never so young.' A few days later he was dead.
>
> (Alvarez 1970: 127)

Alvarez speculated that the very sweetness of Pavese's creative powers had rendered his innate depression all the harder to bear, as if 'those strengths and rewards belonged to some inner part of him from which he felt irredeemably alienated' (Alvarez 1970: 127). For many, the 'last straw that broke the camel's back' may be the deciding factor or, as in Pavese's case, even success or good fortune might merely emphasise the sense of personal failing. Alvarez's classic text, *The Savage God*, is filled with vivid illustrations of the complex developmental story of the suicidal person; a story that needs to be told at length, and re-authored carefully, over time, if the risk of suicide is ever to be seriously addressed. Such careful exploration of the suicide story belongs within the 'developmental care' aspect of the Tidal Model. Our 'immediate care' responsibility is to open a dialogue with the suicidal person; one that might begin to address the deep emotional insecurities that make suicide more likely. Such a dialogue is the medium for the emotional rescue that forms the interpersonal basis for the development of the *Security Plan*.

## Assessing suicide risk

Generally speaking, evidence of a previous suicidal attempt is one of the best indicators that another suicidal attempt is possible, and an analysis of the circumstances surrounding the event may help to gauge the degree of the person's 'intent to die' (Beck *et al.* 1974). Various scales have been developed that appear useful in assessing the presence of suicidal thinking or hopelessness, both of which are often associated with suicide (e.g. Beck *et al.* 1974, 1989). These measure and predict the likelihood of self-harm, but appear only to *inform* the process of care, rather than predicting the likelihood of suicide in any absolute sense. In the light of our experience, the most profitable approach to assessing the risk of suicide is simply to *ask the person*. Two simple questions offer, arguably, the most powerful assessment (see box).

---

*Q.* Have you ever thought about killing yourself?
(If the answer is 'yes', the next question is):

*Q.* Would you tell me more about that?
(If the answer is 'no', the next question is):
*Q.* Why not?

---

More than anything else, the person who is suicidal needs an opportunity to talk about the motives for dying and the expected 'benefits'. These simple questions, which need to be asked at some point in the therapeutic conversation, are drawn from our appreciation of Viktor Frankl's work. Indeed, Frankl believed that these questions were probably the *only* questions that needed to be asked of the suicidal person:

- If the person answers 'yes', then the opportunity arises to have a thorough discussion of the whole context of the person's suicidal motivation: when and how often the person has contemplated suicide and what specific thoughts the person has had as to the 'how' of suicide as well as the reasons 'why'. Most importantly the person can be asked what (s)he thinks would be the 'gain' in suicide and who would be the 'losers'; and especially to what extent the person still believes in the suicidal rationale.
- If the person answers 'no' then the question 'why not?' should elicit the story of the person's anti-suicide philosophy. In our experience people most often say 'It is against my religion (or God would damn me)'; 'I couldn't do that to my family'; 'I haven't got the courage'; or 'I have thought about it but something just stops me'. This question provides an opportunity to open up a discussion about the virtue and value of continuing living, and the abstract power owned by the person that either

keeps him or her going through adversity, or which acts as a censor against self-killing.

Of course the person may elect to deceive us, denying thoughts of suicide when these have indeed been part of the person's experience. Such denials may deceive the novice, but usually the experienced professional will notice some subtle sign of discomfort – a sudden averting of eye contact, a shift in position indicative of 'discomfort', or a change in voice tone. In principle, the 'practised' liar would find no difficulty in deceiving even the most sophisticated professional. However, suicidal people are rarely 'practised liars' and often appear to welcome the opportunity to talk about the despair, hopelessness or self-blame that fuels their suicidal thoughts.

---

**NB** The most experienced member of the professional team should conduct the assessment of the person who is thought to be suicidal. Similarly, the care of the suicidal person should be offered by (or at least led by) a sophisticated professional who is not uncomfortable with addressing the difficult issues that lie behind the threat of suicide.

---

### Caring for the person during the assessment process

Providing appropriate care for people who may be suicidal or self-harming is a complex process, not least because the intent to commit suicide, or to self-harm, is usually covert. However, the emotional effect of caring for suicidal people is also significant (Busteed and Johnstone 1983). Traditionally, much of the responsibility for the care of suicidal people has fallen to nurses. It is increasingly recognised that nurses need many years of experience before they can effectively manage the stress involved in caring for the suicidal person (Barker and Cutcliffe 1999; Cutcliffe and Barker 2002). Traditionally, nurses have employed specific 'observation' procedures (Briggs 1974; Duffy 1995). However, only recently has the negative experience of being 'under observation' been studied (Fletcher 1999). There is increasing evidence that not only are nurses dissatisfied with the philosophy and practice of 'observation', but also the people who are 'observed' find the experience controlling, custodial and punitive (Cutcliffe and Barker 2002; Duffy 1995).

Clearly the nursing care of people at risk of self-harm or suicide, whether delivered by professional nurses, auxiliary staff or family and friends, needs to refocus on providing more manifest forms of support, rather than simply keeping the person out of harm's way. If such care is to develop its full therapeutic potential, then the person who is in receipt of the care needs to be fully cognisant of the decisions and actions of professional staff, and the staff members need to be aware of the powerful emotional dynamic that is generated in the actual caring process. Wherever possible, the emphasis of all such care needs to be on fostering the active collaboration of the person, in a search for solutions (however provisional) to the person's current distress. Once this has been established (the Security Plan) then it may be possible to begin the necessary 'developmental care' work needed to explore the deeper threats to the Self that lie within suicidal intent.

---

**NB** Although the care of suicidal people is often focused on care in hospital settings, similar challenges face professionals working in various community settings. The guidance notes that follow emphasise the kind of support appropriate in a hospital context, but the principles apply to caring for suicidal people in any situation.

---

## The dimensions of assessment

The assessment of suicide risk has three dimensions, which are interdependent and interactive (see Figure 7.1):

1   A focused *Suicide Risk Interview* is conducted, which attempts to establish a working relationship with the person. Within this interview attempts are made to understand more clearly, the thoughts, feelings, beliefs and immediate life circumstances of the person, which might

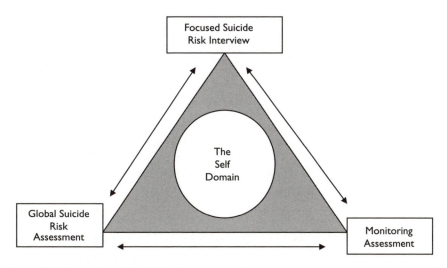

*Figure 7.1*  The process of suicide risk assessment

predispose to suicide. This assessment also attempts to identify what might be done immediately, or in the future, to help the person.

2   A *Global Assessment* is conducted in an attempt to judge the potential influence of a range of *psychosocial factors* on the person. This assessment contributes to a judgement of the appropriate level of *engagement* necessary to provide appropriate supportive care to the person. (The concept of bridging is described in Chapter 8.) This assessment (the *Nurse's Global Assessment of Suicide Risk, NGASR*)[1] requires input from various people who bring different perspectives on the person and her/his world of experience; e.g. medical background and social history, as well as current presentation.

3   An ongoing *Monitoring Assessment* attempts to evaluate the subtle changes in the person's experience, judging whether more or less care is required; and what *specifically* might need to be done to meet the person's needs. This assessment is the most collaborative aspect of the whole process, allowing both the person and the nurse to compare their views on progress and the 'need for care'.

All assessment needs to be carefully and sensitively conducted, but the first two stages of this assessment require very careful coordination, as each is interdependent on the others. Issues raised in the *Global Assessment* of psychosocial factors will have implications for the *focused interview*, and vice versa and issues from each of these will likely emerge in the *Monitoring Assessment*.

Although, it is useful to work from the *general* (the Global Assessment) to the *specific* (the focused interview), an exception may be indicated here. Since the primary aim is to establish a rapport with the person and to begin to appreciate what is 'happening' from the person's perspective, this is best achieved through a focused interview, which would be followed up by the completion of the Global Assessment. However, in some instances the professional team may decide that it is more appropriate to gain a general sense of the person's situation, through the Global Assessment, following this up with the interview.

---

It is inappropriate to make rules about the order of events in the assessment process. Rather, the team should make careful decisions based on their appreciation of how best to balance the needs of the person in care with the demands of the specific setting, and the needs of the professional team members within it.

---

The Suicide Risk Interview and the NGASR may be repeated, at appropriate intervals, to help evaluate changes in either the person's presentation or perception of her or his circumstances. The information from both these assessments provides a basis for deciding the kind of care needed by the person. Where the person is deemed in any way to be *at risk*, the Monitoring Assessment provides a vehicle for involving the person in exploring the changing need for care, day by day. As soon as possible following the completion of the first two assessments, the person is encouraged to begin to frame the basic elements of the *Security Plan*.

### Interdisciplinary teamwork

The three assessments will likely identify a wide range of issues – from the deeply private world of beliefs or memories, to social issues like redundancy or debt. If such issues appear to be significantly linked to the risk of suicide, then they should be addressed. However, decisions need to be taken regarding timing. If the person has been admitted to hospital, the focus of *immediate care* will be upon establishing and maintaining 'emotional security', and engaging the person as an active participant in the caring (and self-care) process. In most mental health care settings, much of the responsibility for organising this will fall to nurses. However, once the person appears to be moving along the care continuum towards the transitional and development care domains, increasing emphasis will need to be put on including community support – professionals as well as family and friends – in addressing the issues that might be relevant to preparation for discharge and return to the natural community.

## The Focused Suicide Risk Interview

The *Suicide Risk Interview* (see Figure 7.2) provides a framework for developing a compassionate relationship with the person.[2] The framework includes a core list of direct questions, which focus on the potential for serious self-harm and on identifying the kind of support that might be appropriate.

In preparation for addressing the issues raised in these questions, the interviewer should aim to:

1  Arrange a quiet setting without distractions.
2  Take as much time as necessary.
3  Develop rapport and trust from the outset.
4  Use simple language, respecting cultural, ethnic and religious background. The person's own language should be used, wherever possible, and the use of professional language and jargon avoided.
5  Open the interview with non-directive questions (open) that will allow the person to express feelings.
6  Follow the person's lead, addressing all of the issues raised.
7  Avoid appearing to challenge or judge anything that is said.
8  Appear sensitive, compassionate and genuinely interested.

## The Suicide Risk Interview

This interview aims to provide the person with an opportunity to access and reflect upon thoughts and feelings that might have a bearing upon her/his personal safety.

The questions here serve as a *guide* to the wording and sequence of the inquiry process. The interviewer should be prepared to rephrase these questions, so that they express genuine and compassionate curiosity. The interviewer should also provide supplementary questions, to help the person amplify answers and clarify meanings. The interviewer seeks to establish the extent to which the person harbours thoughts or feelings, which might contribute to serious self-harming or suicidal acts.

- **(Current emotional state)** Tell me about how things are for you now.
- **(Optimism/Pessimism)** Do you hope that your situation will improve, get better? (If so, how will that happen?)
- **(Pleasure)** Do you still gain pleasure from life? (How do you do that?)
- **(Hope)** Would you say that you are, generally, hopeful, from one day to the next?
- **(Motivation)** How do you feel about facing what each day brings?
- **(Meaning)** [If the person acknowledges distress] Do you see the point of your distress, or do you see the point of life in general?
- **(Desperation)** Have you ever felt desperate? (About what in particular?)
- **(Social burden)** Have you ever felt that you were a burden? (In what way and to whom?)
- **(Suicide)** Have you ever thought about killing yourself?
- (If 'yes' – tell me more – especially)
- How often do you have these thoughts?
- Do you think about how you would actually end your life?
- Have you ever made an attempt to kill yourself? (How did you do that?)
- (If suicidal thoughts are present) How do you resist acting on these thoughts? What do you do to control them?
- Do you think it is likely that you will kill yourself?
- (If person says they have 'never' thought of suicide) Why not?
- **(Death)** Have you ever wished that you were dead? (Tell me why you feel this way. In what way would 'being dead' be better than how things are for you now? Look for a *reason for wishing to be dead*).
- Have you ever wished that it would all end?
- What does that (all ending) mean for you?
- Have you ever felt it near impossible to face the next day? (What was it that you found so hard to face?)
- **(Harm to others)** Have you ever felt that you might harm someone else? When? Who? Why?
- **(Managing Risk)** To what extent should I (or others) be worried about your safety?
- How confident are you that you can keep yourself safe (state specific period of time)?
- How do you feel about asking for help when things get really bad?
- What kind of things makes life more difficult for you, right now?
- What might be helpful for you right now? What might help you feel a little better right now?

*Figure 7.2* The Suicide Risk Interview

9   Pay careful attention to what is said.
10   Encourage the person to repeat important issues by way of clarification.
11   Note any non-verbal behaviour that might suggest suicide risk.
12   Discuss recent events and evaluate their importance.

### Recording the interview

Wherever possible, a summary of the key points raised in the interview should be recorded with the agreement and support of the person.[3] If the person is distressed this may prove difficult, in which case the professional should acknowledge the gist of the interview and advise the person as to which aspects will be summarised in the record.

A concise summary should be entered in the person's care plan. This should detail the main points raised in the interview, providing the basis for a discussion about appropriate care by the rest of the team (see below). The details of the focused interview will also be integrated into the Nurse's Global Assessment of Suicide Risk (NGASR). The summary should emphasise the following points, *using direct quotes* wherever possible:

* general observations on how the person appeared to the interviewer
* overall sense of *hopelessness* or *hopefulness*
* expressions of *thoughts* of suicide or self-harm
* *reasons* for suicide (if present)
* indication of any *previous* suicidal or self-harm *attempts*
* personal and interpersonal *resources* for resisting suicide or self-harm
* *feelings* about seeking support
* possible forms of *immediate help*
* possible risk to *others*.

---

*Summary of Focused Suicide Risk Interview*
2.30 pm, 01.10.2003

Harry appeared very low. Speech limited and halting. Little eye contact. Hunched up in chair. Gains 'no pleasure at all' and 'can't see the point in anything any more'. Admits to feeling 'quite desperate at times'. Says that his 'time has come' and that he is 'being called to the Father'. Has not made any suicide attempts but does think about 'jumping off a bridge or something'. Presently, he 'prays for guidance' and 'generally doesn't feel up to it'. Thinks that 'nothing' will help him and we are 'wasting our time'. Would 'never' harm anyone else as it is 'not in my nature'. Says that he 'won't do anything just yet' but doesn't 'feel at all confident about that'. When asked about accepting help repeated: 'you are wasting your time on me'.

---

## The Global Assessment

### Overview

The unique experience of the person is set in a wider context with the completion of the *Global Assessment of Suicide Risk* (Figure 7.3). This seeks to identify the presence of specific psychosocial stressors that appear to be strongly associated with suicide (Cutcliffe 2003). Originally developed as a method for estimating the present level of risk of suicide or serious self-harm, the Global Assessment provides a practical means of establishing the level of *engagement* appropriate to the care of the individual. This bridging process is the primary means of supporting the suicidal person, providing the basis for the development of collaborative attempts to resolve the problems that make suicide more probable.

The Global Assessment is first completed as soon as possible after the person is admitted to crisis care, or after any indication of a serious crisis in the community. The assessment may be repeated at intervals to evaluate change in the person's circumstances and overall suicide risk status. The items in the assessment represent factors associated with suicide risk, which have been reported repeatedly in the research literature. The assessment is used initially to establish the levels of engagement. The higher the level of estimated risk, the higher is the required level of engagement. As the person begins to show evidence of improvement and lessening of risk, the level of engagement may be reduced, thereby allowing the person a greater degree of autonomy, as part of the rehabilitation process.

> **NB** Like other forms of actuarial assessment (where there is an attempt to 'calculate' risk) the *Global Assessment of Suicide Risk* offers no more than an indication. For this reason it should never be used as the sole form of assessment. The focused assessment (interview), the ongoing evaluation of the person (the Monitoring Assessment) and the opinions of other members of the clinical team need to be incorporated to form an overall assessment of the risk status.

### The necessary knowledge base

The Global Assessment of Suicide Risk can be completed in two discrete ways. It may be used as the basis for a structured interview with the person, or members of the interdisciplinary team may complete it. Our experience with

Name................................................. Date ...........................

Assessing Nurse ....................................... Signature.........................

☐ 1. Presence/influence of hopelessness [3]

☐ 2. Recent stressful event (e.g. chronic insomnia, financial worries, pending court action) [1]

☐ 3. Evidence of persecutory voices/beliefs [1]

☐ 4. Evidence of depression/loss of interest or pleasure [3]

☐ 5. Evidence of withdrawal [1]

☐ 6. Warning of suicide intent [1]

☐ 7. Evidence of plan to commit suicide [3]

☐ 8. Family history of serious psychiatric problems or suicide [1]

☐ 9. Recent bereavement or relationship breakdown [3]

☐ 10. History of psychosis [1]

☐ 11. Widow/widower [1]

☐ 12. Prior suicide attempt [3]

☐ 13. History of socio-economic deprivation [1]

☐ 14. History of alcohol of substance abuse [1]

☐ 15. Presence of terminal or seriously debilitating illness [1]

Total Score ☐

Level of Engagement ☐

Figure 7.3 Nurse's Global Assessment of Suicide Risk (NGASR)

the Global Assessment in various international Tidal Model projects, suggests that the latter is particularly useful, since it provides a forum for team members to discuss and review a wide body of information about the person's interpersonal and social context. Ideally, the person should participate in all discussions regarding the need for supportive care. However, each team must decide in advance whether or not it is appropriate to invite the person to participate in this assessment. The team's decision will be influenced by various factors, such as the person's capacity and motivation to participate in what might be a lengthy and involved *group* discussion, and the need for a professional discussion *in camera*, from which the appropriate professional response might be developed. Given the pressures on professional staff to be seen to *involve* the person in her/his own care and to make informed, independent professional judgements as to the kind of care that might be appropriate, the private completion of the Global Assessment, supplemented by the information from the focused interview, seems like a fitting compromise.

Ideally, the primary nurse or key worker, along with colleagues with access to the information needed, should complete the assessment. Given the range of medical, psychological, social and historical information required, a professional team that can comment intelligently on these aspects of the person's life is vital. If a formal team meeting cannot be convened, then the key worker should attempt to access the necessary information by contacting team members, by telephone if necessary.

---

**NB** Ideally, professionals should be able to bring information from a range of encounters with the person – from the formal encounter of the Focused Interview, through longstanding, more informal caring contacts, to the informal observation and conversation only possible in the milieu of the ward.

---

### Completing the Global Assessment of Suicide Risk

The influence of each item on the assessment should be considered carefully and then scored. In an interdisciplinary team setting, the team members should discuss the possible relevance of each item, drawing on their knowledge of the person's history and information collected in the focused interview. One team member, preferably the person's key worker, should manage the discussion with a view to gaining consensus.

Five of the items offer a weighted score of three, acknowledging their significance as a critical factor in suicide risk. The other ten items, which are less powerfully related to suicide risk, all carry one point. After completion, the total score, and the appropriate level of engagement indicated, are noted.

1 *Hopelessness* is highly correlated with suicide risk (Weisharr and Beck 1992; Young *et al.* 1994). Although often associated with depression, people with recurrent forms of mental or physical distress, personal or social problems, may develop a sense of hopelessness. This item may be rated independently (e.g. through the use of the Hopelessness Scale, Beck *et al.* 1974). Often, however, the extent of the person's hope for the future can be established through sensitive and careful interviewing. This item is normally scored from the information drawn from the *Focused Interview*. (If present = *3 points.*)

2 *Recent stressful events* create specific problems of living, which can deplete the person's coping resources (Khalkhali *et al.* 2001). These stressors may be social (e.g. discrimination, unemployment), interpersonal (e.g. relationship difficulties) or medical (such as chronic insomnia). Details of such events should be elicited from the *Focused Interview*, or from recent professional reports, especially from the social worker. (If present = *1 point.*)

3 *Persecutory voices or beliefs* may also contribute to a sense of powerlessness or hopelessness (Romme *et al.* 1992). Although not exclusively associated with psychosis, they may carry discrete messages about potential for self-harm. Details should be carefully elicited from the *Focused Interview* or the person's social and clinical history. (If present = *1 point.*)

4 *Depression and loss of interest or pleasure* are not only manifest in people with a formal diagnosis of depression, but may be evident in people with other severe forms of mental or physical distress (Barraclough *et al.* 1974). This item is completed from the *Focused Interview* and personal history. (If present = *3 points.*)

5 *Withdrawal* is often one of the first signs that the person is experiencing difficulty in maintaining the pattern of everyday living (Charlton *et al.* 1992). This may be evident in a change in the level of social interaction, more time being spent isolated from others. This item is completed from observations made within the ward milieu and from the reports of the person and significant others. (If present = *1 point.*)

6 *Any warning of suicidal intent* needs to be acknowledged, especially when made more than once (Morgan 1993). Many 'cries for help' go unnoticed and become suicides. However, such warnings may be positive, showing evidence of help seeking. This item is scored from details of the person's history, the *Focused Interview* and reports of the person and others. (If present = *1 point.*)

7 *Any evidence of a plan to commit suicide* represents a major risk factor, especially if the person sought to keep the plan secret (Motto *et al.* 1985). The person may have made an attempt to stockpile drugs, other materials or implements that might be used in a suicide attempt. This may have been noticed/discovered by family, friends or professionals. This item is

scored from the person's history, reports from significant others or from the *Focused Interview*. (If present = *3 points*.)

8   *A family history of serious psychiatric problems or suicide* is significant as the presence of this history may compound the person's sense of hopelessness (Powell *et al.* 2000). If significant family members have committed suicide or been unable to deal with psychiatric problems, they may serve as role models for the person's hopelessness. This item is scored from family history and social background. (If present = *1 point*.)

9   *A recent bereavement or relationship breakdown* represents a very significant risk factor (Fawcett *et al.* 1987). The person may experience recriminations over the loss, or may feel a sense of isolation, especially if the person was their primary source of human support. This item is scored from the family history or *Focused Interview*. (If present = *3 points*.)

10  *Where the person has a history of psychosis* the risk is slightly increased (Powell *et al.* 2000). Although not all people in psychosis experience suicidal or self-harm thoughts, the person's reasoning processes may be impaired, and there is also a risk of impulsive acts of self-harm. This item is scored from the *Focused Interview* and the history. (If present = *1 point*.)

11  *Where the person is a widow/widower* the risk is slightly increased, especially if the person does not appear to have adapted to the loss (Motto *et al.* 1985). This item should also include 'common law' and 'same sex' relationships. It is scored from the *Focused Interview*, medical and social history. (If present = *1 point*.)

12  *Any indication of a prior suicide attempt* represents a significant risk factor (Gunnell and Frankel 1994). This may be derived from the history or the *Focused Interview*. (If present = *3 points*.)

13  *The effects of poverty* are increasingly recognised as a factor in suicide. A history of *socio-economic deprivation* may be associated with long-term unemployment, financial difficulties or poor quality of life, all of which might engender hopelessness and add to the overall risk (Gunnell and Frankel 1994). This item is scored mainly from the social history. (If present = *1 point*.)

14  *A history of alcohol or substance abuse* is significant as some people appear to have used alcohol and drugs to acquire the courage to complete suicide (e.g. Hawton 1994). In others, sustained abuse of alcohol or certain drugs may impair judgement. This item is scored mainly from the medical and social history. (If present = *1 point*.)

15  *Some people with a terminal illness* consider suicide, either as a means of dealing with physical pain, or to deal with the prospect of further deterioration and loss (Hawton 1994). This item is scored mainly from the social and medical history. (If present = *1 point*.)

## Determining levels of engagement

The Global Assessment is used to determine the general kind of supportive care that the person needs in the first instance if the threat of suicide is to be averted. This supportive care is described as *engagement* and is defined in the next chapter. The higher the person's score on the Global Assessment, the greater is assumed to be the risk of suicide or serious self-harm. Consequently, the higher the score, the greater is the need for sustained engagement with the person.

---

**NB** The score on the Global Assessment is used to set the *initial* level of engagement. However, this score merely indicates the appropriate level of support necessary and may require adjusting in the light of new information or changes in the person's presentation.

---

Expert clinical nursing opinion[4] suggests that levels of engagement should be set as follows:

- Score 5 or less = Level 4
- Score 6 to 8 = Level 3
- Score 9 to 11 = Level 2
- Score 12 or more = Level 1.

The clinical team will be involved in monitoring the person's perceived need for support and level of risk daily, using the *Monitoring Assessment*. This assessment, which represents the third strand of the complete Suicide Assessment process, is used to gauge the need to increase or decrease the level of engagement. The Monitoring Assessment is described in Chapter 8.

# Bridging

## Engaging with the Self in crisis

When one thinks, 'Now I have touched the bottom of the sea–now I can go no deeper,' one goes deeper.

(Katherine Mansfield)

## Introduction

The assessment of risk is only the first stage of an ongoing process of action and evaluation. Risk assessment is part of the overall caring process. In that sense, it is the first action designed to reduce the likelihood of the person coming to harm. Whenever any risk to self or others is believed to be present, the professional team needs to adapt its caring relationship, to focus more specifically on what needs to be done to minimise this. In a more constructive sense, the team is beginning to think about the kind of support that might be needed to uphold the 'self in crisis'. How might the team members[1] nurture the conditions – physical, personal, interpersonal and social – that could comfort the person, or otherwise reduce the raging distress that threatens, metaphorically, to drown them?

Nursing involves engaging with people. Other disciplines such as medicine or psychology frequently channel their influence through other people, often through nurses. Nursing is, however, invariably a direct access discipline, focused on nurturing the growth of the person. However, the *effect* of nursing is indirect. The person changes not because of any direct influence from the nurse, but as a function of various changes in the nurse–person relationship and the environment, which are organised by the nurse.[2]

At least in hospital or residential settings, nurses have a responsibility for managing the physical and social environment, so that nursing cannot be done from a distance, but is implicitly an interpersonal encounter. Traditionally, nurses have been expected to 'observe' people in their care, reporting on the state or presentation of the patient to the supervising physician. However, to provide meaningful nurturance it is necessary to engage with the person. *Engagement* includes observation. It is not possible to engage a person in an interpersonal interaction without being in a position to make observations about what the person is doing or saying.[3] The primary aim of engagement is to identify:

- *how* the person is at any point in time
- *what* is the nature of the person's experience
- *how* the nurse (and others) should respond to provide the optimum conditions for meeting the person's need for security – both physical and emotional.

The nursing team identifies the appropriate level of engagement following a full consideration of the evidence that suggests that the person might be at risk of harming her or himself, either through direct action – like an act of self-harm or suicide – or poses some threat to the welfare of others. Usually, decisions concerning the appropriate level of engagement will be made at an interdisciplinary team meeting, following a review of all the available evidence.[4]

---

**NB** The deployment of the principles of engagement are most appropriate to the immediate care setting, where the person is in crisis and requires the intensive support of the professional team alongside family and friends. The guidance provided here illustrates the kind of interactions needed to support the Self in crisis. However, the general principles of engagement apply in any care setting, where the Self is in any way vulnerable or insecure.

---

## The process of engagement

### Engagement: A definition

There are four levels of engagement. These define the general supportive conditions within which more specific care is offered. When people are in residential care they will be in receipt of at least one level of engagement. As the person's needs change, the level of engagement will also change, allowing either more or less opportunities for direct caring contacts.

### Level I

The person who is deemed to represent a *very high risk* of suicide, self-harm, self-neglect or harm to others, clearly needs the fullest support possible from the professional team. This does not mean that a nurse, or other member of the therapeutic team, will be engaging *actively* with the person at all times.

However, this level emphasises that the person needs constant *access* to a nurse, or other professional, for support. This support might include the discussion of specific problems of living, engaging in other one-to-one or group activities, conversation or simply 'being with' the person. It should be taken as read that the ongoing support of someone deemed to represent such a risk, is a taxing and sophisticated professional responsibility.[5]

*Level 2*

The person who is deemed to represent a *high risk* requires regular support from the nursing team throughout the day and night. This means that some-one will contact the person on some regular, though not fixed schedule (for example, approximately every 15 minutes, varying between 10 and 20 minutes). The nurse will make a judgement of the appearance of the person. If the person appears in any way distressed, the nurse will ask how they are and if they need anything. Arrangements will be made, as appropriate, to attempt to meet the person's needs.

*Level 3*

The person who is deemed to be an *intermediate risk* will be engaged formally at least three times per day – morning, afternoon and evening – to establish their needs. The aim of these brief contacts is to remind the person that support is available, and to monitor the person's own management of the Personal Security Plan.

*Level 4*

The person who is deemed to be at *no apparent risk* should be engaged on a structured basis daily, in a one-to-one session, a group or a family meeting. This level of engagement is used to provide the active care required to address the person's specific need for nursing care, identified in the original and ongoing assessment.

---

**NB** People who are deemed to require levels of engagement 1, 2 and 3, will also receive level 4 engagement, which is the medium for one-to-one and group sessions. Where people are deemed to be 'at risk' in their own homes, their care will include a consideration of the support (engagement) available from family members and friends.

---

## Organisation of engagement

- Keyworkers, or primary nurses, will take responsibility for organising the delivery of care, on a daily basis.
- The appointed nurse-in-charge is responsible for ensuring that the delivery of all such care is coordinated.
- Individual nurses who undertake to engage with the person (across all levels) are responsible for recording any points of note deriving from the process of engagement, in the person's care plan.
- The nursing team will review the information emerging from the process of engagement daily, so that some summary report may be made for the benefit of other members of the interdisciplinary team.
- Each day people receiving engagement levels 1, 2 or 3, will be encouraged to complete the Monitoring Assessment, a copy of which will be entered in the person's care plan, and a copy made available for the person's own reference.

# The levels of engagement

Given that care is a creative process, and involves regular revision in the light of experience of the person, engagement cannot be defined *exactly*. However, some guidance can be offered as to how it should be organised and presented.

## Engagement level I

Where the person is deemed to be at a *very high risk* of coming to harm or causing harm to others, care is focused on providing the person with the highest level of support possible.

- The nurse responsible for the person's care should advise the person of the nursing team's view of their current state of vulnerability, discussing the team's rationale and listening to the person's view, especially if this is in any way in conflict with the team's view.[6]
- The nurse should advise the person about the general structure and organisation of her/his care over the next 24 hours (or until the next review of engagement is undertaken).
- The nurse should ask the person if they wish to ask any questions or comment.

In keeping with the principles of the Tidal Model, it is important that this process is collaborative. If the person appears to reject the need for this level of engagement, the nurse should acknowledge and note the person's views, as appropriate. An attempt should then be made to explain, perhaps with different examples, why the team members consider this to be the most appropriate form of care, at this time (see box).

---

**Example**

'I've been thinking about how you are doing. A few things that you have said suggest that you are feeling a bit vulnerable at present. For the time being I think that my colleagues and I should give you as much support as we can, to help you through this difficult patch. I'll arrange for either myself or one of the other nurses to be with you at all times, so that you can feel supported. We shall try not to be intrusive, but we want you to be able get help as and when you need it. We can help you talk things through or just help you get through the day. We'll meet together tomorrow to review how you have found this kind of support and how you are feeling in general. How do you feel about that?'

---

### Engagement level 2

Where the person is deemed to be at a *high risk* of coming to harm, or harming another, care is focused on providing the person with regular support throughout the day and night.

- The nurse responsible for the person's care should advise the person that the team believes they need regular support.
- The nurse should explain that someone will be in contact with the person regularly throughout the day, to ask how they are doing, and whether or not they need anything.
- The person should be advised that, wherever possible, the nurse will try to arrange for any specific needs to be met either then or at some later appointed time.
- The person should be advised that someone will also contact her or him regularly during the night, to ensure that (s)he is comfortable, or check if (s)he needs anything.
- The person should be asked if (s)he has any comments or questions.

The nurse will make visual contact with the person approximately every 15 minutes. If the nurse believes the person to be in distress or likely to be a cause of distress to others, the nurse will make contact with the person directly, to assess the situation further, establishing what action if any, is required. A note should be made as appropriate in the person's care record. The nurse should, however, make direct contact with the person *at least once*, in the morning, afternoon and evening, to assess their situation.

---

**Example**

'You seem to be doing fairly well at the moment, but maybe you still need a bit of regular support. I'll arrange for someone to check out how you are doing during the day and at night. That way we can find out if you need anything – perhaps to talk something through, or maybe organise some activity. However, if you need anything at any time, just let me know, or one of my colleagues. How do you feel about that?'

---

### Engagement level 3

Where the person is deemed to be at an *intermediate level of risk*, to self or others, care is focused on providing intermittent support throughout the day and night.

- The nurse should advise the person that the team believes they might benefit from some support.
- The person should be advised that someone will contact them at points during the day, to ask how they are doing, and whether or not anything is needed.
- The person should be asked if (s)he has any comments or questions.

An identified nurse will make contact with the person at least three times a day – during the morning, afternoon and evening – to assess the person's situation.

---

**Example**

'You seem to be doing really well at the moment. I'll see that someone keeps in touch during the day to see how you are getting on with your Personal Security Plan and to see if there is anything needing attention. How do you feel about that?'

---

### Engagement level 4

Where the person is deemed to be at *no apparent risk*, or at low risk, care will focus on engaging the person daily in one or more of the following relationships:

- A one-to-one session, focused on addressing the specific problems that brought the person into care, or which stimulated a crisis. These sessions will focus on establishing what needs to be done to reduce or resolve the *immediate* effects of the problems or crisis (see the one-to-one session in Chapter 11).

- A family meeting, involving appropriate family members (or friends) who are in some way involved in the person's current difficulties, or who might be able to help ameliorate these difficulties. The focus of this meeting should be to address what needs to be done (or to happen) to reduce or resolve the problem or crisis, and the part each person can play in achieving this.
- A group session, involving other people in care. These sessions may have a general focus, such as raising self-esteem; a specific focus, such as discussing how group members are presently addressing discrete problems; or an information focus, providing details about medication, therapeutic services, or forms of community support (see groupwork in Chapter 12).

At an appropriate point after entry to the care programme, the person will be advised of the various forms of support available. Specific details will be offered of the nursing team's approach to care, including details of the various options available in the form of individual, family and group support.

Where care is delivered within the community, either in the person's home, as part of a partial hospitalisation or 'out-patient' programme, this level of engagement with the person will be negotiated by arrangement.

## Bridging: The proper focus of engagement

Originally, the necessary process of reaching out to people in acute distress, who might represent a risk to themselves or others, was called engagement. All of the Tidal Model projects around the world base their work on the materials developed in the original pilot work in England, and the subsequent revisions made following the initial research evaluations. All our previous publications on the Tidal Model and the one hundred or so practice projects refer to and understand the concept of engagement. Consequently, we have maintained use of the term *engagement* here. However, through discussion with colleagues and service users and consumers, we have come to realise the problematic nature of the term engagement. Not only has it been widely appropriated for use in various policy documents, but its widespread use has led to a blurring of its meaning. Engagement may not mean all things to all people, but it certainly does not mean the same thing to everyone. Given our interest in the politics of language we are also aware that 'engagement' can mean a 'moral commitment', which fits neatly with the value base of the Tidal Model. However, it can also mean 'an encounter between hostile forces'. Clearly, many of the criticisms of the process of 'observation' in mental health care, which the concept of 'engagement' sought to displace, revolve around the inherently hostile or defensive nature of the practice of observation. Gradually, we came to consider alternative titles for this necessary process of reaching out to people in distress, in an effort to connect with them, meeting them at least halfway. Consequently, we have renamed this process *bridging*.

'Bridging' is a creative endeavour. It involves constructing a means of crossing some threatening water, so that we might reach something of importance on the other side. In the context of mental health care, what we wish to 'cross' is the threatening waters of madness, and what we aim to 'reach' is the person in distress. The bridging metaphor aptly summarises the necessary creativity required and the effort that is likely to be involved in 'bridge building'. It also acknowledges that the activity is not without its inherent dangers. The bridge builder needs to undertake this activity skilfully and carefully, acknowledging that risks might be involved. The metaphor also acknowledges that the bridge might be made of almost any sort of material, and might be built to last or be a highly temporary structure. This also conveys something of the character of the 'bridging' activity in mental health.

The creative practitioner might well use a preplanned structure to reach the person, such as the guidelines mapped out above. Alternatively, the practitioner might use any available means to build some kind of a bridge to cross over and make contact with the person in distress. Although we appreciate that using a 'ready-made' system has its attractions, we suspect that in ordinary everyday practice there is likely to be a need for creative 'bridging', and that such a creative form of practice is likely to be most rewarding, especially to the more accomplished practitioner.

## The Monitoring Assessment

### An overview

The Monitoring Assessment is the third strand of the approach to Risk Assessment illustrated in the previous chapter. Where the person is deemed to be at *any significant risk* to self or others, the Monitoring Assessment is completed on a *daily basis*. Where the person is deemed to be at *low risk* of harm to self or others, the Monitoring Assessment should be completed as appropriate, to provide the basis for the development and revision of the person's *Personal Security Plan*. The Monitoring Assessment has, therefore, a dual function: representing a collaborative means of monitoring subtle changes in the person who may be a risk to self or others; providing the basis for development of the *Personal Security Plan* for all people in care.

### Distinguishing features

The Monitoring Assessment has three discrete objectives:

1   To engage the person in assessing her or his own risk status. This helps to reduce the person's sense of disempowerment, nurturing their awareness of 'personal power'.
2   To provide a simple rating of the perceived level of risk – from the perspective of both the person and the professional.
3   To identify specific actions that might help to reduce further the level of risk and begin to promote the person's sense of emotional security.

Although the Monitoring Assessment may enhance greatly the person's sense of emotional security, hope and general self-esteem, the process of completing the Monitoring Assessment differs greatly from a typical counselling or therapy interview:

- By focusing on the paper template of the assessment the person may be lifted, momentarily, 'out' of her/his lived experience and may have an opportunity to look at her/himself *as if* from a distance.
- If the person can be encouraged to write in her/his answers to the half dozen question, (s)he may feel a powerful sense of ownership of the whole process and may feel a degree of control over the proceedings.
- The conversation between the person and the nurse is focused and practical: what is happening *now* and what might help improve the situation in the *future*. This may enhance greatly the sense that the nurse is 'caring with' the person – developing a genuine collaborative relationship.
- The process of completing the assessment emphasises that the person is the expert. The nurse is trying to find out 'what works' for the person, or what 'might work'. In that sense the process of completing the assessment helps validate the person's sense of personal worth.

The *Monitoring Assessment* should be completed by an identified nurse, preferably the person's Primary or Associate nurse. The Assessment, which need take no more than 10 minutes to complete, should be conducted in private. The outcome of the Monitoring Assessment should be signed by the assessing nurse and the person and then entered in the care plan record (Figure 8.1).

### Administering the Monitoring Assessment

The Monitoring Assessment (see Figure 8.1) aims to engage the person in a conversation about some of the very superficial aspects of Selfhood.

- What is happening, emotionally for the person right now?
- To what extent might this represent some kind of vulnerability, or emotional insecurity?

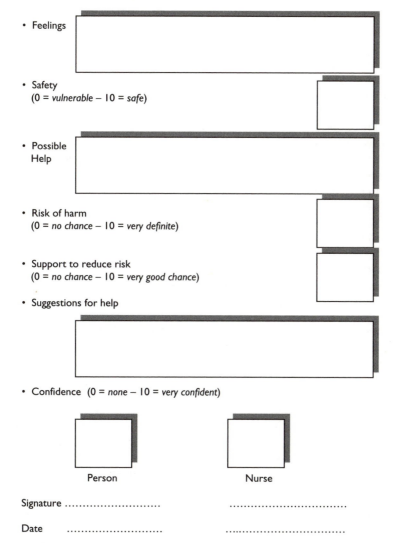

- Feelings

- Safety
  (0 = *vulnerable* – 10 = *safe*)

- Possible
  Help

- Risk of harm
  (0 = *no chance* – 10 = *very definite*)

- Support to reduce risk
  (0 = *no chance* – 10 = *very good chance*)

- Suggestions for help

- Confidence  (0 = *none* – 10 = *very confident*)

Person                           Nurse

Signature ...........................          ..................................

Date    ...........................          ..................................

*Figure 8.1* The Monitoring Assessment

- How might the person – together with the professional team, and perhaps others – try to redress the balance, realising a degree of 'emotional security'?

---

**NB** Wherever possible, the person is encouraged to complete the Monitoring Assessment, filling in the boxes and ratings with support from the nurse. This will help the person develop further awareness of her/his thoughts and feelings, and sense of control and personal power.

---

The nurse opens by providing a rationale for the Monitoring Assessment:

'People often find it useful to talk about how they are feeling and how we might go about making things at least a little better in the short term. So let me begin by asking "How are you feeling today?".'

After a brief discussion the nurse encourages the person to make a note of her/his feelings on the assessment. (If the person is unable or unwilling to write, the nurse will check with the person what (s)he would like entered on the assessment.)

The nurse then focuses on the person's feelings of security/insecurity or vulnerability:

'To what extent would you say that you feel safe or secure, in yourself, today? On a scale from 0 to 10, where 0 meant you felt really vulnerable, not at all safe, and 10 meant you were as safe and secure as you could be, where would you say that you are now?' [Person encouraged to enter rating.]

The aim of the assessment is to develop an understanding of what might promote a sense of emotional security for the person. Using the ratings, the nurse helps the person *imagine* what it would be like to 'feel more secure':

'So, what would help you feel more safe? You have rated yourself at 2. What would be different if you were at 3? [The nurse encourages the person to identify what the person would be *doing* or what other people might be *doing*. This helps identify specific *actions*, by the person and others, that might help promote a greater sense of emotional security.] Would you like to write down those examples now?'

It is important to get a sense of the extent to which the person might *feel* that (s)he is a risk to her/himself or others, *now*:

'If we stay focused on how you are feeling right now, to what extent do you think that you might harm yourself (or someone else)? Using the same kind of scale, with 0 being "no chance at all" and 10 being a "very definite chance", how would you rate yourself right now? [*It is important to use the language used by the person. If the person says 'hurt myself', 'end it all' or 'just lose it completely', then these expressions should be used to represent the risks of self-harm, suicide or harm to others.*] Would you like to write down your rating now?'

If the person rates *any* chance of self-harm/suicide/harm to others, the nurse explores the extent to which the person might be amenable to influence:

'To what extent do you think I, or anyone else, could help you change your mind about that? A score of 0 means that there is "no chance" that I could do that and 10 means that there is "a very good chance". Where would you put yourself right now? Would you like to put your score in that box, where it says "support to reduce risk"? [If the person believes that there is 'any chance', however small, that (s)he might be helped to feel differently about the risk of self-harm/suicide/risk to others, the nurse would explore this further.] So, what would I (or anyone else) be *doing* if I was helping you to feel differently about all of this?'

Even if the person says there is 'nothing' that can be done to help, the nurse tries to explore possible avenues of help:

'OK, so you don't think there is anything that I could do, specifically, to help you feel differently about this. So, how could I be of more help to you *in general*? How might I help you feel even just a bit different about this?'

Even if the rating of risk of harm is low it is important to explore possibilities for support beyond the confines of the therapeutic team, especially among friends, family or even other people in care:

'Who do you think could help you feel more safe? [and then] What would they [naming the person/people] be doing that would make you feel more safe than you do right now?' [Encourage the person to summarise and then record the help that might be offered by the team or others.]

Finally, both the nurse and the person will offer 'confidence ratings' related to 'staying safe and secure'. This offers the person an opportunity to judge her/his overall sense of emotional security and also provides the person with an opportunity to appreciate how others might view her/his circumstances:

'So, before I ask my last question, is there anything you want to ask, or maybe to say about what we have been doing here?

'OK, then let me ask, how confident are you that you can keep yourself safe and secure until [specify a day/time]?[8] A score of 0 means that you are "not at all confident" and 10 means that you are "very confident" [and] would you like to record your rating?

'People usually find it helpful if the nurse also scores this "confidence" rating. It gives us an opportunity to compare notes if you like. So I guess I would say that I was fairly confident that you can keep yourself safe over the next day or so, so I would rate you at 7. Could I borrow the form for a moment so that I can put my rating on it?'[9]

---

**NB** If there is any discrepancy between the confidence ratings given by the person and the nurse, this should be opened up for discussion:

'It is interesting that you rate your confidence in keeping yourself safe pretty highly – a 9 – whereas 1 gave you a 7. So I guess I am a little less confident than you. Maybe we could talk about that for a minute. I wonder why you think I am less comfortable with things, than you are? Do you want to talk about this or shall we do it later?'

It is important that the nurse invites the person to comment on this discrepancy. It is vital that every attempt is made to avoid a power clash. Instead, in the spirit of collaboration and 'learning from the person', which underpins the Tidal Model, the nurse seeks some counsel on this discrepancy. Ultimately, however, it may be important simply to acknowledge that there are two different views (stories) about the confidence rating. This may also help the person appreciate that other people rarely 'see' us as we see ourselves.

---

Before concluding, the nurse should thank the person for her/his assistance with the completion of the Monitoring Assessment:[10]

'Well, I would like to thank you for doing this assessment. I know that these things are rarely easy but I found it really useful and I hope that you did too. I am going to make a copy of this for you, for your own reference, and then I'll file this one in your notes. Maybe we can pick up some of these ideas you have raised here, later, when we take another look at your Personal Security Plan. OK?'

## Summary

From the person's perspective, the Monitoring Assessment provides a medium for the examination of personal perceptions of risk (to self and others) and the construction of alternatives, which represent the important 'next step' on the recovery journey.

For the professional team the Monitoring Assessment provides an important record of the team's commitment to collaborative care. Although this commitment is important for all people needing the support of the therapeutic team, this is especially important in the case of those deemed to be 'at risk' of harming themselves or others. The Monitoring Assessment provides a valuable record of the team's efforts to engage the person in the process of minimising risk. Although valuable as part of the general therapeutic programme, this is also a valuable record of part of the team's efforts to fulfil its 'duty of care'.

## The Personal Security Plan

The three approaches to assessment undertaken within the *Self Domain* aim to identify any major risks of neglect, self-harm, suicide or harm to others. The person's care will focus on addressing those risks, by trying to arrange or foster the conditions that might reduce the risk of harm to the person or others, especially those identified as meaningfully useful by the person her or himself. Various approaches might be employed to help reduce risk in the short term, from the provision of simple support to time-limited and carefully selected drug therapy, or more active forms of social support. In the longer term such risks are best reduced by an integrated, collaborative care programme, which capitalises on the available support networks of family, friends and the person's social and community network.

The main focus of Risk Assessment within the Tidal Model is to develop a collaborative approach to minimising risk through the development of a conjoint *Personal Security Plan*, produced by the primary nurse and the person. The Personal Security Plan aims to identify what (exactly) the person might be able to do for him or herself to reduce the likelihood of coming to harm, or harming others. The Personal Security Plan also identifies the kind of support that the person might need at present to enact the plan. This is the simplest possible of care plans. A single sheet of paper should suffice; indeed, the simpler the better from the perspective of ownership by the person in care. Figure 8.2 shows an example of a completed Personal Security Plan.

The Personal Security Plan is the bedrock of the person's contribution to his or her own care. Perhaps more than any other aspect of the person's involvement and collaboration in their own care, the Personal Security Plan is something that manifestly *belongs* to the person.[11] Given that the person's experience of Self is, by definition, private, the professional focus needs to be on trying to access, as much as the person is willing, the thoughts and feelings related to emotional vulnerability and security.

The importance of the Personal Security Plan cannot be overemphasised. If the person does not feel secure – emotionally as well as physically – then all

## Personal Security Plan

What can **I** do that might help me feel more **safe** and **secure**?

*I will read over letter from my friends, every day. Doing this bolsters my self-esteem.*

*I will make a note every day of the people who value me for who I am and what they say about me.*

*I will listen to music on my walkman and talk to people. This usually helps me deal with my voices.*

What can **others** do that might help me feel more **safe** and **secure**?

*The nurses will ask me how I am doing at least four times a day.*

*The nurses will be happy to talk to me whenever I feel the need.*

*Someone will ask Dick to come see me and bring Mo his dog. I like Mo — he is a great dog.*

| Signature | Date | Signature | Date |
|-----------|------|-----------|------|
| *Tony Smith* | *17/7/03* | *R. Jenkins (StN)* | *17/07/03* |

Copy to be given to the person and original to be retained in nursing notes.

*Figure 8.2* Personal Security Plan

other interventions, however sophisticated and appropriate, may have little positive effect. Indeed, if the person cannot be helped to *feel* more secure then they may be unwilling to advance further into the therapeutic process and instead withdraw further inward. The Personal Security Plan aims to do exactly what it says: produce a plan that might foster a sense of personal security. Given the shifts that occur in the person's sense of emotional security from day to day if not from moment to moment, it is vital that the Personal Security Plan is updated regularly. Where the person has been assessed as being at high risk (for neglect, self-harm, suicide or harm to others), the Personal Security Plan may need to be updated daily. Where the person has moved into *Transitional Care,* or where the level of risk has been assessed as low, then the review and revision of the Personal Security Plan will need to be less frequent.

### Minimising risk: General considerations

The team needs to ensure that the person's physical and social environment is as safe as possible. Arranging this degree of security ranges from removing or monitoring access to parts of the built environment that might represent a risk to removing access to objects, materials and other people that might prove harmful. These common-sense precautions are part and parcel of the Personal Security Plan but are invariably the responsibility of the therapeutic team charged with assessing risk within the wider environment, and usually become the practical responsibility of the nursing team.[12]

### The focus on the interior

The Personal Security Plan focuses specifically on the knowledge concerning risk or threat to self or others, which lies 'within' the person or at least is known only 'to' the person: the thoughts, feelings and beliefs that might precipitate a harmful interaction with some aspect of the physical or social environment. For instance, alcohol or illicit drugs are not of themselves harmful. However, they risk becoming harmful when someone has a desire to consume them in large quantities. Similarly, open windows can afford fresh air and a good view and swimming pools can provide exercise and relaxation, but both can also be used for the purpose of self-destruction.

Consequently, the Personal Security Plan focuses on what is happening within the person's thoughts, feelings and belief systems. The aim is to iden-tify how the person might be able to manage the thoughts, beliefs or feelings that might contribute to a risk of harm to self or others, by using her or his personal resources and enlisting the direct support of others. In developing the Personal Security Plan the nurse assumes that the person already pos-sesses the personal resources necessary to manage the risk, but needs some help to clarify how (s)he might do this on a regular daily basis. The nurse also assumes that if the person can be helped to feel more emotionally secure, then (s)he will also feel more safe and the net effect will be that the person will also become less of a risk to self or others.[13] The development of the Personal Security Plan involves asking the following four simple questions:

1   What has the person done *in the past* that appeared to help them feel

more emotionally secure and reduced the risk of possible harm to self or others?

2   What is the person doing *now* that might be helping them feel more emotionally secure and reduce or offset the risk of harm?

3   What does the person think that other people have done in the past, or might do in the future, that might help them to feel more emotionally secure?

4   How might the person develop these personal and interpersonal 'resources' to form a Personal Security Plan?

### Developing the Personal Security Plan

These four questions 'presuppose' the presence of a willingness to collaborate in the care plan, and to develop a sense of 'personal security and empower the person. Such *presuppositional* questions[14] help the person realise that they have the capacity to manage their own risk of harm, albeit assisted and supported by the nursing team and others. By adopting this positive approach to the Personal Security Plan, the nurse instils a degree of hope in the future, while at the same time validating the present difficulties of the person. The following example (see box) illustrates the conversational nature of the process of clarification and negotiation involved in the development of the Personal Security Plan.

---

*Nurse*:   So you feel that you might harm yourself again?

*Person*:   I guess. It goes around in my head – the thoughts I mean – it goes round in my head most of the time. I just feel that it's all so pointless. I'm going to do it again. I know I am.

*Nurse*:   So how do you deal with that? How do you deal with those thoughts going round in your head? [*Note:* the nurse does not ask 'if' the person can deal with these thoughts, but by asking 'how' (presuppositional question) assumes that the person already does.]

*Person*:   Well, I'm not sure I do. I mean, I hadn't thought about it really. They seem to have a life of their own . . . the thoughts. I mean.

*Nurse*:   Well, you must be doing something to deal with these thoughts, something really powerful, because you haven't harmed yourself since you came to us [validation of the person's resources].

*Person*:   Yes, but that's because I'm here, isn't it?

*Nurse*:   Well, maybe we should talk about that, when we look at your security plan.

*Person*:   Personal Security Plan? What's that?

*Nurse*:   Oh, sorry, that's what we call one of the care plans. Let me

---

show you what I mean [offering copy of the blank *Personal Security Plan* – see Figure 8.2]. Let's talk about how you deal with your thoughts about harming yourself. Are you OK doing this just now?

*Person*: Well . . . OK.

*Nurse*: I'd like to talk about two things – two very important things. First of all, what can *you* do to help yourself with your present problems? And, how you can continue dealing with these thoughts about harming yourself? Secondly, we need to talk about what I might be able to do, or the rest of team, or anyone else that you can think of?

*Person*: I dunno. I don't know if I can handle that.

*Nurse*: Let's give it a go and see what happens. Yes?

*Person*: Alright.

*Nurse*: So tell me, what kind of things have you done *in the past* that seem to have helped you to deal with thoughts about harming yourself? . . . What can *we* do to help you to deal with these thoughts? How do you feel about talking about that?

*Person*: Well . . . I have sometimes talked about it to someone. That sometimes helps . . . well just for a short time. Not completely, you know, they still are there – in my head.

*Nurse*: Uh huh. That's really interesting. So talking to someone can be helpful. Anyone in particular?

*Person*: Well, maybe Rosemary – my friend, She really understands me. We go back a long way.

*Nurse*: OK, so Rosemary can be helpful to talk to . . . anyone else? [The nurse proceeds to help the person to identify all the people who might be 'useful supports' for this part of the *Personal Security Plan*. The nurse proceeds to explore other possibilities.]

*Nurse*: Right, so what else have you done in the past *that has been helpful in any way*? [*Note:* The nurse assumes (presupposes) that the person has done *something*. This encourages the person to explore personal resources that may not be immediately apparent to him or her.]

*Person*: Well it seems silly but sometimes I just tell the voices to fuck off!

*Nurse*: [Laughing] And do they . . . 'fuck off' I mean? [Although some may find the use of straightforward Anglo-Saxon English a little 'unprofessional', this is part of the rapport building, respecting and valuing the person's natural language.]

*Person*: Well for a little while maybe.

*Nurse*: Hmm, seems like that's a good one too, maybe you should include that in your Security Plan too. So what things seem to make matters worse? [Note that everything that the person

> comes up with is accepted as a 'good idea' – providing that it works for the person and is not obviously harmful to the person or anyone else. The nurse is learning from the person about what works and perhaps also what doesn't work.]
>
> [Later]
> *Nurse*:    This is going well. So what else do you do that seems to work?

## Conclusion

Working together in this way, the nurse and the person build up an idea of the kind of *practical things* that the person might do to help to reduce the risk of harm. The Personal Security Plan is an elegant method of distilling these details of what 'needs to be done' (see Figure 8.2 for completed example). The Personal Security Plan provides a simple reminder of what (s)he needs to be doing on a daily basis, and also details the kind of support that the person needs to help promote her or his emotional security.

# Chapter 9

# The World Domain

## Planning holistic care

> Paternalism: the moral principle, which allows people to give others everything except respect.
>
> (Thomas S. Szasz)

### The story of the problem: The problem in the story

The problems of living that we call 'mental distress', 'mental illness' or 'psychiatric disorder' involve expressions of a human crisis. Even if we believe that distress involves some disturbance of the physical *body* (such as a hypothetical biochemical anomaly) it remains a highly complex, and potentially bewildering state of affairs – to the professional as well as to the person. What is commonly referred to as the mind (psyche or soul) must, of necessity, incorporate the body, especially the brain. In the respect that the brain is the location of all that is experienced through the body, the brain is the body. It is impossible to experience problems of living without involving the body in a major way. The philosophical split, between *mind* and *body*, holds no currency in the world of mental health where all our abstract ('mentalistic') experiences, which we call thoughts, feelings, emotions, etc., are experienced through or reside *in* the body.

Problems of living involve the myriad ways that people feel about themselves and others, and their associated beliefs about life in general and the various meanings. People who have had extreme or disabling problems of living experience major threats to their personal identity and to the values they hold about themselves and life in general. For most, the experience represents a signal that something needs to change – at the very least in terms of accepting help to address current or longstanding difficulties in relating to oneself, others or life in general. For some, the experience can appear to open a doorway to the soul, alerting the person to the presence of the spiritual in everyday life; the problem of living being a symbolic representation of the call to change or to develop awareness of the meaning of one's life. For some people, the experience of something that is commonly viewed as a curse (so-called *mental illness*) might be interpreted, even if only in the longer term, as a blessing; an opportunity to change or grow, born of crisis.

However we interpret or define problems of living, whether as forms of mental illness or spiritual emergence, these problems are framed by the same thing: the person's *story*. In the *World Domain*, the Tidal Model practitioner tries to give maximum respect to the story framed by the person's autobiography.

## The World Domain

### Aims of the Holistic Assessment

The Holistic Assessment is focused on the person's 'world of experience' and on providing a formal opportunity for the person to tell the story of what has been happening recently, and how this is anchored to the established story of the person's life. The Holistic Assessment aims:

- to give the person an opportunity to *describe*, *discuss* and *examine* her/his *present* experience of illness and health.
- to establish the basis for developing a *Personal Care Plan* focused on the person's unique needs, as (s)he perceives them
- to enable the development of a *collaborative* relationship between the professional and the person – one that emphasises joint exploration of the person's needs and problems
- to develop an *empowering* relationship within which the nurse aims to assist the person in making informed decisions and choices
- to begin to *clarify* 'who' the person is.

Despite its many attempts to reinvent itself, the mainstream psychiatric service is dogged by its concern to classify the person as one kind of a 'patient' or another.[1] However, in addition to 'what' people might be called – anxious, manic depressive, borderline personality disorder, etc. – we need to be conscious of 'who' the person is. Within the Holistic Assessment we hope to begin to ask 'who are you?' Given the inherent complexity of the question, any response will represent no more than a provisional starting point. However, the mere act of begging the question might suggest that we (the professional team) are more interested in the person than in any putative disorder or 'illness' that might presently be troubling the person.

### Objectives of the Holistic Assessment

The Holistic Assessment has four dimensions and seeks to clarify the following:

1 What does the person believe are her/his *present* 'problems' or 'needs'?
2 What is the *scale* of these problems/needs? How *big* are they?
3 What aspects of the person's present life might play a part in helping to *resolve* such problems, or meet such needs?
4 What needs to *happen* to bring about what the person would regard as *positive change*?

### Problems or needs

The first objective involves an exploration of the person's problems/needs:

- identifying the main *problems* or *needs*
- describing these in the person's *own language*
- gaining an understanding of how these problems or needs *affect the person*, and how the person's life has changed *over time*
- clarifying the *personal meanings* attached to the problem or need by the person.

### Problem evaluation

The second objective involves an *evaluation* of the person's problems or needs:

- How much *distress* is generated by the problem/need?
- To what extent does the problem/need *disturb* the person's experience of everyday living?
- How much *control* does the person have over the problem/need?

### Personal resources

The third objective involves a description of the person's *resources*, emphasising the role and importance of:

- *personal* supports – family, friends, etc.
- *material* supports – money, possessions, home, etc.
- *spiritual* supports – beliefs, values, faith, etc.

### Problem or need resolution

The fourth objective involves a provisional description of how the problem/ need might be *resolved*.

- How will the person *know* when the problem is resolved or the need met?

- What *needs to change* – in the person or others – for this resolution to happen?

### How does the Holistic Assessment differ from other forms of assessment?

Traditional assessments invariably break down the 'whole' problem (or person) into constituent parts or 'subproblems'. The Holistic Assessment is focused on the person's experience of problems and needs, health and distress *now*.

As a rule, people do not talk about different *aspects* of their problems. Usually, a problem of living – however named or labelled – is experienced 'whole' or 'complete'; it is an expression of the whole 'lived experience'. The Holistic Assessment tries to draw together, as far as possible, the person's experience of different aspects of life problems into something that approximates the 'lived experience'. The Holistic Assessment tries to produce a representation of the person's problems in a way that appears *real* to the person.

Traditional assessment is invariably written in professional language or terminology. The results of the Holistic Assessment are presented in the person's *own* '*voice*', using the person's own *natural language*. By giving the person back her or his own voice, (hopefully) this will be received as an 'empowering gesture' – showing the extent to which the person's own words are valued by the professional team.

Traditional assessments are usually based on a highly professional relationship, where the nurse is the 'expert'. The Holistic Assessment emphasises *collaboration* and *dialogue* and recognises that the person in care is the 'expert' on her/his problems or needs.

### When should the Holistic Assessment be completed?

The aim of the Holistic Assessment is to establish the person's perspective on their need for nursing. The Holistic Assessment may therefore be used in *any setting* – acute hospital ward, own home (community care), day care, etc.

- The Holistic Assessment should be completed *as soon as possible* after the person's entry into the service.
- Where the person is unable (for whatever reason), or unwilling to collaborate in assessment, this should be deferred until later, and a provisional supportive care plan introduced, designed by the primary nurse or keyworker.

### How should the Holistic Assessment be undertaken?

The assessment should be conducted in a setting where privacy and the minimum of disruption can be guaranteed.

- The nurse should start by aiming to put the person at ease, before beginning the assessment process.
- The person should be given a copy of the assessment to refer to (and where appropriate, complete) during the interview (see Appendix 1 at end of book).
- The nurse should explain the purpose of the assessment, referring to each page in turn.
- The person should be invited to write their responses to each of the main questions, as the assessment progresses. This will emphasise the empowering nature of the whole process.
- If the person is unable or unwilling, for whatever reason, to complete the summary, the nurse will complete the recording of the responses to the questions on the person's behalf.
- Before recording *anything*, the nurse should check with the person that they have understood correctly what has been said. Such constant checking will develop further the collaborative nature of the assessment and will enhance the person's trust in the nurse.
- Each page of the assessment should be signed at the bottom by the assessing nurse to comply with legal and professional requirements.[2]

## Completion of the assessment

### How should the assessment be recorded?

Traditionally, assessment information is summarised and presented in the professional's voice (e.g. 'The patient *reported* that she had difficulty sleeping ...' or 'she *said* that the voices were telling her she was worthless'). The Holistic Assessment is focused on the person's immediate understanding of her or his problems and needs. Consequently, the details of the assessment are presented in the person's voice. (See example of a page from the Holistic Assessment in Figure 9.1.)

### Who should complete the assessment?

The Holistic Assessment should be completed by one of the qualified nurses in the service. Ideally, this will be the person's assigned primary nurse or keyworker, responsible for the overall design, development and management of the person's care plan.

**How this all began:** *I have been called by God. He says that I am his Messenger. I need to get out of here. I must do the work that has been set for me.*

**How this affected me:** *Nobody believes me. I have been in hospital before. They give me drugs. I don't want them. They make me tired and I can't think straight.*

**How I felt in the beginning:** *I felt great. I could hear God talking – it was like nothing I had ever felt before. I have repented all my sins. I have been a very bad person. I am saved. Now I am saved.*

**How things have changed over time:** *Nothing much has changed. I have a lot of other voices now – like interference. I am not doing much. It's the drugs. I stopped taking them, then they gave me this needle.*

**The effect on my relationships:** *My family never had much time for me. I am the black ~~goat~~ sheep. My brother is OK. He gives me some money and takes me to the hills sometimes.*

**The Holistic Assessment**

**Entry to the service:** 'What has brought you here?'

1. **Problem origins:** 'so when did you first notice ... or become of aware of ...?'

2. **Past problem function:** 'and how did that affect you at first?' etc

3. **Past emotions:** '... and how did you feel about that at the time?' etc.

4. **Historical development:** '... and in what way has that changed over time?' etc.

5. **Relationships:** 'and how has that affected your relationship with people?' etc.

*Figure 9.1* Completed first page of the Holistic Assessment

### Should anyone else be involved in the assessment?

The nurse will usually conduct the assessment with the person alone, ensuring privacy and confidentiality. In some cases the person may request the presence of a relative, friend or advocate, *for moral support*. Such requests should be honoured wherever possible. In such instances, however, the friend or advocate will usually not contribute to the assessment process. On occasions it may be appropriate to involve a friend, partner or family member. Where such a conjoint assessment is conducted, the nurse should ensure that the assessment reflects the perceived problems, needs and wants of the person in care.

### How often should the assessment be repeated?

Traditionally, assessments are repeated at intervals to measure change or identify new problems. The Holistic Assessment is used, primarily, as a way of introducing the person to the Tidal Model's emphasis on 'story' and the collaborative nature of the relationship with the nurse with regard to care planning. The care plan will take over, seamlessly, from the end of the Holistic Assessment. The care plan identifies how the nurse and the person are addressing specific problems, and also provides an ongoing assessment of changes in the nature and function of specific problems of living. Consequently, repetition of the Holistic Assessment is unnecessary. However, the primary nurse should ensure that the care plan emphasises a *continual* ongoing assessment of the person's experience of the problems that brought them into contact with the service, and awareness of ongoing changes.

## The process of the assessment

### Introduction

Each page of the assessment should be completed in the presence of the person (and any significant other).[3] This will increase confidence in the collaborative relationship between the nurse and the person in care, from the very outset.

The first page of the Holistic Assessment (see Appendix 1, p. 247) should include the names of the person and the nurse completing the assessment, along with the date and time of the assessment, and the names of anyone else present. A brief summary of the circumstances of the person's admission to the service (ward, unit or programme) should be noted along with details of the primary nurse or keyworker.

The assessment should be begun as soon as possible after the person's entry to the service. A brief explanation of the purpose of the assessment should be given and the person should be encouraged to participate as fully as possible. Before entering any of the details noted above, the nurse should check their accuracy with the person and should provide supplementary information as appropriate.

If the person is in any way reluctant to participate, the nurse should negotiate the beginning of the assessment: 'I appreciate that this is difficult. Well how do you feel about just beginning with the first page or two, we can

[After making the person comfortable] 'We are really interested in your understanding of what's been happening for you recently and how it has been affecting you. We use this assessment [offer copy] – the Holistic Assessment – to get a summary of all of this down on paper. We use this as the jumping off point for your care plan – trying to make sure that we offer you the kind of help you need, right now. Do you feel OK about beginning this now?'

stop any time you like and come back to this later? OK? Well perhaps we could begin with checking some of these details.'[4]

### Overview of problem or need (Appendix 1, pp. 248–9)

The formal part of the Holistic Assessment begins by trying to establish the person's perception of what has brought her/him into hospital or, alternatively, what the person needs or wishes to talk about. Before beginning this section, the nurse would offer the person an opportunity to record the story in her or his own hand. (Figure 9.1 shows how the most important elements of the person's story are summarised.)

'As I said, we are really interested in hearing your story about everything that has been going on for you. We have some questions here that usually provide a useful starting point. We can summarise the main details of each answer here, on these pages. Would you like to write down your answers as we go along, or would you rather I did this?'

It is important, from the outset, to avoid asking specifically about 'problems'. (Some people do not believe that they have any problems. Indeed, for many, being in psychiatric care against their wishes *is* the problem.) Instead, the nurse should ask more open questions, which will allow the person to talk about what is important, in their own words.

### Examples

- 'Tell me then, what have you brought with you, that you want to talk about (or *feel* that you need to talk about)?'
- 'So, what would *you* like to talk about?'
- 'What's on your *mind*?'
- 'Where shall we *begin*?'
- 'What has brought you into hospital (the unit, programme, etc.)?'

- 'Why do you think I have been asked to see you?'
- 'What has been happening with you recently that you would want to talk about?'

Naturally, the nurse will add supplementary questions to encourage the development of a conversational dialogue, a proper exchange of thoughts and feelings.

### Problem origins (How this all began)

The *focus* of the assessment is on the person's experience *now*. However, people often expect, *or want*, to spend some time putting their present situation in context. For this reason it is important to begin at the beginning. People usually want to begin the story at the beginning. Ask the person about the background to whatever it is that has brought her/him to the service. The 'beginning' of the story is wherever the person begins the story. The person constructs the beginning. This is a fundamental 'given' (fact) of the Holistic Assessment.

---

'I see. So clearly you are not happy about being here and, as you say, you were brought here very much against your wishes. People had been trying to hurt you and take you away, so you locked yourself in your flat. Yes? . . .

So, all of this . . . people trying to hurt you and take you away . . . when did all of this first start?'

---

*Alternative opening questions*

- 'When did you first *notice* (the problem)?'
- 'When did you first *become aware* of . . .?'
- '. . . and this all started, *when*?'
- 'Tell me a bit about what was going on in your life when all this started.'

### Past problem function (How this affected me)

The next set of questions aims to explore the person's direct experience of the problem – what *effect* did this have on the person's life? A useful way to introduce these questions is by summarising (briefly) the origins of the problem. This also shows the person that the nurse has been listening and paying careful attention to the unfolding story.

*Examples*

- 'So [summarising the 'origins of the problem'] how did that *affect* you at first?'
- 'Tell me a bit more about how that affected you.'
- 'So, what effect did that have on you and your life, in general?'

### Past emotions (How I felt in the beginning)

The next set of questions examines the *emotional* impact of the problem *in the beginning*.

*Examples*

- 'And how did you feel about that *at the time*?'
- 'How did you feel about all of that *in the beginning*?'

### Historical development (How things have changed over time)

The nurse now has a good idea of *where* the problem first emerged into the person's world of experience, *how* it affected the person and *what* feelings were associated (then) with the problem. Now the nurse tries to bring the situation 'up to date'.

*Examples*

- [Summarising briefly the problem origins, effect and feelings] '*So*, that was then. In what way have things *changed* for you?'
- 'In what way have things changed over time – between then and now?'
- 'How would you describe things *now*? What is different, *now*?'

### Relationships (The effect on my relationships)

Highly personal problems are experienced interpersonally, even if other people who share the person's world are unaware of the fine detail of the problem, they may well be affected by it and even contribute towards it. The nurse now explores briefly the effect of the problem on the person's *relationships*.

*Examples*

- 'And how has all of that [the description of the problem or need] affected your relationships with other people?'
- 'Tell me a bit more about how that has affected your relationships – with

friends, family [work colleagues if appropriate] or just "other people" in general?'
- 'So what do other people say about all of this [the problem or need]?'

The nurse reaches the end of this page and (as with each successive page) takes the opportunity to ask if the person is ready or willing to continue.

### Current emotions (How do I feel now?)

The next stage of 'bringing the problem up to date' involves exploring the current emotional context – how does the person feel *now*?

### Examples

- 'And how do you feel about all of that [the problem] *now*?'
- 'What feelings do you have about [the problem] now, *at this very moment*?'

### Holistic content (What do I think this means?)

Now that the nurse has a very good idea of what is the nature and function of the problem or need, it is time to explore its *meanings*. The nurse might ask the person directly, what they think all of this means, or might choose to preface this question with a simple summary.

### Examples

- [Brief summary] 'You first became aware of this [time] . . . and at the time [event] was happening in your life, and it affected you by [effect] and you felt [emotion]. Now, you think that it has had [effect] on your friends and [effect] on your family and now you feel [emotion].'
- So, given all of that, what does all of this *mean* for you?'
- 'I'd like you to think about this next question. It's an important question. For I would like to know what you *make* of all this. You have told me your story of what has brought you here (or what has *happened* to you? what you think is *wrong*), and how you feel about things. Clearly you have been trying to make sense of all of this. So what does it all mean for you – *on a personal level*?'

### Holistic context (What does all of this say about me as a person?)

Taking the exploration of meanings one stage further, the nurse invites the person to think about what 'all of this' might mean for them 'as a person'.

*Examples*

- 'So, given what you have just said [brief summary] what do you think that this says about you, as a *person*?'
- 'Given all that has happened to you, what does this say about you, what does it say about you as a person?'

### Needs, wants and wishes (What needs to happen now/what do I want or wish would happen now?)

Having gained a detailed picture of the problem and its wider context, the nurse now moves on to consider what might need to be done, by way of a nursing response. The answer to the final two questions in this section will help the team decide what kind of support the person thinks might be appropriate.

*Examples*

- 'And what would you hope would be done about all of that [summarising the problem]?'
- 'And what would you want to happen *now*?'
- 'If I was able to grant you one wish, in relation to what we have been talking about, what would you wish for?'
- 'And what *else* might you wish for?'

### Expectations (What do I expect the nurse to do for me?)

Finally, in this section, the nurse tries to establish what the person's expectations are of the nursing team. What does the person expect that the nurse or other members of the team will or might *do* for her or him?

*Example*

- 'This is the last question in this section, and it is also an important one. What do you expect me to do for you? Or, to put it another way, what would you hope that I might be able to do for you? What do you think that my colleagues might be able to do to help you?'

### Evaluating the problem (Appendix 1, p. 250)

In the next section, the nurse will try to *evaluate* the problem using a simple rating format. Again, before moving on to this next stage, the nurse should ask for permission to proceed.

*Examples*

- 'I'd like now to get an idea of how "big" a problem all of this is for you, right now.'
- 'I want to ask you three questions. They are at the top of the page. They are very important questions. Indeed, all these questions are important. However, these three questions will help my colleagues and I get an idea of how *distressing* you find all of this [the problem]. Also this will tell us to what extent this problem *upsets* the living of your life. And finally, this will tell us how much *control* you think that you have over the problem – to what extent you can deal with it. Does that sound OK?'

Before beginning the rating, the nurse needs to know if the problem should be evaluated 'as a whole' or if there are different 'parts' to the problem:

- 'We can use this format to get an idea of how "big" the problem is. Do you want to talk about the problem *as a whole* or do you want to split it up into some of the bits that you have been talking about? We can either write down "the whole thing" or we can break it up into different parts. What do you say?'

The nurse should then invite the person to record either "the whole thing" or each "part" of the overall problem in the boxes provided, before moving on to evaluate these with the person.[5]

- 'Using this rating scale here (see Appendix 2, p. 253), where 1 means you have "none" – "you are not at all distressed" and 10 means it is "extreme" – "you couldn't imagine being any more distressed", where would you say you are right now? How much distress, (between 1 and 10) is the problem giving you now?[6]
- 'And, using the same scale, to what extent does [name problem] affect or disrupt the living of your life? (1) means it doesn't disrupt your life at all, and (10) means you couldn't imagine your life being any more disrupted.'
- 'Finally, I would like to get an idea of the extent to which you think that you can exert some control over this [problem]. (1) means that you feel that you can do nothing to influence, or control, the problem and (10) means that you have complete control over it. Where would you put yourself right now?'

The ratings should be entered into the boxes for each aspect of the problem before proceeding to the final stages of the assessment.

### Personal resources (Appendix 1, p. 251)

The nurse now opens the assessment out to consider some of the personal 'assets' or 'resources' of the person – identifying the people, things and beliefs that are important to the person, and the part they play in the person's life. Given their personal significance, these will play a vital part in the subsequent care plan.

#### People who are important

• 'Tell me a bit more about the people who are important to you in your life. Who are they, and in what way are they important to you?'

The names of each person should be entered in the box, alongside a brief note that explains *why* the person thinks they are important. It is especially important to seek clarification on what it is that the person *does* that makes the person *feel* their importance.

#### Things that are important

• 'Tell me about the things that are important to you. What "things" would you miss if suddenly they weren't there any more?'
• 'And why is this [naming the thing] important to you?'

The name of each thing – along with a brief description of its importance – should be entered in the box.

#### Ideas or beliefs about life that are important

• 'Tell me a bit more about the beliefs you have about life in general that are important to you?'
• 'People often have certain values, or rules, by which they live their life – a personal philosophy, or code if you like. What would you say is your personal philosophy? What values or rules are important in your life?'

Again, these ideas, beliefs or values should be noted, along with an explanation of why they are important.

### Resolution of the problem need (Appendix 1, p. 252)

In the last stage of the assessment, the nurse asks the person what it would be like *not* to have the problem, to have the problem resolved, or the need met. The answer will help to identify the final goal of any intervention or support, *in the person's own words*.

*How will I know that the problem has been solved, or the need met?*

The nurse invites the person to 'imagine' what it would be like if the problem was no longer present, or if it disappeared *magically*. In framing these questions, it is important to assume that this *will* happen. Framing the question in this way will help the person to imagine a future without the problem.

- 'How *will* you know that this [name problem] has been solved?'
- 'What *will* life be like for you when the problem is no longer a problem for you?'
- '*If* – when you were asleep tonight – some kind of miracle happened, and your problem disappeared, what would you notice first when you woke up in the morning?'
- 'If I could wave a magic wand and make your problem disappear, which of course I can't, what would be different?'
- '*When* you no longer have this problem, what will be different?'
- 'What else *will be* different?'

*What needs to change for this to happen?*

The final question invites the person to *reflect* on what might be necessary for this change to occur.

- 'What do you think *needs to happen* for this [name problem] to be resolved?'
- 'What can *you do* to help resolve this problem?'
- 'What can *anyone else do* that might help resolve this problem?'
- 'How will you *know* when such changes show themselves – in you, or other people in your life?'
- 'When this [name problem] is gone or at least not so much of a problem for you, what will other people notice that is different about you?'

### Conclusion of the assessment

Before concluding the assessment the nurse should offer the person an opportunity to make any final comments, or to comment on the process of the assessment itself:

- 'I think that is just about all that I have to ask you. Is there anything you would want to add? Is there anything else you would like to say? Maybe you have some questions for me?'

Any comments that the person wishes to be added, or any amendments that the person wishes to be made, should be accommodated immediately.

Similarly, if the person has *any* specific queries, an effort should be made to respond to these immediately, or the person should be advised when a response is likely to be forthcoming.

The nurse should then advise the person 'what happens next' and thank them for their help with the assessment.[7]

- 'Well, now that we've completed the assessment I shall make a copy of this for your reference. I shall put the original in your notes, and the team will use this as the basis for planning the development of your care.'
- 'Before we go I would like to thank you for your help with this. I know that these interviews can be difficult and sometimes we seem to be going over the same old ground. However, I have to say that I found it really helpful. I think I have a better understanding of what you see as your problems and what we might do, together, to deal with them. I think I have a better appreciation of who *you* are. I hope that you found this helpful. I am sure that my colleagues will find the completed assessment *really* helpful. So, once again, thanks very much!'

### Illustrations of the holistic narrative

These two narratives represent the stories that the nurse took during the Holistic Assessment.

'Jack' is in his late thirties and has spent the past ten years working on the North Sea oil rigs. This is his third admission to hospital and he has been attributed a diagnosis of paranoid schizophrenia:

> I was on the oil rigs a couple of years ago. It put me in a bad mood and the lads started to get on my nerves. In the beginning I felt weird. I felt stressed and cut off from friends and stuff. Over time, I know that I got radiation sickness on the rig, know that they are targeting me. Now Louise (my girlfriend) has left me and my sister has got fed up with me, but I don't tell my mates about this. Now I feel confused. I don't understand what is going on. This means that there is no way that I can avoid this because they will target me wherever I go. I don't know what this says about me as a person. I need help with the sleeping. I know that nothing can help out with the radiation. I expect you to get me a change of sleeping tablets. I'll talk with Bill about other things. I have rated my difficulty with sleeping as 7 for distress, 7 for disturbance and 5 for control. I have rated getting targeted with the radiation sickness as 10 for distress, 7 for disturbance and 1 for control. The people who are important to me are Mary, my sister who is my flesh and blood, and Andrew and John who I have known since school – we know one another really well. The things, which are important to me are my house and my bike. It's a Harley-Davidson. I like to fix it and clean it

and get away on it. The pub is also important to me. It's my local. I believe it's important to make time to relax, to find the time to relax, to forget about work. I'll know that the problem has been solved when I notice I am getting some proper sleep. If things were different I'd notice they wouldn't be chasing me any more. They would leave me alone. What needs to change for this to happen is that I need to change my sleeping tablets. I don't think anything can be done about the other stuff.

Marie has a long history of mental health care, stretching over many years. She has a diagnosis of schizophrenia and she was admitted to hospital a few days before this interview:

I've been brought here under a Section because I complained to the police about a doctor and I want to see him charged. Nobody believes me, and they treat me like a crazy woman. Also, I have skeletons of my dead baby in my head. This has caused friction between me and my man and my father. Nobody believed this has happened.

At first I felt wiped out, devastated. I felt cut off from everybody. Alone. I also felt possessed by demons. Nothing much has changed over time, but because things should be better it is actually worse. This has affected my son who has been fostered out. He thinks I am a crazy person and I think I have been a bad mum. Maybe if he had had a better start he'd have turned out differently.

Now I feel saddened and despondent. What a wicked world this is, but I'm still hopeful that something will show through. This means that I am special. I had a past life when I was a doctor and there has been a book written about my life history. This means that I am a lovely person. I want to help people. I am a kind person.

I want help to get the doctor charged who killed my baby and I want help to get rid of the skeletons. I would like some help with accommodation – somewhere bigger for me. I would like the nurses to look after me a bit and help me relax. I would like help to look at getting this doctor charged at least. I would like some sleeping tablets. I have rated the whole thing (everything that has happened to me) as 10 for distress, 9 for disturbance and 1 for control. I have rated the need to get the doctor charged as 10 for distress, 10 for disturbance and 5 for control. I have rated the skeletons in my head as 10 for distress, 10 for disturbance and 1 for control.

The people who are important to me are David, who is my flesh and blood; Alan because we lean on one another; mum and dad who help out with my son – they're always there; Muriel because I rely on her a bit; my CPN as I see her as a friend; the church because Jesus looks after me; and granny for I can look after her. The things that are important to me are my picture of Jesus and my cross. They are enough to look after me, a reminder when things get bad. The ideas about life that are important to me are that Jesus will help me cast demons out of my head like Mary Magdalene. I believe that I have had a past life and I know this because I have been regressed.

I will know that the problem has been solved when the skeletons in my head will be gone and I can sleep at night, and people will believe what I am saying. What needs to change for this to happen is that people need to take me more seriously.

## Flexibility and creativity

The approach described here is merely an example of how the nurse might go about exploring these various dimensions of the person's story within the Holistic Assessment. In every situation the nurse should frame each question using a form of words that suits both her or himself *and* the person being interviewed. The examples offered here represent the kinds of questions that we, and many of our colleagues, have found to be useful during the Holistic Assessment. Others should generate their own alternative questions, as appropriate.

However, the approach described here has been shown, in general, to be a useful way of beginning and developing the person's story. In our experience, most people like to begin their story 'at the beginning' – wherever they believe that to be. Also, most people like to talk about the thoughts and feelings that are embedded in their story, and the meanings they attach to various events. Given that this story is unfolding in a formal therapeutic context (a care setting) most people are not surprised by the invitation to 'rate' or 'evaluate' the problem, and to identify their personal 'resources'. Similarly, the invitation to 'envision' a future *without* the distress associated with specific problems of living appears to make sense to many people. Indeed, many people make the comment that this is the most 'obvious' question to ask, since it provides the most personal context for the framing of any 'goals' of care and treatment. From the professional's perspective, it is worth noting that this kind of 'envisioning' not only makes any 'goal setting' personally significant, but strengthens the person's awareness of the power of *imagination* in the whole recovery process.

However, if the person is especially reluctant to engage in developing the kind of detailed narrative outlined here, the nurse would respect this and invite the person to skip to the very end of the whole process and talk about 'what needs to be done, *now!*' In our experience, this kind of reluctance is often shown by people who do not believe that they have any 'problem', and especially those who have been brought into mental health care against their stated wishes – those committed within the Mental Health Act under some 'compulsory treatment order'.

'OK. I hear what you are saying. You don't want to go through this assessment. You don't want to be here and you just want to go home. Right?

As I said before, I haven't got the authority to just "open the door" and let you walk out of here. So, before we wind up, let me ask you just one question. What do you think would *need to be different* for whoever has that authority, to let you go home?'

Persistence, tempered with patience, is a vital quality for any professional seeking to offer constructive, person-centred help in mental health care. If the person is unable or unwilling to open out her or his life story, and after the offer of 'options' is still unwilling to talk, the respectful nurse would accept this and withdraw, noting that the offer to 'talk' remains open and that (s)he will return again, in a specified time period. If this conveys nothing else, the person may get the message that the nurse is *genuinely* interested in what (s)he has to say and this, in itself, might represent a powerful therapeutic message.

# Chapter 10

# The Others Domain

## An anchor in the social world

If one does not know to which port one is sailing, no wind is favourable.
(Seneca)

### No man is an island

Were he alive today, doubtless John Donne would acknowledge that both women and men need other people, and that the virtue of independence, which we have trumpeted so much in health and social care, is an illusion. We are social animals. Even when we feel the need to retire from the social world, thoughts of friends, family and relationships, invariably preoccupy us. The true hermit is a rare animal indeed.

Towards the end of his life Freud pondered on the essence of humanity. What might it mean to be 'sane', to be in some sense 'fully human'? What, practically, might this involve or require? His elegant conclusion appeared simple: '*Lieben und arbeiten*' – love and work.

> The communal life of human beings had, therefore, a two-fold foundation: the compulsion to work, which was created by external necessity, and the power of love. (1930)

We assume that when he said 'love' Freud meant sharing true generosity of spirit and intimacy with another, rather than simply sexual love; and when he said 'work' he might have considered productiveness, in terms of living a meaningful life, not simply occupation, employment or the often obsessive earning of money. In our view, people need some sense of vocation, within which they might be able to love through work, and be socially productive through an expression of generous, platonic intimacy with others.

### *Drowning in our success*

Few of us today have much opportunity to experience such a vocation in life, far less to enjoy the simple platonic love and noble work to which Freud referred. Western society may be enjoying considerable economic affluence and an unprecedented level of comfort and convenience, courtesy of all manner of technological wizardry, but spiritually we are at a low ebb. In principle, we should be enjoying unequalled levels of well-being. However, despite our creature comforts, few of us are contented and many of us are not even at ease. Anxiety, alcoholism, suicide, aggression and impulsive violence, gambling and drug abuse, chronic fatigue and depression are commonplace. Over 20 million British people take antidepressants, double the number from a decade ago. Violence has increased fortyfold and suicide rates have trebled in the past 30 years (James 1988). Time off from work with stress-related illness has increased by 500 per cent in the past 50 years, with a huge knock-on effect in terms of social costs and general social instability. The situation is, arguably, even worse in the USA, which might be cast as the scriptwriter for this painful social drama of soulless, miserable affluence.

These crude statistics suggest the creeping realisation that there is little correlation between material wealth and emotional (far less spiritual) well-being. Fifty years ago, Erich Fromm anticipated the damaging effects of affluence and the emergent post-modern culture (Borgmann 1993), where all is surface and people pledge their allegiance to the logo and the brand name, rather than to human family, with whom we share the planet:

> In the end, such a civilisation can produce only a mass man: incapable of choice, incapable of spontaneous, self-directed activities: at best patient, docile, disciplined to monotonous work to an almost pathetic degree, but increasingly irresponsible as his choices become fewer – the ideal type desired, if never quite achieved, by the advertising agency and the sales organizations of modern business, or by the propaganda office and the planning bureaus of totalitarian and quasi-totalitarian governments . . . The human being who has resigned himself to a life devoid of thinking, ambition, pride, and personal achievement, has resigned himself to the death of attributes which are instinctive elements of human life.
>
> (Fromm 1956: 77–8)

Even Fromm might have been thrown by the emergence of the 'brand culture' that has become such a part of late twentieth and early twenty-first century life. Labels – from fashion to food and drink – have become the key signifiers for membership of an amorphous group, underpinned by global capitalism, which worships daily at the altar of materialism, the shopping mall. Our parents' generation, to whom Fromm issued his dire warning, would not have understood why young (and not so young) people would want to display labels on their clothing, and 'be seen' consuming certain brands of food or drink. They were still embedded in a culture where food, drink, cars, clothing and housing were merely the processes for living life, not the point of life itself.

Western society has become increasingly desperate in its 'search for mechanical and rational and symbolic securities, which substitute for the spirit-confidence of the Nature [humankind] has lost' (Hughes 1994). A more critical view would suggest that the incessant rounds of shopping, drinking, 'texting' friends, flicking through magazines, clubbing and numerous other 'diversions' are illustrations of how people anaesthetise themselves; people whose lives have grown increasingly meaningless. Although there is nothing specifically 'unhealthy' about any of these things, individually, the apparent addiction to trivia or sensation (or 'trivial sensation') may simply lead to further discontent, or even be a sign that such discontent is already deeply rooted.[1]

What relevance has all of this for the recovery process for people in mental health care? It seems ironic that so many so-called 'sane' or 'normal' people are so plainly discontented with themselves and their lives. Apart from the horrendous catalogue of human misery noted already, this is witnessed also by the groaning bookshelves in the self-help, personal development or New Age sections of the high street bookstore. Mental health appears to be an elusive proposition for just about everyone. It is also ironic that many of those deemed, formally, to be patently 'mentally unhealthy' are obliged by their circumstances to explore the meaning of their own lives, as a way of rescuing themselves from the sea of madness and, perhaps in so doing, beginning to find a way back to the shores of humanity. Describing his own experience of psychotic breakdown and the long, slow journey of recovery, Gary Platz wrote:

> For me spirituality wasn't a factor in recovery from madness toward some form of sanity. Rather, madness was essential in the recovery process from a spiritual crisis.
>
> (Platz 2003: 201)

In that sense, arguably everyone is faced with the same challenge: to make sense of life; to find or construct meaning in or from the experiences we have in life. We can divert ourselves from this challenge through all manner of pleasure seeking, or even by immersing ourselves in work, but ultimately the question comes back to haunt us: Who am I?

### Self-esteem and connection

As we noted in Chapter 6, who we are as persons is largely a personal construction. We invent ourselves through the process of thinking and talking about 'who' we have been and who we think we are becoming. However, this takes place within a social context, and much of what we have to say about 'ourselves' is either directed towards other people, or in response to something which others say or do. Berger and Luckmann (1967) called this the 'reality of everyday life':

> The reality of everyday life further presents itself to me as an intersubjective world, a world I share with others . . . I am alone in the world of my dreams, but I know that the world of everyday life is as real to others as it is to myself. Indeed, I cannot exist in everyday life without continually interacting and communicating with others . . . I also know, of course, that the others have a perspective on this common world that is not identical with mine. My 'here' is their 'there'. My 'now' does not fully overlap with theirs. All the same, I know that I live with them in a common world. Most importantly, I know that there is an ongoing correspondence between *my* meanings and *their* meanings in this world, that we share a common sense about its reality . . . Common-sense knowledge is the knowledge I share with others in the normal, self-evident routines of everyday life.
>
> (Berger and Luckmann 1967: 37)

People who experience serious, disabling problems of living become detached from this 'everyday reality'. The experience of becoming a psychiatric patient (or even a user/consumer/client of mental health services) requires the adoption of a role that essentially sets the person apart from the common-sense knowledge that once framed the experience of everyday reality.

The psychiatric system, whether bounded by the walls of the hospital or the timetables, meetings, paperwork and arcane language of 'care in the community', is not part of the everyday reality. It is a foreign land, a place shunned and avoided at all costs by most of the 'normal' population. If the recovery journey in mental health involves recovering a sense of human identity through reclaiming the story of one's life, it also involves charting a strong course in the direction of that symbolic place called 'everyday reality'. Indeed, the physical act of trying to sail towards the dry land of 'everyday reality' is a vital part of the whole recovery of identity that takes place in the private domain of the Self.

### Overview of the Others Domain

The Others Domain illustrated in Figure 10.1 is focused on three interconnected dimensions:

- the 'living world', where we conduct all of our social affairs and where all the support we receive from others, is presented
- 'supportive care', where we find specific sources of support to address our problems of living

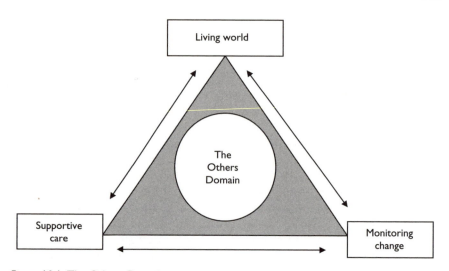

*Figure 10.1* The Others Domain

- the social process through which we become more aware of and monitor change in our life circumstances.

Each of these dimensions involves further exploration of what is happening in the life of the person, and the development of practical responses to the various environmental, social and interpersonal aspects of the social world of others.

## The living world

The care that a person needs is invariably multidimensional in character, especially where the person is experiencing grave personal and social difficulties. In addition to the specific care offered by the nursing team, the person is likely to require support, advice, information and direct help with various other aspects of life, from a range of health and social care agencies. Although health care may be the central focus of the care plan, an integrated care plan should acknowledge the importance of personal and social areas of life, for the recovery process.

The professional team should ensure that the care offered in the Self and World Domains is coordinated with inputs from other appropriate agencies in the Others Domain: medical care, social work, psychology, occupational therapy, user advocacy and psychotherapy, as required by the person. Information about the person's needs should be coordinated with the identification of who might be able to meet these needs, and what they should or could offer by way of specific support.

---

**NB** It is vitally important that the person in care (and where appropriate family members or advocates) knows the names and different responsibilities of all the agencies involved in the care planning and delivery process.

---

### Dimensions of assessment

To provide the necessary context for the development of appropriate care, within the Others Domain further assessment may be needed in the following areas:

- finance
- housing
- legal support
- medical care and treatment
- advocacy
- social and community support
- occupation and leisure
- education
- employment.

Information concerning the person's needs in any or all of the above areas may be drawn from focused interviews, or globally from existing sources of information.

Most of these areas will be addressed in the *Transitional Care Plan*, when the person is being prepared to return to the natural community, or when moving between one care setting and another. These areas usually become the discrete focus of the *Developmental Care Plan*, where the wider context of the person's life is being addressed and a broader base established for the development of a genuine sense of recovery.

### Membership and belonging

Despite the various social and media campaigns conducted in recent years to educate and inform the public about mental health, stigma remains a major problem for anyone with an experience of 'mental illness' or any serious 'mental health problem'. The commonest consequence of stigma is the sense of alienation from family, friends and wider society. In many instances, this perception is translated into a physical reality, as ties with established friends or acquaintances, and sometimes even family, are stretched and broken.

Arguably, the most vital function of care within the Others Domain, is to provide the conditions under which the person might begin to reconnect with 'others', establishing the kind of relationships that might provide the basis for friendship, natural social support and a sense of belonging and membership to some *community* of others. (An important part of this work is undertaken through the groupwork described in Chapter 12.)

It should not surprise us that stigma remains such a potent force in post-modern western society, or that it is often extremely difficult to negotiate the 're-entry' of people into society, following any period as a 'psychiatric patient'. The concept of 'mental illness' is used to contain all the uncertainties of post-modern life; a receptacle for the 'dark side' and the general anxieties of so-called 'normal' people, for the madness that lies latent within us all. Viewed from this perspective, society maintains the concept of alien madness – the classic 'us and them' scenario – as a way of discriminating Self from Other: we are sane because they are crazy.

At the same time, the traditional social ties and networks that frame and support the traditional society are fading or have already collapsed (at least in most parts of the western world). In addition to the loss of much of the human contact and support that people used to enjoy (literally) at the hands of friends, neighbours and families, the stress experienced by the lack of such a supportive infrastructure compounds the person's sense of alien-ation – the feeling that (s)he has drifted too far from land ever to be able to return.

Ironically, the most powerful sense of connectedness, membership and belonging comes from the sharing of stories with 'fellow travellers', whether other people currently sharing the care system with the person, or others who have recovered from an episode of mental distress (see Barker *et al.* 1999a; Campbell 1996; Leibrich 1999). People who have negotiated their recovery, whether wholly or in part, are powerful role models, illustrating the possibilities of the recovery journey and helping realistically to boost the person's hopes. Helping the person learn about and make links with local groups, such as the Hearing Voices Network, Depression Alliance or a local Club House, provides rich opportunities for rekindling the person's sense of membership and belonging, and begins also to challenge the damaging effects of stigma. Information about the availability of such supports, or direct contact with representatives of such organisations, may be arranged either through the Individual Care Plan (described in Chapter 11) or through the Information Group (described in Chapter 12).

## Supportive care

The needs of the person in care are invariably complex and wide ranging. It is unlikely that any single professional agency will be able to meet all the person's needs. The Self and World Domains focus specifically on the person who is relating to these problems of living or needs, and how the person relates to the 'others' within their world of experience. In the Others Domain, this focus includes all the other people who make up the system that might help address the person's discrete problems of living. These may be both professional agents as well as lay people – family, friends, members of support groups, etc. – who might also have an important part to play in the ultimate resolution of the person's problems, or who might otherwise contribute to their story of recovery.

The Others Domain is wide ranging. From a care perspective, the interdisciplinary professional team lies at its heart. This team is charged with the responsibility for coordinating care and treatment in one or more of the care settings across the care continuum. Supporting the core team, which usually comprises nursing, medical, OT and social work, are a range of other professionals who make contributions to the ongoing care plan. This list of possible agents includes:

- clinical psychology
- housing
- social services
- pharmacy
- legal services
- further education
- chaplains and religious or spiritual advisers
- psychotherapy and counselling
- complementary therapists
- occupational counsellors.

Not least, this list of possible supportive agents should include friends, life partners and family. However, as with the list of professional agents, care needs to be taken over the identification of what role such lay people might play and what exactly might be the form of their support. It should not be assumed that status – whether as friend, family member, therapist or counsellor – necessarily equates with helping potential. The person must be the final arbiter and judge as to who might offer support in relation to which particular needs and what that support might entail.

Ideally, there should exist only one care plan, within which all details of the necessary care and support can be recorded. This should integrate the different contributions of the various team members. In the immediate care setting, especially in hospital, the nursing team usually leads the delivery of care. Given the nurses' responsibility for managing the overall therapeutic environment of the ward and their proximity to the person in care, it is appropriate that the plan of nursing care should incorporate all other directions for care and treatment, especially from medical and therapies staff.

However, in transitional and developmental care settings, the person who is most closely involved with the person and their family may not always be a nurse. Here, the professional who carries the designated responsibility for supervising the delivery of the person's care and treatment should manage the core care plan.

## Monitoring change

The central focus of the Tidal Model is the development of awareness of change. How does the person come to *know* (experientially) that (s)he is moving through the critical experience of distress, and what options for charting a course of recovery lie before her or him? Given this core assumption, the experience of care can and indeed should ultimately be reviewed by the person receiving the care. Only the person can know if the care provided has 'worked', since the person will define what (s)he means by 'worked'. However, at least in the early stages, the task of reviewing the process of change usually falls to specific members of the professional team – hopefully supported and augmented by the person themselves. Usually this takes the form of a review meeting within which the professional team members occupy enviable positions of authority, irrespective of the review meeting's location across the care continuum. Given the focus on collaboration and empowerment within the Tidal Model, the person should not only be a *participant* in this process, but specific arrangements should be made to ensure that the focus is on meeting the needs of the person, rather than the professionals or the service, during this review. To this end the review should be focused on the person's agenda rather than a traditional professionally focused 'case conference'. The person is and should always remain, literally and figuratively, the 'point' of the meeting.

### The structure of review meetings

The following overview of the organisation of review meetings is in no way exhaustive, but is relevant to the monitoring of change across the care continuum. Given the context of (for example) routine ward rounds, case conferences, Mental Health Act Section Review Meetings, and Care Programme Approach (CPA) meetings,[2] the following suggestions might help refocus the attention of such meetings on the proper 'subject' – the person themselves.[3]

### Rights of attendance

The review meeting is convened to discuss the person's care. Consequently the focus of the meeting is the person's needs. It should be taken as read that the person should be present and that every effort should be made to ensure that their comfort and dignity are guaranteed and safeguarded.

The person's presence at the review meeting should always be entirely voluntary and a formal invitation to participate should always be extended. The person should also be advised that if (s)he does not wish to attend alternative arrangements will be made to discuss the person's care.

If the person declines the invitation, arrangements should be made to meet privately with the most appropriate member of the therapeutic team to review progress at some later time, by arrangement. In such circumstances, the person should be given a choice as to which member of the team they would like to meet with.

### Participants

The number of professionals present should be kept to a minimum – no more than three or four. All workers should introduce themselves and explain why they have come to the meeting. Professionals attending the review should clearly be there for the person's benefit.

### Students

Students from different disciplines need to learn about the conduct of review meetings. However, this should not be at the expense of the person in care. Students should only attend the meeting if the person has given explicit approval in advance. Asking the person as the review meeting is about to begin, or even as the person enters the room (an all too common practice), is not acceptable as this places pressure on the person to give consent.

### Advocacy

The experience of being 'reviewed' by a team of professionals can be traumatic. To offset the natural feelings of insecurity and isolation, the person should be asked (well in advance of the review meeting), if (s)he would like to bring a partner, friend, family member or advocate to the review. Arrangements should be made to make any such 'support person' comfortable, and ensure that this person also feels part of the proceedings.

### Timing

The person (and family member or advocate) should be notified well in advance of the schedule of the review. Team members should make every effort to adhere to this timetable and should attend punctually. Latecomers should apologise and offer an explanation to the person, rather than to professional colleagues. Similarly, should anyone need to leave before the end of the review, an explanation should be offered, and the professional should leave when his or her departure will cause the least disruption.

*Seating*

Seats should be arranged to encourage informal communication with the person who is the subject of the review, situated at the heart of the group. The seating arrangements should encourage the person to feel that (s)he is a participant in the discussion, rather than the focus of a cross-examination.

*Refreshments*

If refreshments are considered desirable, an offer of a choice of refreshment should be made *first* to the person and any advocate, friend or family member (if present), and then to professionals. Indeed, there may be a virtue in taking refreshments as a precursor to the formal discussion. This may help to put people at their ease and foster informal conversation.

*The process of the review*

The review should be conducted in a sensitive and respectful manner. Consideration should be given to which member of the team is the appropriate person to ask any particular question. Professionals should not discuss the person amongst themselves. Every attempt should be made to ensure that decisions are made conjointly with the person and team members.

Particular care needs to be taken over all questions which are posed in a public setting. Unless absolutely necessary, questions should not be asked about distressing or intimate aspects of the person's life. Similarly, questions that might test the person unduly should be avoided. Finally, professionals should not ask questions to which they already know the answers.[4]

## The caring destination

As the Roman philosopher Seneca affirmed, aimless progress is just aimless progress. We need to have some sense of a destination, even if this is metaphorical or symbolic in character. Our efforts to support the person on the recovery journey may represent more wind in the person's sails, but to what *end*? Clearly, both the members of the professional team and the person must share an appreciation of what the port might be like; whether this is the final destination or merely another port in a long drawn-out storm. The current fascination with doing everything at speed or more quickly has encouraged the idea that people should be admitted and discharged from services as fast as possible, whether or not this clashes with the need to slow down the pace of the madness going on within the person.

If we are doing nothing else in helping the person through the experience of mental distress, we are helping that person become aware that (s)he is more than a 'patient' or client or user/consumer. We are helping the person to reclaim the appreciation that (s)he is a person, first and foremost, and that this human identity (as distinct from the psychiatric identity conferred by the mental health system) belongs in the everyday reality of life beyond the mental health system. In so doing, we help the person appreciate how (s)he might regain the position lost in the social world or local community, or we might help the person develop an appreciation of some alternative position, perhaps complete with a new identity, that might be an important part of the recovery journey.

The specifics of all of this are, necessarily, vague. We are only too well aware of the extent to which we have 'drifted' during our life journey. We never had any specific intention of being 'here' at this point in our lives: we drifted here, albeit by dint of trying to get to somewhere else. Why should it be any different for the people whom we call the service user or mental health services consumer? The important thing is to be aware of making an effort to travel somewhere; preferably somewhere which at the time seems like a good destination. Whether this will be our ultimate destination, or even will turn out to be all that 'good', is to miss the point. To paraphrase the Chinese sage: there is no destination – all is journey.

These sentiments may appear a world away from the goal plans, framed within case conferences by teams of distinguished and highly qualified 'do-gooders', all intent on guaranteeing the best possible outcome for the person defined as the 'patient' or 'client'. Often these professional goals are painfully modest, with much anguish and argument devoted to the best way of ensuring that the person 'continues to take their medication' or 'avoids relapse'. It does not take a philosopher to beg the question 'for what ultimate purpose?' What is to be the point of all this striving if the appropriate port is not clearly within our sights, having been identified by the captain, the person who is in receipt of our care.

The Others Domain is the place where the professional team, family members and friends begin to splash around on the shoreline, knowing that at some point the person will need to push off in the boat and begin to head for the open seas. It is here in the Others Domain that we need to ask all the important questions about the kind of supports – physical, intellectual, emotional and perhaps also spiritual – that the person might need as the wind begins to billow the sails, and the comfort and security of the immediate 'Others' are left on the shore. Hopefully, by the time we get to that metaphorical shoreline we shall have addressed most of those concerns. Before the person gets anywhere near the transitional care phase of discharge, (s)he will have explored some of the options that lie in the world of 'everyday reality'; will be more aware of what challenges lie ahead and who might be available to help confront them; and will know what other 'supplies' might be needed for the journey ahead and where (s)he might obtain them.

The Others Domain, perhaps because it is located specifically in the shallows of the Ocean of Experience, can be an uncomfortable place for the professional team. In the Others Domain the professional team members discover that they are only some of the many who make up the social world of the person in care. Here they come face to face with their responsibilities for letting go of the person and, importantly, their responsibility for preparing the person for the journey, which will always be taken alone.

# Chapter 11

# The lantern on the stern

## Individual Care

> The light which experience gives, is a lantern on the stern, which shines only on the waves behind us.
>
> (Samuel Taylor Coleridge)

## Helping the person to need help less

### Guided by the experience of the expert

How can we proceed without experience? Yet we are full of experience – it flows through us, moment by moment. If only we could appreciate the experience that is happening for us, right here and now. If only we could become more aware of what we have, as opposed to what we have not got. Awareness is the lantern on our stern, and gives us the gist of the approach to individual care within the Tidal Model.

Over 25 years ago, when we worked in the field of rehabilitation, we used to discuss with our colleagues how we could 'make ourselves redundant'. We had not long since embarked on our professional careers and were working with people with serious problems of living and multiple disabilities, many of whom had experienced years of continuous institutionalisation, Naively, we were aware that the whole 'point' of professional service was to make ourselves and the service we offered, redundant: 'no longer necessary', 'superfluous to requirements', something that could be 'omitted without any loss of significance'.

A quarter of a century later, we think that we are more aware of why becoming redundant remains the highest possible professional ideal. All around us are people trying to convince us that we need their services, from financial advisers to lifestyle gurus. Few of these 'consultants' will settle for a one-off consultation. Most aim to be involved for as long as they can, since 'having clients' is at least one of the critical measures of professional success. However, exactly why anyone would need this advice and what exactly it amounts to are two of the most impertinent questions that might be asked of the ambitious professional. All are selling something, if only themselves. Indeed, for many of them, this is all they have to sell – themselves.

More than a century later, George Bernard Shaw's dictum still holds water: professionalism is a conspiracy against the laity. If people understood exactly what the professional was doing, there would be much less need for 'the professions'. People would become aware of how much they could do for themselves, with the minimum of assistance, if not entirely unaided. In the Shavian sense, the Tidal Model is an anti-professional approach to mental health care. It does not believe that there is any special knowledge concerning mental health, known only to the professional, that can bring about the resolution of serious problems of human living, or speed the person's recovery.[1] The Tidal Model proposes that only the person can ever own such knowledge. However, this does not mean that task of helping people through the course of their mental health recovery is simple. The person is the supreme 'consultant'; the one who will be the final judge as regards what *needs to be done* and whether or not it is working. However, the person needs sophisticated support to plan and execute the process of recovery. The traditional idea of 'professionalism' may be a distraction. Perhaps we need a different construction of the 'helpful helper': how might others be genuinely helpful to the person in need?

### What's on the helping menu?

As we argued in the opening chapters, the process of offering meaningful help to someone in distress is more akin to craft than it is to science or art. The business of helping is more of a noble trade than an obscure professional art or science. The 'helpful helper' has to work out how best to shape what needs to be offered to fit the person's needs: tailors, dressmakers, photographers, cooks or hairdressers might be better role models for the helper in mental health – all are skilled and knowledgeable, but all are aware that the customer is boss.[2]

> When Milton Erickson was asked about the models on which he based his therapy, he would say: 'I design a new model for each patient.' If asked about the role of theory in his work he would add: 'I create a new theory for each patient.'

In the tidal metaphor, the professional often acts more like a life-saver who, realising that the person is drowning, organises a rescue. However, life-savers do not restrain or overpower the drowning person. Invariably the life-saver 'joins with' the thrashing movements of the drowning person, gradually slowing these down until the person is either helped to swim or float alongside the rescuer on the journey to shore. The life-saver offers an important analogy for the concept of the helper within the Tidal Model. For most of the working day the life-saver 'does nothing' – or at least nothing dramatic – all the while maintaining a vigilant watch over the beach or pool, in a state of constant *preparedness*. To the idle observer, this work is easy. However, the relaxed presence of the life-saver belies the demands of maintaining a calm state of high alert; ready to launch into action; knowing enough about oneself to avoid being sucked into the whirlpool created by the drowning person.

Mental health care has many similarities to the work of the life-saver. For much of the time the professional does 'nothing special' and often appears to be calm and relaxed; active listening being just one such example. Of course, many adopt the view that 'anyone could do that'. But the apparent simplicity of much mental health care belies its inherent complexity and necessary skill. In an age where we have become obsessed with professionals having the 'right skills' we often forget the importance of the *qualities* of the individual practitioner. What kind of *person* does the practitioner need to be to become helpful? What kinds of qualities does the person need to possess to be able to facilitate the recovery journey? We mapped out most of these attributes in Chapter 2. However, here it is worth recalling some of the critical features of the helpful helper. The helper needs to:

- *believe that recovery is possible* – otherwise that first step, out onto the recovery path will not be taken
- be able to *contain the fear* that inevitably comes as we move slowly out into deeper water, feeling for our own safety as well as that of the person whom we are guiding
- be *creative* and *resourceful*, looking for and trying out alternatives when difficulty is encountered. There is no one perfect way to help, but an infinite number of possibilities. Finding what would be helpful by looking for it is 'the way'.

These assumptions are problematic in a professional world that stands in the shadows of the twin towers of science and research. We are encouraged to believe that we should only use 'methods' that have a proven track record of efficiency or effectiveness; methods that have been 'tested' scientifically through research and have been shown to 'work'. Of course, there is value in discriminating the 'good' from the 'bad', distinguishing the blatantly 'toxic' ways of treating people from those that are 'gentler' or more compassionate. However, beyond that we doubt the wisdom of generating lists or menus of 'effective methods' or 'research-based technologies' of human helping.

The kind of help that people *need* is similar to their food menus. At any dinner table there will be a few vegetarians, perhaps a strict vegan, some who choose the fish, others who shun the soup, everyone taking wine but some suffering for it in the morning. Take another evening with the same group of people and the choices may be similar but not entirely identical. Each person is trying to make a judgement as to what would be the 'right' choice *now*. At different times of day, on different days, at different times in the person's life, different food choices will be made. There are some foods, or all if taken to excess, that are unkind or downright 'bad' for the individual digestion. These need to be treated with caution. Similarly, there are some simple foods like bread or rice that are generally 'good', but individual exceptions to this rule can and do occur. We need to be aware of such possibilities. However, ultimately, eating and drinking is about identifying what would be 'right' for the person 'here and now'. After a spell on a desert island we all might hunger for the simplicity of a piece of fresh bread or some mashed potato. The grand banquet might smell and look sumptuous but will it meet our needs, here and now?

Helping people deal with their problems of living involves the exercise of much the same judgement and restraint as that needed by the perfect host or the *maitre d'hôte*. We try to offer what the person appears to need, want or wish for right now, providing that we believe this will not be bad either for the person, our reputation, or that of our service.

### Begin with the end in mind

The focus of the care is to do whatever needs to be done – *and no more* – to meet the person's immediate needs (actual problems). The professional also needs to continue listening carefully as the person's story unfolds, with a view to preventing or anticipating the occurrence of potential problems, either associated with our offer of help or coming from some other source. As we noted at the end of Chapter 10, the rule of thumb for the plan of care is 'always begin with the end in mind'. To that end, the professional team should be focused on helping the person to return to the world of everyday reality as soon as possible, *but no sooner*. Judging when this might be of course, is an art in itself.

When someone enters any mental health service – whether as a 'patient' entering a psychiatric intensive care unit or a 'client' entering a community 'walk-in' centre – the first question that needs to be asked is: 'What needs to happen for this person not to need this service?' Whether asked directly, as we illustrated in our discussion of the Holistic Assessment in Chapter 9, or asked implicitly as part of the general approach to determining appropriate care, this is the primary focus of Tidal Model care. The answer to this question will, at the very least, *signal* the resolution of the person's present difficulties (what brought the person to the service in the first place).

The means for actively pursuing the answer to this key question involves identifying and building upon the person's existing personal and inter-personal resources. To this end, the Tidal Model emphasises the importance of encouraging the person to become aware of the part they might play (or indeed already *are* playing) in identifying actual and potential problems, and in working out what might need to happen to resolve or at least reduce the effects of those problems. To what extent does the answer that the person seeks (or which the professional seeks on the person's behalf) already lie nestled within the person's story?

The key focus of all individualised care is to emphasise the development of the person's *awareness* of change, however small or gradual. The development of this awareness began in the Holistic Assessment, when the person was helped to discuss what it would be like *not* to have the problem, and what might need to change, or to happen, to help bring that change about.

## The structure of Individual Care

The approach to the provision of Individual Care reflects the principles covered in earlier chapters (see Figure 11.1).

1    The *ultimate aim* of Individual Care represents the state which the person will experience when (s)he no longer needs the service. In the case of someone admitted to a psychiatric intensive care unit, this would involve experiencing the state necessary to achieve discharge from *this particular unit*, even if this involves a transfer to another mental health service.[3]

2    The *immediate aim* is the necessary 'first step' that needs to be taken *away* from the present circumstances, which hopefully will lead in the general direction of the ultimate aim. In effect, the professional asks: 'What

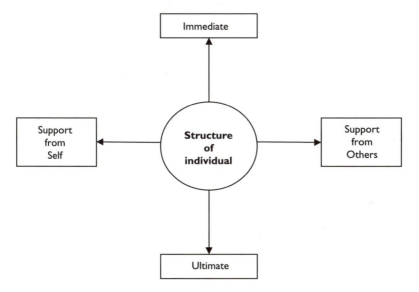

*Figure 11.1* The structure of Individual Care

would *signal* (in however small a way) that the person is moving away from the state that necessitates entry to the service in the first place?'

3   The person needs to identify what are the 'personal and interpersonal resources' that can be drawn upon, which might be used as *support from the Self*, as (s)he takes these necessary steps on the recovery journey.

4   The person can also identify what *support from Others* might prove helpful, in the short term. This will involve emotional, practical and social support from family and friends alongside discrete offers of support from different professional team members.

Individual Care within the Tidal Model is, as a rule, focused very much on the short term: what needs to be done to facilitate the taking of *this* small step, and *then*, what needs to happen *now* to facilitate the taking of the next step? This approach echoes the ancient wisdom of the Chinese sage when Lao Tsu proposed that 'the journey of a thousand miles *always* begins with a single step'.[4] Indeed, any journey, whether short or long, involves a succession of steps. The next big step is always a series of very small steps. The key to a successful journey is to be aware of whether or not the steps taken appear to lead to the desired destination.

### Orientation to Immediate Care

Efforts are made to engage the person directly in the process of Individual Care from the moment of entry into the care setting.[5] As the person moves across the *immediate–transitional–developmental* stages of the care continuum, the kind of care will of necessity change. However, the focus on awareness, and especially awareness of change, will remain a constant feature of the caring process:

1   As the staff member provides the person with an orientation to the care setting, a brief introduction will be made to what services are available and how these might be relevant to the person's immediate needs.

2   The person is invited to identify, broadly, what her or his immediate needs might be, and how these might represent what brought the person into the care setting in the first place.

3   Having clarified the person's understanding of 'why I am here', some discussion takes place about what *needs to change* to allow the person to return home or believe that the service is no longer necessary.

In an effort to involve the person actively in the process, the nurse should encourage them to write down a summary of their understanding of what has taken place:

•   What brought the person into care.

- What the person believes (s)he can expect in terms of support.
- How the person will know when (s)he is ready to leave.
- Who might be able to support her/him during the period of care.
- Finally, to ensure that the orientation has been fully completed, the person is asked to acknowledge that (s)he has been advised about the general care on offer, as well as the specific therapies that are available, concluding with an acknowledgement of 'who' has helped the person through the orientation process.[6]

During the orientation conversation, which may take as little as ten minutes to complete but depending on the person might take much longer, the nurse provides the person with some information about aspects of the model and tries to identity *when* it would be appropriate to begin work on the problems that have brought the person into care:

- The nurse records brief details of the assessment 'plan of action'.
- The nurse makes a note for the rest of the team concerning how the person appeared during the orientation process.
- The nurse makes a note of the issues that *the nurse* thinks need to be addressed soon.
- The nurse states what kind of support (s)he thinks that the team need to offer the person in the short term (Figure 11.2).

By using this simple format, the team hopes to achieve a degree of *transparency* in the whole approach to care. By involving (or at least inviting the involvement of) the person, an important first step has been taken in negotiating the process of collaborative care. By inviting the person to sign the record, the nurse gives a clear message that, although the conversation may be informal and relaxed, this is an important process of which the person is a vital part.

> **NB** Figure 11.2 illustrates the kind of information that would be recorded by the person and the team member following introduction to the care setting. This example uses an acute care setting, but the principle of 'orientation' to the care on offer and the reasons for the person needing care would apply across all care settings.

## The one-to-one session

The individual or one-to-one session is well established in mental health practice, especially in nursing, where it has come to represent the period of time when the nurse dedicates her/himself completely to the person in care,

| Sunny View<br>Mental Health Unit<br>Anytown | Name: *Clare Sweeney*<br>Key worker: *Mary Brown*<br>Medical officer: *Dr TP McKenna* |
|---|---|
| **Immediate Care Plan** | **Date:** *17/07/03* **Nurse:** *P. Buller* |
| **Person** | **Staff** |
| What brought me here:<br><br>*I am worthless.*<br><br>I can expect the following support:<br><br>*Talking with a nurse and going to groups.*<br><br>I will be ready to leave here when:<br><br>*I can ~~to~~ see some future for myself. I need to feel different?*<br><br>People who might support me are:<br><br>*Tom - my brother*<br>*Siobhan - my friend*<br><br>I have been advised of the care I shall receive<br><br>I have been advised about the specific therapies available<br><br>The nurse who provided this information was:   *Patrick* | **Proposed Further Assessment**<br><br>Self Domain: *17/07/03 : 4pm*<br><br>Others Domain: *18/07/03 : 4pm*<br><br>World Domain: *18/07/03: 10am*<br><br>Comments<br><br>*Clare seems very low in spirits, and found it very difficult to concentrate. Said she was very tired.*<br><br>**Specific Issues Identified**<br><br>*Dog (alone) at home?*<br>*Finances*<br>*Medication*<br><br>**Immediate Staff Support**<br><br>*1. Support*<br>*2. Develop Security Plan*<br>*3. Introduce to others*<br>*4. Arrange 1-1 session* |
| Signature          Dated<br><br>*Clare Sweeney*      *17/07/03* | Signature          Date<br><br>*P Buller*          *17/07/03* |

Figure 11.2 Introduction to Immediate Care

focusing on the particular issues of the day raised by the person. The one-to-one session is a vital part of Individual Care within the Tidal Model, since it affords a context within which the person can reflect on her or his experience, supported by the professional's careful respectful inquiries (Figure 11.3).

*Figure 11.3* The organisation of Individual Care

### One-to-one in Immediate Care

When the person is in Immediate Care such sessions should be arranged daily, focused on providing continuity of support alongside that given within general care in the unit. Initially, this contact may be very informal as the professional (usually the nurse) tries to gain the person's confidence, and the person tries to get a sense of what is expected of him or her in this unusual encounter. However, the professional will quickly try to develop the collaborative nature of the session, building on the person's experience in the orientation meeting described above. The focus of the session is very simple, but perhaps because of this it is important to provide a structure that will help the person develop the awareness of 'what is happening' discussed at the beginning of this chapter. We illustrate this structure, or at least one way of providing such support, later in the chapter.

   The aim of the session is to provide a quiet, confidential arena within which the person can explore (briefly) where (s)he finds herself, here and now; and can begin to get a sense of how she might move (or indeed already is moving) forward on the recovery journey. In general, this involves:

*   exploring how things *are changing* in the here and now
*   imagining how things *would be different* if (or when) the person's situation changes, or
*   how things *were different*, in the past (recent or distant) when the person was free (either partially or wholly) of the present problem.

The one-to-one session should appear like an ordinary conversation. The aim is to help the person become aware of the changes that are *already going on*, and how the person might help *develop* these changes, and how the

**Avoiding problem talk**

The one-to-one session avoids problem talk as much as possible. We acknowledge that for many people talking about the past is important, as part of making sense of the life journey to date. However, this can distract from developing awareness of what is happening here and now and, more importantly, can block the creative anticipation of the journey ahead. However, it is important not to make rules about this, as this would be disrespectful. The following extract from a one-one-one conversation illustrates how, with careful use of metaphor, the professional can validate the person's concerns for the story of the past, while helping to focus on the immediate future.

*Helper*:   So what have you brought with you that you would like to talk about?

*Person*:   Oh, I can't stop thinking about how it has all gone wrong. I mean things were never great but why me? That's what I ask, why me? There's got to be something wrong with me – deep down like. I got to get to the bottom of that before I can move on. My last doctor said that. Got to get to the bottom of it all.

*Helper*:   You are right, of course. The past is powerful isn't it? The past writes our life story all over us, like the lines on your face, or maybe it goes right through us, like the lettering on a stick of rock. It's also like the journey we have taken down all the days of our life right up to here, where we are now. You have sailed a long way to get to here and you have survived a lot of storms. Maybe some of those storms were so terrifying that you can hardly believe that you have come out of them with everything intact. Right now you are sailing in calmer waters but the memory of those storms is still anchored deep within you. It is part of your wisdom about yourself. You might have wished for a calmer passage but here you are now, having emerged from the storm. So what's it like to be here and now? What is different?

nursing team, or others, might play a part in promoting small, but steady changes in how the person feels, how the person thinks, and what the person is able to do, on a daily basis.

Although people often 'wait' for change to come about, change is an ongoing process. Change flows through the person invisibly, like water. The nurse aims to help the person begin to notice these small changes, which represent the tiny steps that are being taken on the long road to recovery. The journey of a thousand miles truly begins with a single step.

## Clare's story

Clare was admitted to an acute psychiatric ward two days ago. She had a long history of treatment for depression in hospital and in the community. Her community psychiatric nurse, who had been seeing her regularly, thought that she was suicidal and encouraged Clare to come into hospital for further assessment and support. (Figure 11.4 provides an overview of Clare's first three days on the unit.)

Clare is given a very simple introduction to the staff and ward surroundings after admission so that she can get her bearings and feel a little less disoriented. Following the standard interview with the medical staff member, the staff team prepare a *provisional plan of care*, which will serve as a general support for Clare until a more focused plan of care can be negotiated. Normally, this would be undertaken independently with the staff team, which is trying to establish the basic supportive conditions necessary to assist Clare through her introduction to the programme.

For the rest of her first day, Clare is allowed 'free time' under the general supportive care condition determined by the team (Engagement Level 2). She is introduced gradually to the collaborative approach and encouraged to have some 'sitting in' experience of the available groups held on the unit.

On days 2 and 3 Clare is introduced to more active involvement in group-work and further focal assessment of her needs. As more information becomes available, the team adjust Clare's general plan of care, usually doing this at least once each day, in the evening, in anticipation of the next day's care programme.

---

**NB** The sooner the person can begin to participate meaningfully in her or his own care, the sooner they will begin to gain meaningful supportive care, and the sooner the person will be able to relax her/his dependence on formal mental health services. Consequently, the programme of care involves a careful balance between 'active' engagement in activities that hopefully will generate the kind of support the person needs, and 'passive' periods within which the natural recovery and healing can take place. Judging how much *activity* should be balanced against how much *peace* and *recovery time* is invariably complex. However, it seems clear from many studies, especially of mental health care in hospital settings, that people experience too little activity and too much enforced passivity.

Day 1
- 10 am: Clare admitted to the unit by her CPN
- 11 am: General orientation to her accommodation and unit layout.
- 11.30: Interview with medical officer
- 12.30: Lunch
- 13.00: Staff review Clare's provisional care plan and determine necessary level of support – Engagement Level 2.
- 13.45: Orientation meeting – introduction to concept of care and clarification of ultimate aims and summary of available professional support.
- 14.00: Free time (all free time under Engagement Level 2)
- 16.00: Self Domain Assessment – Suicide Risk Interview
- 17.30: Tea
- 18.30: Information Group – Sitting-in experience
- 19.00: Staff complete Global Assessment of Suicide Risk
- 19.30: Staff review conditions of general care – maintain Engagement Level 2
- 19.30: Free time

Day 2
- 8.00: Free time
- 10.00: World Domain: Completion of Holistic Assessment
- 11.30: Recovery Group: sitting-in experience
- 12.30: Lunch
- 14.00: Free time
- 16.00: Others Domain: Interview focused on possible support role of friends, family and specific members of professional team.
- 17.30: Tea
- 18.30: Monitoring Assessment – and support with development of provision Personal Security Plan
- 19.30: Free time

Day 3
- 8.00: Free time
- 11.30: Recovery Group: encourage active participation
- 12.30: Lunch
- 13.45: One-to-one session
- 14.15: Free time (encourage review of Personal Security Plan)
- 15.00: Solutions Group: Sitting-in experience.
- 16.00: Free time
- 17.30: Tea
- 18.30: Information Group
- 19.30: Free time

* The illustration here shows the almost immediate engagement of the person in the various processes of care and treatment. If the person is *unwilling* or *unable* to engage with care at the outset, then supportive general care is established until the person is able or willing to begin to explore collaborative care.

*Figure 11.4* Clare's story: Overview of the development of Immediate Care*

On the morning of day 3 Clare completed the Holistic Assessment described in Chapter 9. This is the summary of Clare's story that was recorded in the Holistic Assessment:

Four or five months ago I noticed that I couldn't be bothered and that things were such an effort. John (my partner) started to nag me and things got worse. I felt that I wanted to go to sleep and when I woke up it would be alright, but it never was. Now John has gone (left me), the flat has gone and I've had to move in with my friend Janet. Now there is no one to care for me I've lost touch with people. My mum can't help me because of how she is. I would like someone to care, but I know that they know that I can't be bothered. I feel all coiled up tight inside, especially when I think about what has happened. It means that there is no future and it is my fault that there is no future.

All of this says that I'm not very nice, because I'm the kind of person that wrecks everything. I don't think that anything can be done for me but I wish the last six months could be rubbed out and I could start again and have someone to love me. I don't expect you (the nurses) to do anything for me, because you can't do anything.

I have rated the 'whole thing' as 10 for distress, 10 for disturbance and 1 for control.

The people who are important to me are: Janet (my friend) because she tolerates me, and she lets me live in her flat; my mum, because she cares for me (because mums do, don't they?); and a girl I met last night on the ward. She was interesting and seemed interested in me.

The things that are important to me are a pair of earrings my grand-mother gave me; a radio which I can listen to by myself; a picture of my gran, which reminds me of when I was little – she used to cuddle me; and a ring that John gave me, but I don't wear it.

The idea about life that is important to me is that I used to feel that if I was kind to people they would be kind to me – but it all has changed.

If I could be bothered I would know my problem has changed because I would go out with Janet and go for a drink. If the tight feeling wasn't there I could talk to people and I might find myself interested in people again. What needs to change for this to happen is that if someone came to visit me that would be nice. It would show that somebody cares. But I don't think that it's going to happen and I don't think it would make any difference anyway.

When the nurse returned with Clare's copy of the assessment, she negotiated the one-to-one session for later that day. This allowed Clare an opportunity to reflect on the proceedings of the Holistic Assessment, and to think through some of the issues raised about herself and her needs in the assessment.

### Clare's first one-to-one session

When Clare discussed her 'ultimate aim' during the orientation interview, she said that she wanted to 'feel more relaxed'. This was addressed again in the Holistic Assessment when Clare talked about how 'If the tight feeling wasn't there I could talk to people and I might find myself interested in people again'. Provisionally, Clare's 'ultimate' aim is identified as 'to feel more relaxed'.

The one-to-one session is focused on a conversation between the nurse, Mary, and Clare, in which the nurse tries to help Clare develop her awareness of any small changes in her experience of herself and her circumstances; and how she might use this awareness to negotiate a practical 'assignment' that she can carry out by herself. The aim of the session is to empower Clare, helping her to become aware of what she can do for herself, and what untapped capacities she might possess. In the first session the nurse would offer Clare an opportunity to complete the record of the session. If Clare was in any way uncomfortable about this, the nurse would complete the record on her behalf, by way of a rehearsal for the next session, when Clare might take the reins and complete the record herself. The nurse also aims to support Clare, by working collaboratively throughout the session, identifying what role the team might play in helping her to develop and enact her assignment.

*Mary*:   Hi Clare, what have you brought with you that you need to talk about? What's important for you today?

*Clare*:   Well . . . I don't know. I'm . . . I'm still so coiled up, like I said to the other nurse, yesterday. I just can't settle.

*Mary*:   That must be difficult. Would you like to talk some more about that?

*Clare*:   I don't know. I don't know what good talking is going to do.

*Mary*:   I know what you mean. But are you willing to give this a go . . . say just for ten minutes or so . . . then we can check how you are feeling? Yes?

*Clare*:   OK.

*Mary*:   So if you could just 'magic away' this coiled-up feeling, with a magic wand or something, what would it be like . . . in relation to this coiled up feeling? What would be different?

*Clare*:   Well . . . I wouldn't be coiled up, would I?

*Mary*:   Yeh and what would you be like if you weren't coiled up? What would be different?

*Clare*:   Oh, I suppose I'd be more at ease, y'now.

*Mary*:   So should we put 'being more at ease' here in this box [pointing], to suggest what you would prefer to be experiencing?

*Clare*:   You can if you like. It won't make any difference.

*Mary*:   OK. Would you like to write in 'being more at ease'?

*Clare*:   I suppose so . . . but it won't do much good. I'm so useless.

*Mary*:   OK. But tell me . . . when did you first notice this coiled up feeling?

- Mary acknowledges Clare's distress but continues with the focus on the 'being more at ease' feeling. She asks when Clare first became aware of this feeling, and goes on to ask how it has changed over time, helping her to become aware of the subtle changes that occur – apparently naturally; how what she finds difficult, or problematic or distressing, changes over time.

- Mary encourages Clare to make notes – as appropriate – on the record of the session, encouraging her to feel that this is her work; a major part of her contribution towards her recovery.
- In encouraging Clare to explore and become more aware of her resources Mary continues.

*Mary*: Feelings are a bit like clouds, always changing their shape and colour. Tell me, Clare in what way is the feeling of 'being all coiled up' changing for you? How is it different – in any way – for you today, right now?

*Clare*: I don't know that it is any different. I just feel the same. I'm stuck. It's useless. Maybe that's how it is for other people but not for me.

*Mary*: OK, so tell me about the last time you felt *in any way* different? What were you doing?

*Clare*: *In any way* different? What do you mean?

*Mary*: Well, how coiled up do you feel now on a scale 1 to 10: 10 being the most coiled up you could possibly *ever* feel and 1 being 'I don't feel coiled up at all – I'm at ease'.

*Clare*: Uhm, well I'm probably about 7. I mean I've felt worse than this, you know.

*Mary*: I see, so tell me about the last time you felt 6 or less. When was that?

*Clare*: 6. Oh I don't know. 6. Probably yesterday.

*Mary*: Right, so tell me a bit more about yesterday. What was different? What was going on?

---

**NB** If Clare was unable to recall a time when things *were* different (this is highly unlikely but not impossible) the nurse would encourage her to imagine or visualise things being different.

*Mary*: If I could magically 'uncoil' you . . . [laughing and pulling] what would you notice that would be different? What would you be doing? What would *I* notice about you?

---

The session is recorded as it develops. Following discussion, Clare is invited to write a brief summary of her experience of the session (see Figure 11.5). This covers:

- What *is* different (now), or what *would be* different if, or what *has been* different, when the person's experience of the problem changes.

- What the person is *doing*/was doing/would be doing when in that state.
- What the person will do *next*. (in the next hour or two)
- A simple assignment – developing the reflections from the session into some kind of plan for immediate action.
- The person's comments on her/his experience of the session.

Mary then summarises her involvement in the session:

- Brief details of the focus of the session – what the two were working on.
- Any additional 'negotiated assignment' (if appropriate) that provides specific support to the person in the execution of her/his own assignment.
- Brief details of the kind of staff support that the person believes might be helpful, in general.

Finally, both sign and date the record and the person is provided with a copy for reference, while the original is entered is the person's file (Figure 11.5).

### Being normal: sometimes I'm like this – sometimes I'm like that!

It might be worth emphasising what the one-to-one session is *not* concerned with.

- It is *not* focused on changing Clare's mind, emotional state or belief system.
- There is no attempt to identify 'thinking errors', dysfunctional beliefs, or other 'evidence' of psychopathology. These merely represent how others might view Clare's story.

Instead, the emphasis is on helping Clare to become more aware of the range of feelings, thoughts and ways of behaving that are part of her ongoing 'normal' experience.

One of the assumptions of the Tidal Model is that experience is heterogeneous *and* fickle. In any waking day we have literally thousands of mini-experiences, which flow into one another. These experiences, like the weather, change form constantly, but only if we are aware of it. It would take great power and commitment to stay in any one state – emotion or cognitive – for any length of time. (Anyone who has ever attempted to meditate will know this – our minds constantly 'wander' even when asked [or told] to sit quiet.)

The traditional psychiatric and psychological view that people experience states that last periods of time[7] does not square with our view of reality. If we pay close attention we find that our feelings and thoughts change, literally, from moment to moment. Paying attention – noticing – seems to be the key requisite. However, people often do not pay this kind of careful attention or

# One-to-One

| Name: *Clare Sweeney*<br>Key Worker: *Mary Brown* | Date *18.07.03*<br>Time: *3.15pm* |
|---|---|

| Personal Aim: *To feel more at ease* | |
|---|---|

| Person | Key Worker |
|---|---|
| **What is/was/might be different?**<br>*Out walking.*<br><br>**What I did/might do?**<br>*I was looking at birds and thinking about what it would be like to be a bird.*<br><br>**What will I do next?**<br>*Sit around less and be more active — at anything.* | **Focus of Session**<br><br>*Clare feels 'all coiled up' and would like to feel 'more at ease'.* |
| **My Assignment**<br><br>*I'll try to work out some activity plan.* | **Negotiated assignment – Help**<br><br>&bull; *Encourage Clare to engage more with others.*<br>&bull; *Encourage Clare to focus on <u>doing</u> rather than <u>feeling</u>.* |
| **Comments**<br><br>*This is difficult but I understand the point of it.* | **Staff support**<br><br>&bull; *Offer Clare reminders about her assignment*<br>&bull; *Ask Clare how she is getting on — 3 times/day* |
| Signed      Date<br><br>*Clare Sweeney    18/07/03* | Signed      Date<br><br>*M Brown    18th July '03* |

*Figure 11.5* Clare's record of her one-to-one session

develop a stereotyped perception of themselves, as Clare did when she said: 'I just feel the same. I'm stuck. It's useless. Maybe that's how it is for other people but not for me.' People who say 'Clare is *always* like that' employ a similar kind of stereotyped perception. They simply have not been paying attention either.

There is no value in focusing on having an argument with people or 'disputing the facts' since ultimately 'truth' or 'reality' is what people believe it is. Of course, if people ask us for our thoughts on the matter we can talk about how, for what it's worth, we see things differently. Most times, however, we accept what people say. Then, we invite them to tell us 'more' about their experience; assuming that the person's experience will be rich in its diversity, more than a simple one-dimensional representation. In this respect the Tidal Model is 'realistic' rather than falsely 'optimistic'.[8]

We assume that people are 'sometimes like this' and at 'other times are like that'. We are interested to hear about and perhaps see for ourselves this diversity in action. This genuine interest is an important part of helping the person to appreciate the rich diversity of who she or he *is*, has *been*, or might *become*.

## Swimming with sharks – swimming with dolphins

The *concept* of helping people to become more aware of how change is coursing through them – helping them to tell you what they would like to experience as an alternative to what they do not like or what gets them into trouble with other people – is very simple. However, the practice of this principle can sometimes be difficult for all sorts of reasons. Often, offering this kind of help is complicated because the professional does not believe it will be enough, or prior training leads the professional to believe it will be 'wrong' or 'useless'. Clearly, to work within the Tidal Model one must accept, at least provisionally the principles. Only by accepting them provisionally can one begin to try them out for 'goodness of fit' – for the professional as well as the person in care. Some of the suggestions we note here apply to all aspects of testing the 'goodness of fit' of the Tidal Model, but may be most relevant to the working relationship of the Individual Care setting.

### Don't work too hard

Having spent our combined professional lifetime, working within a wide range of psychiatric, psychological and psychotherapeutic 'models' of being human, we have come to the realisation that for much of our professional lives we 'worked too hard'. When we weren't trying to interpret what it 'meant' when the person did this or that, we were trying to anticipate what the person might do next, or work out what we should do next. Although the kind of collaborative style of working we espouse here is not easy, it does involve doing less work. By encouraging people to take ownership of that which is already theirs (the life story), we encourage them to do more 'work'. Hopefully, they will be able to tell us what this or that 'means', what they are going to do, or might do next, and even perhaps what they think we should do next!

### Do enough work

The suggestion above is only half the story. While it is important to resist doing the work that rightfully belongs to the person, or that the person wants or needs to do, that still leaves some work for the professional. Depending on how the person is, that could still be a lot of work relatively speaking. However, if we take note of the points raised above, it will just be *enough* work. We need to provide structure; change the structure if it doesn't appear to be working; ask intelligent questions; be humorous at times; be human at all times; respond to the person's feedback (especially by doing something different when the person didn't like the first thing); give advice if asked; listen long and carefully, if the person just wants to talk; work with the person at all times. The professional is collaborating as much as the person.

### Make assumptions

The old saw suggests that if we assume things, this will make an '*ass*' out of '*u*' and '*me*'. It is a good joke and invariably true. However, every truth has its exception. It is vital – not just important – that you assume that the person has knowledge, derived from experience, which can be used to help repair the leaky vessel and set sail again. This assumption will lead you to ask the person to tell you:

*   'where' they want to go
*   'what' they think would work
*   'how' they might do this or that
*   'what' other people might say or think
*   'why' this or that happened
*   'what' they have learned from this experience.

This assumption is a fast-breeder for the belief that the person is 'working' – rather than 'defective', 'deficient' or otherwise 'invalid'. This assumption is part of the whole validating process that threads its way through the model.

### Give reality its proper place

People with 'mental health problems' are seen, generally, as having 'problems with reality'. Perhaps they do, but probably no more so than the rest of us.

They may simply be engaging with a different reality. However, some 'reality' appears to be true for everyone, everywhere. We believe that *this* (moment) is the only moment we have, and in this moment we act. Indeed, we have no choice but to act. The question is, which act will we perform in this (coming) moment? The idea that we can 'do nothing' is absurd.[9] The emphasis on *action* also helps us put thoughts and (especially) feelings, in their place. People may (and often do) say that certain thoughts and/or feelings made them do this or that. However, there seems to be no way of proving this. Thoughts and feelings may accompany certain actions, but people can (and do) choose to act, despite their thoughts and feelings. We would encourage people to recognise the 'fact' that thoughts and feelings are both private and fickle (they are inside us and come and go like passing clouds). The 'real' question is, given that you 'think' this or 'feel' that, what are you going to do *now*?

### Be supportive

It goes without saying that the person has been having a hard time, which is why they are in care, therapy or treatment. It is also true that the expectations of the care plan can be demanding. Few people in care volunteer for more one-to-one sessions; and some do not even want the ones they are offered. Acknowledge how hard this must seem; acknowledge that this might appear pointless or impossible; invite suggestions as to how it might be made easier or more comfortable.

### Paddle away from whirlpools

People are often drawn to whirlpools or rapids. Indeed, previous therapists may have told the person that these dangers *must* be faced, if the person is to move on. We have no inclination to get into deep or dangerous waters unless the person expresses a desperate desire to go there. Even then, our focus will be on survival – our own and especially that of the person. Self-blame, stories about hopelessness, weakness, 'bad things I did' and 'things I am ashamed of' and '101 reasons to feel guilty' are typical of the dangerous waters of the Self. We see little point in paddling into these experiential hot spots. There may be a lot of value in paddling away from them. Of course, we acknowledge that they exist – they were there, back down the river of time that frames the person's life. But as the philosopher of the ubiquitous bumper sticker put it, 'shit happens'. Everyone has this stuff, but for most of us it doesn't stick, or at least not for long. The act of paddling away from the dangerous waters helps to release us from the metaphorical shit that life throws at us. Perhaps the simplest way to *acknowledge* these enduring pains *and* to paddle away is to ask 'How are you getting over that?' or 'How are you beginning to put that behind you?' or 'How might you put that behind you?'

### Embrace the metaphors in the story

Much of the really important stuff that people want to express about themselves and their lives can rarely be said in straightforward communication.
Invariably it is expressed metaphorically, since what it *is* may not be
altogether clear to the person, but it seems *like* something else that the person
has known. We need to embrace these metaphors and, if possible, develop
them since they represent the significant core of meaning of the person's
experience. When the person confesses to being 'all washed up', we might
acknowledge that all sorts of interesting things get washed up on the beach;
things that other people threw away, but which someone else, maybe on the
other side of the world, finds interesting, valuable and worth holding on to.
Or, when the person confesses to being 'rotten, through and through', we
might acknowledge that decay is a natural part of the body's system. Our
skin sheds dead cells moment by moment and our whole body will, over a
period of a few years, replace all the cells in our organs. We are like plants. We
need to die off to be reborn, to grow new shoots. Maybe that is what happening
for you right now?

### Exploit the person's powers of imagination

Reflecting on what has been learned on the journey so far represents a huge
store of knowledge. However, people are also creative thinkers and can
imagine new worlds for themselves. If the person can imagine what it would
be like to be different, (s)he is more likely to become that difference. We can
help by asking the person to develop the story of this imagined state: 'So tell
me more about what it would be like . . . paint me a picture of this . . . what
do you notice about yourself when you are . . . how are other people relating
to you in this state . . . what do you find yourself doing?' As we said in Chapter 6,
the Self that people *seek* is to be found 'out there' in the future, not in the
past, or buried somewhere inside ourselves. We can help the person grow the
identity of the self through use of the power of imagination.

### Be surprised

People tell lots of stories that represent their futility, hopelessness,
inadequacy and general 'sickness' as a human being. Some will tell quite
different stories, about being descended from royalty, being the Son of God,
or from outer space. For the experienced professional, little of this will come
as a surprise and will remind us of similar stories told by other people we
have met. What should surprise us, however, is how the person has managed,
and continues to manage, with all of this. There is a great value in validating
the person's damning view of her/himself: 'Given all the things that have
happened to you, I'm surprised that you aren't a lot worse (more depressed

. . . dead by now . . . still standing). I don't know how I would have fared with all of that stuff!'

However, curious expressions of surprise might also encourage the person to talk about the subtext of the story: 'So, you are the risen Christ. So, how do you cope with people treating you as if you are crazy?' or 'You have special powers – telepathy and the like. So how does all that stuff work?'[10] Traditional psychiatry and psychology are tainted by the notion that there exists only one truth, which the technology of inquiry will winkle out or somehow 'prove'. In practice, this has usually involved invalidating, suppressing and generally locking up people (and their stories) who do not conform to some anodyne notion of 'normality'.[11] People need to find out for themselves that they are not gods or devils, or that they are no worse (as persons) than anyone else. Even if they should find out that they are exactly what they say they are, the question remains – *what next?*

### Ask for a view of the chart

The journey of recovery is a personal journey. It may share similarities with the journeys taken in the past and presently being taken by others, but we would hope that the person would think that this journey is special. We hope that they would say: 'This is *my journey*.' We are like life-savers, or boat repairers, coastguards or cartographers. We are interested to know something of the journey taken by the person so far. How did the person get to here, whether intentionally or otherwise? But we are mainly interested in where the person is going. When will the person know when (s)he is ready to set sail again? How will the person know that (s)he is seaworthy? Where are they going next? What is the ultimate destination (if indeed the person has one)? What is the plan of navigation, and (if the person does not have one) how will the person manage to deal with the likely difficult waters that lie ahead? It is not our responsibility to map out the person's future journey, but we can at least go over the map with the person, asking more genuinely curious questions, which may help the person to appreciate better what lies ahead.

## The Individual Care Plan across the Care Continuum

The emphasis on the development of awareness within Individual Care extends right across the whole *Care Continuum*. However, at different points on the continuum the person will be developing awareness of different things. In Immediate Care, as described above, the person is mainly focused on working out what to do *next*, which might represent a useful step on the recovery journey; and also who might help in the doing of this next useful thing. When we are lost in the middle of a strange town at dead of night, the last thing we want to be asked is 'Where did you first notice you were lost . . . or how did you feel about getting lost?'[12]

When the person moves into *Transitional Care*, the emphasis switches to the necessary preparation for the journey: What does the person need, by way of support, to begin to undertake the journey? What personal resources can and should the person be drawing upon? Getting ready for any journey – whether it be a foreign holiday or a round-the-world yacht race – requires careful preparation. Regrettably, in many mental health settings this preparation is usually undertaken as part of the 'discharge' process, and often involves the person in only a limited fashion. Given that the person is going to be the one undertaking the journey, (s)he must be at the centre of the operation; being consulted throughout; being the final arbiter as to what will be needed, and what would amount to 'surplus baggage'.

When ready, the person pushes off into *Developmental Care*. Here the emphasis is focused on developing and extending the personal knowledge that has been building up during the period of Immediate Care. In the metaphor of the Tidal Model, the person has been learning to swim, or at least to stay afloat – perhaps repairing the damaged or leaky boat, which brought the person into the safe haven of Immediate Care. This work has either been undertaken on dry land, away from the potential threats of the sea (the natural world), or in the shallows. Now, as the person begins the journey, the psychological and physical threats of the journey ahead become more apparent. As Publius Syrus said: 'Anyone can hold the helm when the sea is calm.' However, who can guarantee a calm sea for any length of time, far less for the whole passage of the rest of one's life? Consequently, it will be necessary to explore the person's awareness of:

- *pirates and storms*: the obvious 'dangers' and 'threats' that the journey will likely present *on the surface* and how the person expects to deal with them
- *currents, rocks and sharks*: the hidden dangers that might exist *below the surface*, of which the person might need to become more aware and anticipate dealing with
- *the trials of the lone sailor*: although the person may have occasional company on the journey, much of it will be taken alone. All people who live with illness, disability, or problems of living, do so alone, since the experience is manifestly a private affair.[13] To what extent is the person equipped for this lonely voyage? How might the person become better equipped?

If Immediate Care is focused very much on finding immediate solutions to specific problems and taking small steps in bite-sized chunks, then Developmental Care looks farther out to sea, anticipating potential threats and hopefully becoming forearmed by being forewarned. The professional must however be guided, even here, by the person:

- Some people are happy to explore beneath the surface – learning more about the world immediately beyond the boat (which is the metaphorical body). Some even want to explore the depths of their lives – going deep-sea diving – trying to understand better why they 'ran aground' in the past; perhaps as a way of avoiding the 'rocks' in future. These people might benefit from more intensive, and sophisticated psychotherapeutic support to develop their awareness of these hidden depths.
- Some are happy only to look into the water – or go snorkelling – becoming aware of the immediate threats that lie just below the surface. These people might wish to develop their knowledge of the surface features of their problems of living, learning to recognise or anticipate when they are getting into 'difficult waters', and developing a personal strategy for dealing with such situations.
- Others have no wish to do either, and merely want help to stay afloat. Such people might simply want a steady supply of medication or regular visits, or even just a telephone number to call when in difficulties – a distress flare! If this is what they want, who are we to disagree? However, if the person repeatedly runs into difficulties under such conditions, we might explore the usefulness of this level of support – and what might be the alternatives.

## Conclusion

The process of Individual Care involves developing a collaborative relationship within which the person can begin to develop awareness of the resources that (s)he currently possesses, which might be used to address the problem of living; what additional resources (support) might be needed; and what needs to happen next, to begin to move off on the recovery journey.

The nature of the relationship between the professional (usually the nurse) and the person is friendly, supportive and businesslike. The professional is not conducting psychotherapy, or at least not in the way it is traditionally practised. Unlike many traditional psychiatric, psychotherapeutic or psychological models, we do not start from the assumption that the person is damaged, weak, flawed, defective or dangerous. They may well be all of these things, but they are also fully functioning human beings. They would not be sitting or standing in front of us now if they weren't. Our task is to find out how the person 'works' (not how they don't work), and to try to channel this knowledge into a process that might be intelligible to the person as well as ourselves.

We make no apologies for working with people's problems of living. After all, this is what brought them to the care setting in the first place. We are not interested in reconstructing their personalities, reconfiguring their bio-chemistry, helping them to self-actualise or do any of the other wizardry that is often claimed by psychotherapy and psychiatry. We just want to help them back on the journey of life: doing this carefully, compassionately and respon-sibly. As we said at the outset, we want the person to need us less, so that as soon as possible the person will not need us at all. This attitude means that the relationship is quite superficial, which does not mean that it is not power-ful, or that it might not engender appreciation on the part of the person. However, we are not entering into a long-term relationship if that can be avoided. We are like the life-savers, boat-builders, coastguards and map makers: we have something to offer that might help with the journey of recovery and reclamation, but we have no intention of becoming full-time members of the crew.

Knowing when to stop is one of the vital skills of the helper, which can only be learned in practice. Most of what we have talked about here involves what would be called, in professional parlance, fairly brief interventions. Each contact should last only as long as it needs to last. There is no point in organising 30-minute or 50-minute sessions and then watching the clock, going over things *again*, or looking for new things, unless this is necessary. If the necessary work can be done in 15 minutes, good. If it can be accom-plished in 10 minutes that will be good too. It is not a race, but neither is it a ritual. Let the working relationship develop its own sense of time, if at all possible. Develop a shared sense of 'outcome' with the person, knowing that 'we seem finished for today' or 'it seems as if we have done all that we can do' as a natural outcome of the work itself, rather than as a function of a case conference with colleagues, or a session with a clinical supervisor.

In the experience of Individual Care the person will begin to reclaim own-ership of the experience of the problem and the knowledge of what might represent a resolution of the problem, which is the first step on the recovery journey. We emphasise the importance of writing their own record of the helping encounter within Immediate Care. As the person holds the paper and pen, the fact that 'this is my life, my problems and my search for solutions' becomes all too clear. This can be scary. Professionals need to be supportive. For some people, taking the pen and writing their own simple summary of the ongoing story can represent a difficult bridge to cross. Patience is all.

In the process of Individual Care the person will begin to understand how the professional team members might help her or him to reclaim the power that has been lost in the storm of mental distress. The person will also dis-cover how hard (or hopefully how relatively easy) this is and will acquire and store away, as an internalised process, some simple ways of dealing with problems of living and working out how to *flow over* or *flow around* life obstacles.

As the person steers themselves out into the calmer waters of Transitional or Developmental Care, different challenges will present. There will likely be less need for the formal structure of templates like the Immediate Care Plan One-to-One Record. However, the person will have learned the importance of writing her/his story, or at least a distillation of its key moments, as (s)he goes. In Transitional or Developmental Care, a notebook or journal can replace the narrow formality of the One-to-One Record. Hopefully, the focus on reflection, awareness and decision making will continue to be valued.

## Acknowledgement

We are grateful to our friend Peter Wilkin for drawing Coleridge's poem to our attention.

# Chapter 12

# All hands to the pumps

## Group Care

> I find the great thing in this world is not so much where we stand, as in what direction we are moving: to reach the port of heaven, we must sail sometimes with the wind and sometimes against it – but we must sail, and not drift, nor lie at anchor.
>
> (Oliver Wendell Holmes)

## Learning in groups

### Sharing experience

Although the specific details of the person's problems of living are unique, most human responses to illness and health have common denominators. People often believe that they are all alone in their experience of distress. However, is this rarely the case. Sullivan (Evans 1996: 18) said: 'We are all more simply human than otherwise.' In Scotland we say that 'we are a' Jock Tamson's bairns'. Crudely translated this means that 'we are all children of the same good god under heaven'. We are all from the same family of man and so we have the capacity to understand our fellow women and men. Whether we use that capacity is, of course, another matter.

Given the common experience of 'being human', group-based support has a key role to play in helping people to prepare and undertake the Discovery journey. Within groupwork people gain an opportunity to:

- share their experiences of difficulty, distress or disability
- obtain natural human support from their peers – people who are, literally and figuratively, 'in the same boat'
- view their problems from a different perspective – through the experienced eyes and ears of the other group members
- enjoy the experience of being the helper, as opposed to being the 'one' who is helped, by the problems of living of other group members
- explore different, potentially new, options for resolving problems of living

- learn from the experience of other people
- gain an opportunity to 'stand back' from problems, by discussing them in the abstract; something which is common to others in the group if not people as a whole.

Groupwork in mental health care has a long pedigree, but has often been seen as a highly specialised undertaking, requiring highly specialised and lengthy forms of professional training. Traditional forms of psychodynamic group therapy would definitely fall under this heading and such groupwork is now usually only available in special settings, rather than, as once was the case, offered as part of routine care and treatment.

Alternatively, groupwork is often seen as only appropriate with certain groups of people: assertiveness groups for the meek among us; social skills groups for the socially inept among us; or problem-solving groups for those of us who are assumed to be unable to solve our problems. These kinds of focused groups do exist in greater numbers, but are often offered only to certain groups of people.

A third kind of groupwork is that which is seen as an optional extra and which operates largely outside of the confines of the care plan. Newspaper groups, craft and other diverting activity groups, provide venues within which the person can 'do' something, but the amount of actual sharing of experience may be quite limited[1].

When the Tidal Model was first implemented in England in the late 1990s the nurses who organised the first pilot projects were less than enthusiastic about the groupwork. Most took the view that they had not been adequately prepared for groupwork, and were apprehensive about handling the 'group dynamics'. Certainly there had been a noticeable decline in the practice of groupwork, especially by nurses, who used to be the mainstay of such groups a generation earlier. Instead, the focus had shifted towards individual work, one-to-one sessions and, in general, a more confidential form of 'case management'. The traditional practice, which prevailed in the late 1960s and early 1970s, of encouraging people (patients) to raise their concerns and problems in either the large or small group meetings which were held twice daily in most psychiatric hospital wards, had certainly gone into decline. Perhaps the image of Nurse Ratched confronting Jack Nicholson's 'Randall P. McMurphy' in *One Flew Over the Cuckoo's Nest* helped consign the potentially damaging dynamics of group therapy to history.

Whether the absence of appropriate training, or the change in attitude towards doing anything in groups, explains this demise remains unclear. One thing does seem clear – many members of nursing staff appear very uncomfortable about leading groups. Perhaps they feel more exposed when expected to perform their professional duties in front of a room full of their charges.

### Group alternatives

All of the forms of groupwork noted above are of value, each in its own different way. However, having reflected on the key principles of groupwork and following consultation with professionals, consumers and user-advocate colleagues, we tried to develop a different and more user friendly framework for groupwork; one that would be open to almost everyone and which would not require major investments of time and effort to acquire the necessary proficiency to lead or facilitate.

The three *core* forms of groupwork developed within the Tidal Model are described briefly in this chapter. The relationship between Individual Care, the core groups – *Discovery*, *Information* and *Solutions* – and other forms of group support, is shown in Figure 12.1.

The three core groups provide a supportive social structure for the Individual Care that forms the key focus of personalised care. The core groups might be seen as providing a jetty or mooring for the other forms of social support that might be available within the service such as traditional group psychotherapy, or in the wider community such as a Hearing Voices Network group. Given that the core groups are gentler and less challenging than some other forms of groupwork, they provide an accessible venue within which

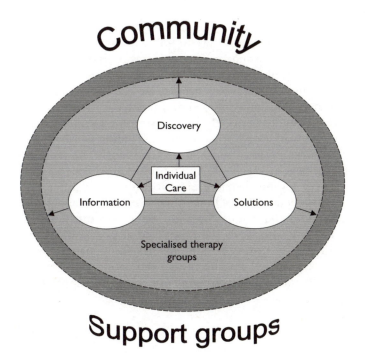

*Figure 12.1* Relationship between Individual Care, Tidal Model groupwork and specialised group and social support

people might begin to rehearse their involvement and exposure to other, perhaps necessary, forms of group experience.

## The Discovery Group

### Aims

Across the estuary from our home in Fife in Scotland lies the port of Dundee where Captain Scott's famous ship *RRS Discovery* was built that first took him to the Antarctic in 1901. Some years ago the *Discovery* was returned to a special dock where it doubles as a tourist attraction and a remarkable symbol for humankind's skill, ingenuity, imagination, courage and appetite for greater understanding of the world in which we live.

Scott's final diaries from his Antarctic expedition ten years later also provide a remarkable record of the humanity and camaraderie of the men who undertook the fateful expedition. Through reading the account of their journey, we learn something more about the journey we all take through life. Despite the many criticisms of the foolhardiness of Scott's expedition, in his diaries we find remarkable illustrations of how Scott and his colleagues maintained their loyalty and compassionate support of one another in the face of adversity.

The main aim of the *Discovery Group*[2] is to provide a setting within which the person can have an opportunity to talk with both peers and staff members, in a supportive atmosphere. The problems of living associated with the experience of mental ill-health invariably are alienating. Whether the experience is new or longstanding, many people step back from ordinary, everyday social engagement and some retire almost completely from the social world because of the stigma or personal embarrassment associated with their problems. The consequent social isolation and alienation can have a major disabling effect on the person's sense of Self, especially the sense of personal value which the person attaches to her/himself.

The Discovery Group therefore aims to provide a setting within which people might experience a boost to their self-esteem, reclaiming in the process some of the personhood that has been lost, either as a function of the experience of mental ill-health, or of the experience of psychiatric care and treatment, or both. The Discovery Group provides an opportunity within which members may reclaim and develop further their ability to share with others, on a simple yet mutually rewarding basis, through simple question and answer sessions.

### Structure

Two members of the professional team normally lead the Discovery Group, but over time group participants may take turns in leading the session. The professional team members should provide a general introduction to the group, advising people that they can, if they wish, just 'sit in' and listen, but hopefully everyone will want to join in. The facilitators might begin the session by asking each other questions and then opening this out to the rest of the group. We have experience of running Discovery Groups in many different countries, with people from a wide range of cultural and social backgrounds. Participants seem to appreciate greatly the active involvement of the 'professional' in the session, especially when the professional team members can laugh at themselves, or disclose some entertaining or amusing detail about their lives. Not only does this provide a powerful form of 'role modelling' for the rest of the participants, but it also seems to strengthen the therapeutic relationship between the people in care and the professional.

### Format

Most commonly, the group is focused on a set of pre-prepared questions that aim to generate simple reflection and light-hearted as well as meaningful conversation. Most of these questions have a simple, accessible focus; for example:

- Tell the group something about yourself
- What would you do if you won the Lottery?
- What is your favourite season and why?
- What is your favourite way of relaxing?

These simple questions will be followed up by other, curious questions about how the person felt, what happened next, what other people made of (whatever they did), and their reasons for saying this or that. Although most of these sessions begin in a very light-hearted manner, if people feel comfortable sometimes they will talk about things that are very close to their hearts. It is interesting, for example, that although many people will talk about how they would spend their millions if they won the Lottery, others (especially those who appear quite poor in a material sense) will talk about giving it to charity, or donating it to some project that might help other people. Such responses can be humbling and very poignant, revealing some of the hidden human depths of people whose true worth has been blocked from view by the psychiatric system.

We usually recommend that there is a balance between simple questions, like those above, and questions that might stimulate some laughter – a powerfully therapeutic event in itself:

- What's the funniest thing that has ever happened to you?
- Tell the group something about yourself that might surprise them.
- What is the nicest thing anyone has ever said to you?

It is also important to include questions that invite the participants to look at themselves in a gentle, non-threatening way:

- If you could give one of your strengths or qualities to a friend, what would it be?
- Tell us about a time when you were happy, contented or felt fulfilled.
- (For the pet owners) How would your pet describe you?
- What would be your first choice – health, wealth or wisdom? (Why would this be important to you?)
- Name one thing that you have done well today.
- What is the hardest thing you have ever done (and how did you do that)?
- What lessons have you learned from life?

These questions can generate a lot of serious searching, but can in our experience generate great warmth and camaraderie among the group members. Most of the questions presuppose the existence of qualities, knowledge, personal wisdom, sense of humour, etc. In that sense, the questions are inherently empowering.

It is important that the professional 'facilitators' try to offer genuine, heartfelt comments in reply to the participants' answers. In our experience the Discovery Group can, and frequently does, generate a powerful blend of gentle humour, self-deprecation, hysterical laughter, moments of sadness, poignancy and short-lived tears. The facilitator needs to afford just enough time, and no more, to the emotional response to the different participants' answers before moving on to the next question.

### Variations

There is no limit to the ways that one might organise a Discovery Group, which would afford an opportunity to reflect at both a superficial and deep level; to laugh at oneself and with others; to learn something about the 'others' with whom we share at least a part of our lives; and to learn something new about oneself. We advocate strongly that everyone who develops a Discovery Group should:

- make an effort to make it distinctive
- ensure that it *belongs* to the setting within which it was developed
- tailor it as much as possible to suit the people who use it
- adapt it as and when necessary to keep up with the changes that are flowing through the service, the people using it and through society in general.

In our work we have used laminated cards, with a picture of a lifebelt on one side and a question on the other (see Figure 12.2). We invite participants

*Figure 12.2* Discovery Group card

to pick a card and offer them the opportunity to answer the question themselves, or ask someone else.[3] At other times we have put the same cards in yellow envelopes (optimistic colour) and this appears to heighten the drama, humour and excitement within the group. It goes without saying that the group facilitators should also participate – allowing the group to learn something of 'who' is this person who is the professional team member.

In many settings the group members generate new questions, which are then typed up and used to augment the basic list. This adds to the sense of ownership, as well as being a fine example of the inherent creativity of the group.

At Rangipapa, a forensic unit in North Island, New Zealand, Ngaire Cook and her colleagues have been working with the Discovery Group for over two years. They run the group once weekly in the morning and have developed a 'sandwich' technique for asking the questions: the first question is general; the next one more personal; the third one general again, and so on. One of the group facilitators begins the session by throwing a soft toy to the other and, when it is caught, asks a question. Each person in the group has an opportunity to hold and throw the toy at whomsoever they please, following this up with a question. The use of the 'flying soft toy' introduces a degree of levity and randomness that otherwise might be missing. However, despite the light-heartedness, the Rangipapa group is highly enlightening, so much so that the residents decided to rename it the 'Discovery Group'. In the spirit of mutual learning, collegiality across oceans, and a sharing of human under-standing, we decided to change the name of our Recovery Group to Discovery Group. Thank you Rangipapa.

### Maintaining the focus

As the name suggests, the Discovery Group is focused on how people are growing, moment by moment, becoming more aware of their personal assets, which are often embedded in their memories or dreams, all the time rediscovering and reclaiming as their own the positive aspects of their lives. Given this focus, it is not appropriate to discuss the participants' problems specifically. If any group members raise their problems within the group and express a desire to discuss them, the group leaders should encourage the person to bring this to the *Solutions Group*, or to raise this within Individual Care.

In settings like Rangipapa, where the people will likely be in care for a lengthy period of time, the Discovery Group may be run only once or at most twice a week; any more often and the group might become too routine, especially if the same group of people are meeting each time. However, in settings where there is a higher turnover of possible participants, like a hospital ward, the group could meet daily.

In all settings, experience suggests that a late morning session is optimal, as this allows participants to fulfil daily routines and do any necessary 'business' before joining the group. It also provides a valuable introduction to the socialising at lunchtime.

## The Information Group

### Aims

A storm-tossed mariner, blown wildly off course, guides his listing ship into harbour, seeking a refit and necessary repairs, looking to refresh his crew, before setting sail again. He wants to know:

- Where has he landed?
- What help is available?
- How much damage is there to his ship?
- Who can help him fix it?
- Where can he obtain new supplies?
- Who can help him plot a new course?
- Who might pilot him out of the harbour when he is ready?

In our experience, people who find themselves washed ashore into the mental health services harbour have a very similar set of questions. If they do not, then some would say they should have.

The mental health field can be a bewildering place for staff, as well as for those required to use the service. In most settings, policies, guidance information and standards change with alarming frequency. New projects spring up, often to fade away and be replaced by a new version of the original. People in positions of authority or responsibility change, as they are promoted, transferred or leave the area. If we add the burgeoning voluntary, charitable and 'non-government' sector groups to the statutory health and social services groupings, then the field grows into a leviathan.

We have always found it extremely difficult to keep abreast of changes in the services with which we have been involved professionally. This led us to wonder what sense the users, consumers and their family members made of such shape-shifting services. To what extent do people:

- know what services are available?
- understand how they might go about obtaining a specific service?
- appreciate what (exactly) the various services represent – in practical terms and in plain English?

The structural organisation and the physical content of many care programmes often bewilder the person, their family and their friends. The language of psychiatry itself presents a huge stumbling block to understanding, especially where jargon is used to conceal or redefine often simple, everyday concepts. As a result, people in care and often their families need information about the nature of their care and treatment and other opportunities for support that might lie beyond the present care setting. Many of these needs for information will be met within the Individual Care offered to the person. However, since many of the information needs are common to whole groups of people, there is a value in organising group sessions to present and discuss information about care, treatment and supporting services. Not only does this make economic sense, but it also provides another valuable opportunity to learn from others, to share experiences and to discuss, meaningfully, issues of common interest or concern.

The *Information Group* aims to provide 'practical' advice to people about services they are presently using, or services that they might consider using. This advice is delivered in 'plain' language, preferably in an entertaining, interesting or otherwise accessible way.

### Structure

Francis Bacon's dictum that 'knowledge itself is power' is the primary motivation behind the Information Group. Without knowledge we are not only ignorant, but also powerless. For too long the people who have used psychiatric and mental health services have often been kept in the dark about many of the services available, and frequently similarly mystified about the services they do receive.

The people who lead the Information Group should be 'in the know' – in a position to provide information concerning what people think is important. They should be people with an in-depth knowledge of specific topic areas who can comfortably answer intelligent and searching questions from people in care and perhaps also staff members. The user/consumer group should, in principle, determine the topics. If the people in care find this too onerous, staff might profitably offer a menu of 'possibilities', arranging session on the topics that prove most popular. In time, the people in care will generate their own list of desired topics.

### Format

There are an infinite number of possible topics for the Information Group, but experience of Tidal Model projects around the world suggests that the following are most popular:

- *Medication*: intended effects, side effects, contraindications (etc.) of particular drugs (identified by the participants).
- *Current care and treatment*: discussion of the specific characteristics of the care and treatment presently on offer.
- *Psychotherapy and counselling*: its aims, availability and appropriateness.
- *Nutrition and well-being*: how to eat well, keep fit and generally stay healthy.
- *Social security benefits*: how to make applications and eligibility criteria.
- *Community supports*: what is available and where to find it.
- *Specialist mutual support groups*: groups that are available locally (e.g. Hearing Voices Network, Depression Alliance, Gamblers Anonymous, Narcotics Anonymous). What special help do they offer?
- *Housing and supported accommodation*: where to look for alternative accommodation. Sources of advice and support.

## Variations

An occupational therapist and a nurse usually facilitate the Rangipapa Information Groups jointly, but other professionals are included to cover specific areas of knowledge and experience. The groups run across a four to six week series, once a week in the early evening. The service users are asked what topics they would like to have included, and the members of the whole professional team are also asked to make suggestions. Before each series begins, all service users are informed of the programme, so that people can identify which sessions they would like to attend.

The topics covered have been very varied: for example, active listening, managing your violence, understanding mood, healthy eating, medication, budgeting, and developing illness awareness

## Links with the wider community

Although all care provided in hospital or other residential settings should be linked in some way to the wider community to which the person belongs, the Information Group can provide a powerful form of linkage. The hospital-based team should encourage members of the community services to run groups focused on 'community support' within the ward, especially as part of the *Transitional Care* programme. Similarly, community staff might invite their hospital or specialist services colleagues (drug and alcohol team members, counsellors, psychotherapists) to address groups in the community about programmes and services available in other settings, or representatives of the Citizens Advice Bureau, Employment and Disability Rights Awareness projects.

## The special voice of experience

The potential contribution to Information Groups that might be made by user/consumer-advocates, psychiatric survivors, or others who have navigated the recovery journey, is inestimable. Apart from the special knowledge of the recovery journey, such people come carrying a huge beacon of hope. Their very presence signals the 'possibility' of recovery, but also frames this within a realistic storyline.

Although many professional staff, especially in hospital settings, can be uneasy about extending invitations to 'non-professionals', the first principle should be to identify the *person with the knowledge*. Clearly, only people who have successfully navigated the journey into, through and out of a psychiatric crisis can talk with any confidence about what this is like; what appeared to help; and (importantly) what help such a person can offer others in a similar predicament. Many user-advocates – like Irene Whitehill and Sally Clay who offered the Foreword to this book – have developed valuable knowledge about services, methods of dealing with various problems of living, methods of self-management, and especially ways of managing medication as part of an everyday living lifestyle that goes far beyond anything that clinical staff and professional researchers can offer. Another old friend, Ed Manos, first facilitated an Information Group focused on psychotropic medication in a hospital ward in New Jersey over 25 years ago. Clearly, Ed had learned a lot about the medication he had been taking and was able to help his peers explore profitably many of the issues they encountered with their own medication regimes.

### Frequency

The Information Group can be offered as often as necessary, or as often as specialist advisers are available. In a setting like an acute psychiatric ward or intensive care setting, there may be great value in providing such groups on a daily basis, such is the need for stimulation, discussion and information. In other settings, weekly session, or, like the Rangipapa example, sessions arranged as part of a block programme, will be more appropriate. In general, however, these groups probably work best in the evenings when people feel more relaxed and are beginning to wind down for the day.

## The Solutions Group

### Aims

The Tidal Model emphasises the necessary search for solution. Given that the problems of living which people experience determine the need for help, both lay and professional, it follows that we should be focused on finding solutions to these problems. However, unlike some other therapy models or treatment systems, we do not believe that the professionals have the answers to the person's problems. As we noted in Chapter 11, the Tidal Model needs to be tailored to suit every person in the programme: Everyone needs a theory of their own to explain how they got here, and how they might move off again, back onto the ocean of experience. So, the pragmatic focus on finding solutions that fit individual people is carried over into the work of the *Solutions Group*.

The Solutions Group is part of the 'heavy work' of care – helping people to learn more about themselves and their problems, and instilling hope in the recovery process. Traditional group therapy is often focused on how people have developed their present problems, attempting to unravel some of the complexity surrounding the genesis of the person's problems. The Solutions Group continues the emphasis described in Chapter 11 on Individual Care – emphasising the exploration of ways that the person already is or might be moving forward; how people might become more aware of their capacity to grow through and out of their current problems of living.

### Structure

The Solutions Group is highly practical and focuses on conversations about change that is already taking place within individual members. What subtle examples of change is the person already becoming aware of? Alternatively, the group will focus on conversations about what change might be like; how participants will know change when they encounter it.

The Solutions Group should be led by suitably qualified professional team members, preferably those who are engaged in the same kind of solution-finding work with people within Individual Care. The professional should lead the group into a discussion of the small, perhaps insignificant, changes that participants notice that which might represent the steps they are already taking on the recovery journey. The group facilitators[4] offer a brief overview of the rationale of the group before beginning:

- 'We'd like to welcome everyone to today's Solutions Group. Those of you who have been here before will know that we talk about change here, and how we all can become more aware of change as it happens within our lives. Here we can also talk about what kind of changes we'd like to see in our lives, especially in relation to things that we find problematic or upsetting. Are we ready to go?'

As with the Discovery Group, there is a virtue in the professional facilitators *joining* with the group. The use of 'we' is not a patronising gesture, but an acknowledgement that the professional team members are also involved in a process of life change, and need to be aware of small changes occurring for them over time. Where appropriate, the facilitators should offer examples of their growing awareness of change as it occurs within their own lives.

The facilitators invite the participants to offer examples of 'things that are different'; specific, real world examples that might represent the seed of recovery:

- 'OK, let's talk about what's different for us. Let's talk about all the changes that we have noticed recently, maybe that we are noticing right now. Maybe small, maybe big changes. Let's talk. Who wants to lead us off?'

The facilitators should be assertive and directive, but supportive and genuinely enthusiastic. They should 'really want to know' what is happening for the people in the group, and should be prepared – outside of the group – to be working on noticing changes in their own lives. If the group is slow to engage, the facilitators will model. Silence is not a virtue in the Solutions Group:

- 'All right, well maybe we could get the ball rolling, Sarah. What have you noticed that is different for you recently?'

The facilitators' job is to open up the conversation, by asking questions, which seek to reveal more and more of the person's experience of the change process. This should be done in a positive, and genuinely curious manner.[5]

*   'Right! So you noticed that it was easier to get up this morning. So what exactly was it that you noticed? What did you find yourself doing that sort of told you – "Hey this feels different"?'

The facilitators try to bring other group members into the conversation as quickly as possible, looking for their constructive comments, approval and declarations of support, for the person who is noticing the change:

*   'Well, that sounds fascinating. I have a real sense of what's going on for you. So what do others think of Sarah's story?'

### Problem surfing

Invariably, people do want to talk about their 'problems' and how they cannot shift them or otherwise get out of the rut. The facilitators' challenge is to try to help the person step outside of the experience, if only for a moment, so that they can begin to work with the experience, from the outside, and become more aware of some of the subtleties of the experiences which they have on the inside:

*Jack*:       I just can't seem to shift this feeling of dread. It's like a weight, like a stone hanging in the pit of my stomach. It's like pulling me under.

*Facilitator*: Uh huh, and how heavy would you say that this dread is for you, like right now? On a scale between 1 and 10, with 10 being like it couldn't be any heavier, and 1 is you can hardly feel it at all – how heavy is it for you right now?

*Jack*:       Oh, I guess, maybe 8 or something.

*Facilitator*: It's 8, good. Could I ask you to stand up for a moment and join me here [indicating her side]? Sarah, would you step up too, please. Now, where you are standing right now Jack is 8 and where Sarah is standing is 10 on this scale of 'dread heaviness'. OK? Can you imagine that 'dread' is like a huge wave underneath you, powerful and, as you say, threatening to pull you under?

*Jack*:       . . . yes. I think so.

*Facilitator*: Now if you turn and look at Sarah, can you feel within yourself what that feeling of 10 is like? The power of it?

*Jack*:       [Looking] Yeh, it's awful.

*Facilitator*: Ok, Jack, now turn and look at me. [Walking] I am now standing

|  | at 1 on this scale of 'dread heaviness'. Can you see me? Can you feel inside of yourself what that 1 thing is like? Where I am now there is no heaviness – no feeling of dread at all. |
|---|---|
| *Jack*: | Uhmm, yes I think so. |
| *Facilitator*: | OK, in a second we'd like you to take just one step towards me. Well maybe I am asking you to walk on water but . . . [laughs]! Hey, maybe we are surfing here. Anyway, just one small step, OK, but it is a step away from 8 and in the direction of 1. OK? You want to take that step now? Sarah, do you want to come and be with Jack while he takes that step? |
| *Sarah*: | You ready to go Jack? |
| *Jack*: | [Stepping] OK. |
| *Facilitator*: | I wonder what Jack is feeling now? Now that he has taken that step, what is different for him, where he finds himself now? |
| *Sarah*: | [Touching Jack on the shoulder] So, what's different for you here, Jack? |
| *Jack*: | It's not so bad here. It's not so heavy. |
| *Sarah*: | Good, and what else do you notice about yourself, here? What else is different? |

The facilitators are helping Jack to have a slightly different experience of Self, one that is fuelled by imagination, but which is anchored in a memory, perhaps of some other time and place.

| *Sarah*: | I see. And this feeling that you are having *now*, it reminds you of a feeling that you have had before, a feeling you had someplace else, maybe recently? |
|---|---|
| *Jack*: | Yes, it is like I felt the other day. Well a bit like that. |
| *Sarah*: | OK. Can you see yourself in the picture of the other day, or do you feel yourself, like being there, the other day? |
| *Jack*: | I see myself. Like, yes, I can see it, well sort of. |
| *Sarah*: | So, what do you see yourself *doing* in the picture? |

The facilitators are working with one of the obvious facts of life – people do not stay in one emotional or cognitive state for any length of time. Our experience is richly diverse, but often we get stuck – like a broken record – on one particular emotional or cognitive groove: I feel bad all the time; the voices never go away; I am rotten through and through; nothing works for me; I have tried everything. The facilitators try to help Jack to surf his present 'tidal wave of dread'. They begin by *not* denying it is there – after all it is – he just told us. Then, they help him to feel himself moving, away from the experience that he brought with him today, in the direction of 'something different'.[6] Then, they invite Jack to develop his story about this 'altered state', this 'different experience': *what* do you notice, *what else* do you notice

. . . and what *else* do you notice? Finally, they invite him to ground the story in the reality of living – *doing*:

- What does he *notice* himself *doing* when things are (were) different?
- *What else* does he see/feel himself doing?
- What he does he hear himself *saying*?
- What does he notice *other people* doing, in relation to him, when things are different?

Although this part of the session is focused on Jack, the other participants can be brought in at interesting points:

*Facilitator*:    What do you notice about Jack just now?
*Participant*:    He looks as if he is smiling.

Jack is serving as a role model for the change process. He is illustrating how change can happen – even when one thinks it is not happening – and this imaginary change is very like other changes the person has experienced; and these changes are tied up with doing different things – usually doing very different things from what the person is doing now.

The Solutions Group aims to identify what kind of 'doing' is associated with thinking and feeling differently *for the individual person*. This 'doing' – in the form of general patterns of behaviour or engagement in specific activities – becomes the focus for a short discussion about what the person might do *next*:

*Facilitator*:    So, Jack you are saying that when you are focused on other people – listening to them, talking about things, noticing what they are wearing, noticing how warm or cold it is and how they sweat or rub their hands – when you are noticing all this stuff, you don't notice the feeling of dread so much. Is that right?
*Jack*:    Yes, it seems so.
*Facilitator*:    Sounds very much like it. A fascinating story. I wonder how you might use this knowledge to help yourself deal with this 'dread' thing.
*Jack*:    I'm not sure.
*Facilitator*:    Has anyone got any ideas as to how Jack might use what he just told us, on a day-to-day basis.
*Participant*:    Maybe you should try to pay more attention to people, Jack, like when you are talking with them, like you just were telling us.

The other group members provide support, encouragement, help ask curious questions, and learn something more about themselves in the process. In a typical one-hour group, three or four of these short 'experiments in experience' might be undertaken, augmenting the general story-telling about small changes that opened the group.

Because this is the 'working' part of the group programme, the Solutions Group is best located in an afternoon, allowing people time to unwind from their efforts. However, the group need not be arduous and should be peppered with humour as well as insightful observations from the facilitators and participants.

### *Variations*

At Rangipapa, the Solutions Group meets weekly in the afternoon and invariably begins with an invitation to acknowledge 'what has gone well, this week'. The facilitators ask the group members in turn so that everyone has a chance to participate. This includes the facilitators, staff members who are members of the group and the service users. If a person wishes to 'pass', other members of the group are free to speak for them, noting what they believe has 'gone well' for the person concerned.

After the first round of questions, the facilitators ask for ideas as to 'what has not gone so well', with a view to talking about 'what might be done about this'. The Rangipapa experience is that group members offer one another support and encouragement in the search for 'solutions'; this applies to staff as well as service users. The group has also been highly effective in helping service users to transfer what they have gained from the group into solution finding as part of the day-to-day process.

## The golden rule of groupwork

We have offered here just a few illustrations of how groupwork can augment the individual focus of the Tidal Model. Within groups people learn that they are not alone; that they have resources, assets and characteristics that are often overlooked; that they can help others; and – most importantly – that change happens, as John Lennon said, when you are busy making other plans.

There is no single way – no golden rule – to running these groups. As George Bernard Shaw said: 'The golden rule is that there are no golden rules.' In our experience, the best groups are those led by the most enthusiastic, creative and resourceful practitioners – or by people like Irene, Sally and Ed, who have graduated from the university of life.

## Acknowledgement

We are grateful to Kay Vaughn, Denny Webster and their colleagues in Denver, Colorado, for their inspiration in the development of our group work.

# Chapter 13

# Making waves

## Theoretical and philosophical undercurrents

When the waters deepen, the sands shift.
(Malay proverb)

## The deep sea of ideas and influence

We have alluded in the preceding chapters to various philosophical and theoretical points of reference, which have helped us map the course of development of the Tidal Model. Here, we acknowledge the principal influences on the model, which have helped us develop our appreciation of the kind of context that is necessary to begin the journey of recovery and reclamation, and the kind of people who also might represent the necessary supports to prepare for and to undertake the journey.

We begin the chapter with a brief consideration of the psychiatric and mental health context into which the Tidal Model was launched at the cusp of the twenty-first century, and go on to acknowledge those theorists and practitioners, some of whom we have known personally, who have been our primary inspiration for the philosophy of the Tidal Model. We conclude with a brief consideration of the philosophical influences on the practical dimensions of the model.

## The shifting sands of the madness machine

The emphasis of mental health care has shifted dramatically in recent years, especially within the USA and UK. Thirty years ago much of the focus was on people with various 'neurotic' conditions and the notion of a humanistic form of behaviour change technology was beginning to take shape. People with more 'serious' forms of madness were still largely invisible, locked up in hospital or in the crazy stereotypes of the silver screen. By the 1990s the tide had turned dramatically, largely due to the deinstitutionalisation programme. Many people entering the health and social care disciplines today will struggle to comprehend what institutional life could have been like a mere thirty years ago. Many also seem to assume that our city streets have always been home to both the 'seriously mentally ill' and the dispossessed vagrant. Certainly, the majority appear to have bought into the carefully constructed and highly politicised concept of the 'serious and enduringly mentally ill', which seems like a long-winded way and clumsy way of saying 'chronic psychotic'. We did not like the term when used in our day, not because it was a pejorative label but because it conveyed a sense of professional futility, hopelessness and inevitability. We have come to believe, largely by dint of our own experiences of people once called 'chronic psychotics', that recovery is possible, but it requires considerable sustained effort on the part of both the professional and the person who has been written off by the system.

The notion of the 'serious and enduringly mentally ill' is a piece of political and economic phrase-making that has no place in any text on helping people make the recovery journey to the land that might be called mental health. We use the term here to locate it in its proper context and, once we have had our say, we shall consign it to the dustbin that houses all the other banal, distorting and judgemental expressions concerning madness that have passed their sell-by date.

The 'serious and enduringly mentally ill' might well be called in some quarters SEMIs, such is the predilection for abbreviations and acronyms in psychiatry, psychology and mental health in general (Barker *et al.* 1998a). Such terms serve a useful function, of course. They help us forget that we are talking about human beings, the complexities of their lives, and the amazing array of fragile emotions and sensitivities that course through the person-hood of these people, now reduced to the stereotype of a SEMI. The concept of the SEMI was generated by the administrators of the mental health machine, many of whom had enjoyed clinical careers, but who found their proper niche in framing strategy, outlining policies, issuing guidelines, writing standards and generally shuffling paper. Where a generation ago the novice mental health professional had to confront a sea of faces, now the first challenge is often to navigate a sea of paper. Our colleagues in every country we have visited and worked in take every opportunity to tell us this, so we thought it worthy of repeating here.

The terminology of 'serious and enduringly mentally ill' was developed, in our view, to provide a linguistic basis for reviving the belief that some forms of 'mental illness' were largely 'untreatable', and to provide a rationale for economic programmes that appeared to favour some people (patients) at the expense of others. Certainly, the despairing rhetoric of 'serious and enduring mental illness' has often although not always been used as a rationale for doing little for people beyond medicating and socially corralling them.

This terminology came in the wake of the infamous 'decade of the brain', where research funding shifted away from social and psychosocial pro-grammes in the USA, and subsequently around the western world, to favour laboratory research in the neurosciences. As genetics and the biological sciences appeared to be on the brink of great discoveries regarding the explanation and amelioration of many disorders of the body, psychiatry hoped that at last it would be able to demonstrate that the mind was merely an expression of the brain, and that all the answers we had traditionally sought lay in the explication of its workings.

As a result, the past 20 years have witnessed a wealth of biological, neuroscientific and genetic hypotheses concerning the origins or bases of various forms of 'serious and or enduring mental illness', and many of these have become increasingly accepted as complete 'explanations' for human distress (Keen 1999; Newnes *et al.* 2000). Despite such popular acceptance, a considerable body of research exists that challenges these assumptions (Dawson 1994, 1997; Lehtonen 1994; Tienari *et al.* 1994). More importantly, there is evidence that viable alternatives to such biological constructions of mental distress exist, suggesting the possibilities for more holistic forms of psychosocial intervention (Alanen *et al.* 1991; Pylkkanen 1997). As Keen (1999) has noted, the public and political anxiety expressed over the 'uncertainty' of ever identifying any single causative factor for serious forms of mental ill-health (such as schizophrenia) has generated a form of pragmatism that risks stifling the continued search for a proper understanding of such problems of human living and how we might help people address them.

Drawing a parallel with our aquatic metaphor, in our search to understand the forces of nature, which generate typhoons and tidal waves, whirlpools and waterspouts, we have abandoned our interest in swimming and shipbuilding, in sailing and white-water rafting. We have featured the mental health equivalent of the mariner's craft here, not in any effort to deny the existence of all manner of physical threats to our personhood which might emanate from the biosphere of our bodies. Rather, we accept that these threats exist, but believe that we – the scientific and human community – still have little understanding of what these are, and how any emergent knowledge might be used to our communal human good. What we do know, from our own experience and from our reading of the work of others, – is that we can improve mental health care by relatively simple means – not by 'rocket science' – and that the means for doing this lie all around us. In this chapter, we shall try to bring together examples and illustrations of that theoretical knowledge, which is the symbolic anchor for the Tidal Model.

## The harbour

### *Ed Podvoll: The harbourmaster*

We believe in the importance of understanding, which can not only provide its own reassurance and comfort, but can also help build the jetty where we can moor the ship of life, taking rest and replenishment; and from which we can set sail again, when the tide is right. Although, as we shall see shortly, we have been influenced by a great many thinkers and practitioners, the work of Edward Podvoll represents a key influence; and one that provides an important link between the (theoretical) search for understanding and the (practical) act of helping.

In Podvoll's most important work, *The Seduction of Madness*, he provided an eloquent description of the process through which people, out of an urge for inner transformation, enter an altered state of consciousness, which entrances, fascinates and ultimately seduces them. This altered state, Podvoll called the 'second state':

> A natural but archaic substratum of mental functioning, built into the nervous system, always available, but accessed only by exceptional circumstances and conditions. Initially, it is a neutral state, but when its rudimentary reflex micro-operations become exposed to awareness, they may come to dominate awareness.
>
> (Podvoll 1990: 152–3)

These lines resonated with our experience of working with people in psychosis and also our explorations of our own states of consciousness. Within the concept of *awareness* – that simple, taken for granted state of being 'here and now' – lies the key to the whole process of addressing madness and negotiating the recovery of mental health.

The concept of 'micro-operations' also held great explanatory power and reminded us of our vicarious witness of the process of entering madness (see Clay 2004). Quoting Henri Michaux, Podvoll commented:.

> Each idea or belief becomes a center of energy – a pulsating machine – and it lashes out from there: as if all the mind asked was to function much, much faster than usual, to function at perhaps its 'free' speed that of nightmares (estimated at fifty times faster than normal) the speed that is born in seconds in the mind of the drowning, the speed that occurs sometimes in the dying and causes delirium.
>
> (Podvoll 1990: 139)

In this state, which can be brought on by stress (or any 'borderline' event), lie the seeds of insanity. The micro-operations involve, for example, enormously accelerated thinking that repeats and multiplies itself; thoughts and pictures uniting as hallucinations as in a dream. Things become mistaken for other things, whether seen, heard or felt. (A simple, every night example is the experience, when falling asleep, of a sudden 'twitch' of the leg, which is linked immediately to the drama of 'stumbling'; which for us always seems to be tripping over kerbs. Presumably for people who live in the country, some other 'meaning' is invoked.) In the emerging psychotic state, the person loses the capacity to doubt and, above all, in the struggle for certainty the person fights against all self-critical impulses, so that soon (s)he loses all grasp of consciousness itself – the ability to watch and reflect upon ongoing experience. In this way, the people increasingly lose their way in an 'ocean of their own projections'.

Soon the person can begin to feel at the mercy of forces which are beyond control; being led by such forces, by ghosts, demons, machines or people. If the forces are of a destructive character, the person may end up in an internalised hell in which even self-destruction is possible: 'Rare are the insane who are able to cope with their insanity' (Podvoll 1990). But even in these states, moments of wakefulness emerge, which Podvoll called 'islands of clarity': moments of consciousness free of the psychotic experience, in which spontaneous rays of hope appear, alongside doubts about the reality of psychotic experience, representing a miniature 'aha-experience'. For Podvoll, these were the decisive elements in terms of recovery. For people drowning in a tidal wave of wildly proliferating, confusing, and increasingly distorted thought patterns, these represent some 'dry land' from which the process of recovery might begin.

Podvoll makes the vital observation – vital in the sense of emphasising its natural flavour, common nature and frequency within the 'normal' lived experience – that psychosis can be a one-off and short-lived experience. He noted:

> Generally, we think of psychosis lasting for years, but there have also been many thousands of psychoses of shorter duration. This applies not only to those who have intermittent bouts of psychosis but also those who have only a single experience.
>
> (Podvoll 1990: 151).

Like children who have a single, never to be repeated, grand mal epileptic seizure, people can have brief psychotic interludes. (Indeed, in drug states this lasts only a few hours.) Podvoll described a dyslexic adolescent who dreaded school. When he was having a particularly difficult time in class, he would 'spontaneously feel that everyone was reading his mind, mocking him. For a few hours afterwards he might feel that messages were being given to him through the television set' (1990: 151).

Podvoll made the vital point, which most 'aware' people would recognise from their own experience, that in terms of subjective reality, when someone enters the 'second state' duration is not the immediate concern. Time appears to collapse into what is universally called 'timelessness' (suggesting that most people have experience of this). Real time (i.e. 'clock time') dissolves into mental time 'where it feels like the experiences of a lifetime can be had in a moment'.

### The safe haven

Ed Podvoll has provided us with the most eloquent and flexible description of the 'necessary conditions' for supporting someone in madness, from which they might be guided, at their own pace, back to the ocean of their own functional experience. More importantly, he frames this guidance within a coherent and, in our view, comprehensive theory of the psychotic process. Although focused on psychosis, we believe that it is relevant to all forms of severe emotional distress and experiences of 'psychic pain'. In our neurotic states we lose our awareness of the frivolous, petty, trifling nature of life problems (or ourselves), inflating these into psychic dirigibles that lift us from the ground of everyday reality. Awareness – and our loss of awareness – seems to be the key. Podvoll made this important observation:

> The difference between guarding and abandoning one's intelligence and sanity during a psychosis has very great consequences, yet only a hair's breadth separates them. The early situation of psychosis is usually very fragile and flickers back and forth between clarity and confusion. The amount of this flickering is often conditioned by *who* one is with and *how* one is being treated. When the environment is a safe one, with healthy friendship and patience, the psychosis may resolve itself in short order. On the other hand, when a psychosis that might naturally last only several hours or days is overreacted to by others in an attempt to suppress it as quickly as possible (as with over-medicating or other subjugating techniques), the disoriented one often fights against the effects of what he feels is an intrusion and a punishing abuse of his already-fragile mind.
>
> (Podvoll 1990: 152).

Podvoll found early success in exploring his hypothesis about 'safe havens' by taking people out of state psychiatric hospitals in the USA and relocating them to safe, supporting, natural home-like conditions that became known as 'therapeutic households' (Fortuna 2000). In such suitable healthy surroundings the experience of 'islands of clarity' may be increased, so that the dissipating, debilitating identifications become less frequent. This zone of awareness or wakefulness is a kind of inner observer. For Podvoll, healing depended on the facilitation, or discovery, of the 'zone of wakefulness' (Podvoll 1990).

Podvoll's thesis was remarkably simple, but socially and professionally radical. The last place any sane person would want to place an 'insane' person would be alongside other 'insane' people. Instead, if someone is 'losing their mind' the appropriate place to locate such a person would be in the company of 'healthy people'. Podvoll asked: 'If *you* were ill, who would you want to have on your team?' Podvoll said that after people got over the shock of trying to imagine themselves in such a state (which says something about their empathy levels, if not also their false sense of security), they would identify the following:

- Someone who is patient with a sense of humour.
- Someone who could simply *be* quietly by their side, when communication is not possible.
- Above all, someone who would not attack them, out of their own frustration when, under the influence of the great speeds of 'micro-operations', they made mistakes or lost the thread of what they though they knew.
- In effect, they would want a calming force, who would not add to the confusion already going on within.

We have asked the same kind of question of literally thousands of people (professional and lay) in different countries and across differing cultures and class systems. We consistently obtain the same answers.

It is a sad indictment of our supposedly sophisticated society, with its complex and elaborate health care infrastructure, that highly trained and eminently qualified professionals scurry and scamper around noisy, often physically unkempt, environments where at least a dozen if not sometimes 50 people, all in much the same state of unhealthy mental disarray, are housed. Often we say that the best we can do is to medicate (suppress) the expression of distress, and hold umpteen, interminable meetings in which staff talk about the difficulty of 'doing anything with this patient'.

We have visited and participated briefly in the Windhorse project in Massachusetts; one of the initiatives in developing 'therapeutic households' which flowed from Podvoll's vision. We know what it feels like to be in such a milieu. More importantly, we have talked to people who were on the journey of reclamation of their sanity with the help of the Windhorse staff.[1] There are few imperatives in professional practice these days and even fewer certainties, such is the influence of political correctness. However, the vision and insights of the Windhorse staff and Podvoll himself helped us to realise that the establishment of a *safe haven* had to be our first priority. Wherever possible, this should be a 'grounded' activity focused on developing awareness of some of the basic principles of being and staying alive.

Jeff Fortuna, who was a long-time colleague of Podvoll, and who led the Windhorse project in Massachussets, has written about the need to 'pay deliberate attention to details: emphasise an earthy simplicity in arranging the domestic environment. Domestic details become the "pull of gravity" or antidote to mental wandering' (Fortuna 2000: 186). Traditional psychiatry, in perceiving the person as 'serious and/or enduringly mentally ill', works too hard in 'caring *for*' the person, with the result that the person's capacities to 'be' and 'become different' wither.

Fortuna emphasised the importance of making choices, with the support of 'caring with', on an almost incessant, daily level. Choices about any and all aspects of the person's ordinary grounded reality. One person described the experience of this process:

> For me, this raised some interest in the outer world, for example, making decisions on the basis of what I would like? How do I want to live? This was in contrast to the flat, institutional environment I came from, in which I had no ability or right to exert myself in this way – a very simple practical, and thus, refreshing task.
>
> (Fortuna 2000: 187)

Ironically – given that Podvoll was a psychiatrist and many of those who followed him, like Fortuna and others, were social workers or psychotherapists – this pragmatic, grounded, reality-reconnecting activity (which Podvoll called 'basic attendance') had more than a hint of 'nurturance' about it. Podvoll asked:

> Does this mean that basic attendance is some kind of glorified nursing? The answer is yes insofar as it involves a genuine 'nursing of the mind.' So imbued is our culture with the notion of psychological treatment as being a white-collar, professional job where the psychotherapist does not have to reveal how he or she walks; eats; handles money; celebrates; does physical labor; relates to friends, children and animals; and so on – or does anything but talk about the past and the present and the future – that we think that anything else is 'merely nursing', or 'case management', something inferior to offering psychological 'insight' or the supposed science of prescribing medications.
>
> (Podvoll 1990: 264–5)

As we have noted elsewhere in this book, sadly even nurses themselves are beginning to shun the 'ordinariness' of 'mere nursing', seeking permission to deliver psychiatric diagnoses (to what effect?) or prescribe psychotropic medication (to an effect we know all too well). At the same time, nurses are less likely to be found doing the ordinary relating, caring with, living with, working with activity that Fortuna has shown to be such a vital part of facilitating recovery. In a recent report (Browne 2001) on the state of psychiatric wards in a part of Ireland, it was noted that the ward was dirty and litter was strewn on the floor and soiled clothing hung from the veranda railing. When asked by the journalist why this was not attended to, a nurse replied, 'It is the patients' responsibility to clean up after themselves, not ours.' The low small voice of 'us and them' had grown into a deafening roar.

The safe haven is an emotional (and hopefully physical) space where people can find some shelter from the storm of their mental distress; a place where they can gain emotional (and also physical and spiritual) nourishment; a place where they can review the damage done to their life-craft; and begin to develop awareness of what 'needs to be done' by way of repair. It may well be a place where the staff do some of their own repair work, at times of low activity – in much the same way as swimming instructors or life-savers will use the pool to maintain their fitness when there is no obvious call on their services. If Podvoll and Fortuna and their colleagues are to be believed, *awareness* is the way to begin the repair. We certainly have good reasons for believing them.

## The crew

Podvoll asked: 'Who would you want to be on your team?' In reflecting on the people we have known personally during our careers, and whom we have encountered through their work, we tried to list our own 'dream team'. Who would we sign up that would represent the best examples of the humanity necessary to represent us as persons? Initially, our list was rather obvious, comprising the great and the good of human inquiry and human helping: Martin Buber, Carl Rogers, Samuel Tuke, Dorothea Dix, William James – all people whom we believed were more concerned with understanding or helping others than understanding or helping themselves. So, we left out Freud, Jung and just about everyone else who had tried to establish a 'school of thought' or a patent psychological/psychiatric method.

Our team would also include many of the friends and colleagues whom we have worked with over the years, but we would reserve a special place for the people we know personally who have undertaken the journey through madness – however it is labelled and categorised by psychiatry – and who returned to tell the tale. Among them would be Irene Whitehill and Sally Clay, whom the reader met in the Foreword; Dan Fisher, Judi Chamberlin and Pat Deegan, whom we first met through the National Empowerment Center in Massachusetts; Peter Campbell, from London, one of the founders of Survivors Speak Out in the UK; Ed Manos, a consumer-advocate from New Jersey who became a personal friend; Paddy McGowan from Omagh, who founded the Irish Advocacy Network; Anne Helm, a user-advocate from Dunedin in New Zealand; Gary Platz, a window-cleaner turned psychotic 'Redeemer' and now a consumer-advocate in Wellington, New Zealand; and Ron Coleman, who has returned to become one of our neighbours in Scotland. All these people braved the storm commonly called schizophrenia or manic depression, so they would be highly experienced members of our team.

However, in the spirit of the model we decided to set ourselves a firmer challenge: to select a crew[2] that would represent our most potent influences, again drawn from among those whom we knew personally, or through their work. The task was surprisingly easy, which suggests either that we had not thought this through sufficiently, or that the crew were essentially self-selected. Bearing in mind that Podvoll waved us off at the quayside, this was our list of critical theoretical thinkers, who have influenced the development of the Tidal Model.

### Harry Stack Sullivan: The old sea dog

The Tidal Model assumes that we need to get close to the people in our care, so that we might explore (together) the experience of health and illness. We have noted how health care is becoming increasingly technical and emotionally distant: e.g. through the use of computers, or the shield of paper system. However, many people with mental health problems are calling for care and treatment to re-emphasise the relationships between themselves and their carers (Barker *et al.* 1999c; Newnes *et al.* 1999, 2000). Although relationships are as old as humankind, within psychiatry their explication has one critical champion.

Harry Stack Sullivan is a little known figure in contemporary mental health care: partly because – as his biographer pointed out – he was such a poor writer; partly because he bucked the Freudian conventions of most of his colleagues; and partly because he was out of step – sexually and perhaps emotionally – according to the narrow mores of the day. He trained in psychoanalysis in the United States, but soon drifted from the specific psychoanalytic beliefs, placing more focus on both the social aspects of personality and cognitive representations. This moved him away from Freud's psychosexual development and toward a more eclectic approach.

Freud believed that anxiety was an important aspect in his theory because it represented internal conflict between the id and the superego. Sullivan, however, saw anxiety as existing only as a result of social interactions. He described techniques, much like defence mechanisms, which provide tools for people to use in order to reduce social anxiety. *Selective Inattention* – now well known to cognitive therapists, many of whom assume that the term originated with Aaron Beck – was one such mechanism first described by Sullivan.

According to Sullivan, mothers show their anxiety about child rearing to their children through various means. The child, having no way to deal with this, feels the anxiety himself. Selective inattention is soon learned, and the child begins to ignore or reject the anxiety or any interaction that could produce these uncomfortable feelings. As adults, we use this technique to focus our minds away from stressful situations. From such observations and interpretations Sullivan began to develop the interpersonal relations theory that made his name (Sullivan 1953). Sullivan was highly influential both on his immediate followers and on later generations:

* Don Jackson (1968), who went on to become a pioneering family therapist, was supervised by Sullivan, and served as a model for the development of Jay Haley's (1979) systems oriented family therapy.

- Irving Yalom (1968) credits Sullivan's theory as one of the most important influences on the development of group psychotherapy.
- Ferster and Skinner's (1957) early work on schedules of reinforcement provided empirical support for Sullivan's notions of the importance of learning by reward and punishment.
- Sullivan's ideas about modelling and vicarious learning, which obviously emerge in group psychotherapy, also influenced theories on child development, especially Bandura's (1977) social learning theory experiments.
- In his attempt to integrate psychoanalysis and developmental psychology, Stern (1985) acknowledged Sullivan's ideas about the interpersonal nature of humans, subjective relatedness (personifications), the development of self and anxiety.
- Sullivan was a critical influence on the development of cognitive-behaviour therapy.

Most notably, for us, Sullivan coined and used extensively the term 'problems of living' as an alternative to 'psychopathology', which was in use at the time. Thomas Szasz was later to promulgate the use of this term, which not only appears more respectful, but also *meaningful* in terms of the interpersonal nature of a person's engagement with the world.

However, our key reason for including Sullivan as part of our crew is because of his honest appraisal of himself and his humanity. There was something of a scandal in Sullivan's day (fuelled by a story that he had been admitted to a psychiatric hospital) concerning his alleged 'schizophrenic' status and homosexuality. Frustratingly for his colleagues, neither of these could be confirmed. However, many doubted his emotional status and adopted the view that this would contaminate his therapeutic relations with patients. Like Ronnie Laing, who was to follow much of his example, Sullivan appeared to embrace his own 'psychopathology' in his dictum, 'Everyone is more simply human than otherwise.' This suggested that the psychotherapist's problems of living might actually come in handy when it came to understanding the 'psychopathology' in others. Although this view scandalised the blank-screen analysts of his day, it lit the torch for the egalitarian form of caring with that we have described in this book, and which is only beginning to make its presence felt in mainstream psychotherapy. Sullivan's biographer suggested that Sullivan's key contribution to psychotherapy and psychiatry was his ever-present awareness of the need to convey respect for the patient and to maintain the patient's own self-esteem. A more fitting epitaph is hard to imagine and one of the very best reasons for welcoming him on board. For a comprehensive review of Sullivan's life and work, see Evans (1996).

Sullivan's influence can hardly be over-stated and he heads our list, not least because he is largely forgotten, or worse unknown, beyond psychotherapy circles. His work paved the way for much of the work that ultimately was to influence us, and his emphasis on understanding the relationship – that people have with others and also have with 'themselves' – is central to the whole thrust of the Model.

### Ronnie Laing: The mate

Much of our thinking about the human condition and how we might begin to understand it, and hence ourselves, is drawn from Nietszche, Husserl, Heidegger, Sartre, Merleau-Ponty, Jaspers, Wittgenstein and Camus. Whereas we only dipped our toes into some of these deep waters, Ronnie Laing immersed himself in the study of these European greats. In our view, three men dominate the history of twentieth-century psychiatry: Freud, Jung and Ronnie (R.D.) Laing. All were visionaries, with loyal followings. Sadly, history also reveals how each had feet of clay. Although much has often been made of their moral frailties, this should not detract from a careful appraisal of the value of their work.

We were reminded of this when we listened again to Anthony Clare's BBC interview with Laing in his radio series, *In the Psychiatrist's Chair*. Laing talked candidly about his isolated childhood, the development of his introspective nature, and the mother who (perhaps) unwittingly nurtured the most controversial psychiatric voice of the past 50 years. Who would have forecast that a solitary child from a middle-class Scots home would have so rocked the foundations of twentieth-century psychiatry? The very mention of his name, more than a decade after his death, is sufficient to trigger vituperative debate. This may of itself be sufficient evidence for the endurance of his influence. But at 61 he died of a heart attack playing tennis – too competitively, as was his wont – in the South of France. In the interview, recorded five years earlier, Laing laughed nervously as he recalled how his mother had told his daughter she had once fashioned a voodoo doll, intent on creating a heart attack in her only son. His weary but still good-humoured voice suggested that Laing was all too aware of death closing in on him.

Laing's influence extended far beyond psychiatry, psychotherapy and medicine. However, the practical application of Laing's thought – by the man himself and some of his most famous allies and former pupils – was largely non-medical. Indeed, we might interpret the application of his philosophy, especially through his frequently revised views on psychotherapy, as a *nursing* approach, focused on *nurturing* the conditions – social and interpersonal – under which people might finally seize their own power and use this, constructively, to define themselves, rather then be subjugated, if not actually driven to madness, by others. Although others have since developed and refined his ideas, Laing was the most important influence on our thoughts about 'caring with'.

Given Laing's focus on the experience of madness, the radio interview reminds us of the inherent value in hearing him talk in the rough Glaswegian brogue, which can be refreshing to the ear. At times he articulated certain words carefully, as when he talks of the den*i*gration of the experience of madness, giving emphasis to the word's root in *deni*al. Like his contemporary, Thomas Szasz, he shared a rare appreciation for the proper meanings of words; although, contrary to public misconception, this was just about all they would share.

In the eyes of many, Laing let himself get too close, empathically speaking, to his patients and risked burning himself in the process. In this regard, he was following very directly in the footsteps of his ideological mentor Sullivan.

Regrettably, the great fuss over his many alcohol-fuelled appearances on television, and his willingness to let his views be politicised recklessly in the late 1960s, have obscured Laing's legacy – much of it not part of his original ambition. Very early in his career, in Glasgow in the 1950s, he created a 'rumpus room' for disturbed patients. This was to become a model of the 'safe space' that acutely disturbed people needed, and where they might give free rein to their disturbed and disturbing emotions. The very name suggests the presence of the maternal in Laing, and of course was a wonderful, practical example of the 'safe haven' of our metaphorical harbour.

Without patronising the people who were nominally in his care, he recognised that, like children, mentally distressed people needed a space within their temporary home (hospital) where they might *be* in their madness. A couple of years later he wallpapered and furnished another of the bleak rooms at Gartnavel Hospital to create a real 'living room' for four 'backward' women patients, who were eventually discharged, much to everyone's surprise. That the women eventually found their way back into institutional care merely attested to the lack of support for them in the so-called 'natural community'. The ultimate failure of this project may well have turned Laing's vision from attempting to remodel hospital care in favour of the establishment of more genuine community-based alternatives through the Philadelphia Association.

These early projects did, however, signal the possibilities of 'nurturing' people into recovery. Later, his experimental community at Kingsley Hall inspired many of his followers and former students to develop the potential of therapeutic households. Arguably the most famous of these – Loren Mosher – developed the Soteria House project in the USA, which demonstrated the possibility of nurturing recovery in people with schizophrenia within an ordinary living environment. And of course another of his disciples, Edward Podvoll, serves a key role in this chapter, as indeed his work does throughout the book.

These experimental projects, which emphasised the value of nurturing emergence from psychosis, through often extraordinarily 'ordinary' forms of human support, represent the nursing legacy of Laing's original work in the 1950s and 1960s. It is ironic that male psychiatrists should have discovered the human virtue – and therapeutic value – of organising a sustainable and sustaining caring environment. (Hilda Peplau might have sometimes questioned their motives, but we think that they would have wanted her to do so.) These often quite extraordinary projects are, however, arguably only the tip of the iceberg of Laingian influence. The contemporary concepts of 'safe houses', supported accommodation, therapeutic households, and especially, the virtue of validating the distress of acutely mad people, owe much to his often eccentric example. Little wonder that he became an icon for the emerging survivor groups like Survivors Speak Out, and indirectly inspired developments like the Hearing Voices Network, which discovered almost 30 years later that experiences dismissed as meaningless symptoms of a hypothetical brain dysfunction could be understood and often represented a coded form of the distress the person had experienced earlier in life.

Laing argued consistently that the 'abyss of understanding' between normal or neurotic and psychotic people that was postulated by Kraepelin, Bleuler, Jaspers and others, was not a given, but an artifact; a result of the failure of empathy and understanding. His early work is full of clinical vignettes in which a person in schizophrenia's sense of the world and their own bodies as menacing, uncanny and fragmented becomes readily intelligible, and the seemingly bizarre delusions of Laing's 'patients' become suddenly fraught with meaning. For a comprehensive review of Laing's life and work, see Burston (1996, 2000).

---

Laing was not afraid to 'get down' and 'be' with the people in his care. He also managed to distil much that he had learned from the great European philosophers, translating a lot of arcane, obscure ideas into a lyrical story that captured the imagination of our generation, and still draws readers a generation later. He formed the bridge between the once distant professional and the person at risk of drowning in mental distress. He showed us that although there was always a risk of drowning oneself, there was nothing to fear in getting wet.

---

### Hilda Peplau: The ship's surgeon

The Tidal Model developed from the five-year study of the 'need for nursing' (Jackson and Stevenson 1998), which generated a substantive theory of nursing practice in mental health care (Barker *et al.* 1999c, 1999d). The *Need for Nursing* study sought to clarify the discrete roles and functions of nursing within a multidisciplinary care and treatment process. Paradoxically, it may have revealed something of the virtue of nursing in the context of mental health care, whoever is the 'carer'.

By translating the theory of the need for nursing into practice, the Tidal Model developed many of Peplau's assertions about the importance of interpersonal relationships for nursing practice, many of which she gleaned from Sullivan, and also incorporated a model of the process of empowerment (Musker and Byrne 1997) developed within a parallel study (Barker *et al.* 1999b). These theory-generating studies continued the tradition of inquiry involving the interpersonal processes of nursing practice (Peplau 1952; Altschul 1972), which sought to clarify further what mental health nurses should do in the name of human caring.

Hildegard Peplau, was one of the world's leading nurses, and was known in the USA as the 'mother of psychiatric nursing', such was her influence over more than 50 years. She received countless awards, honorary doctorates and accolades, which reflected her public esteem, but which said little about who she was and why we would want her on board.

Peplau's theoretical and clinical work led, at least in the USA, to the development of the distinct specialty field of psychiatric nursing. Her seminal text, *Interpersonal Relations in Nursing* (1952), was completed in 1948 but delayed for several years because at that time it was considered too revolutionary for a nurse to publish a book without a doctor as co-author. Peplau's book has been widely credited with the transformation of nursing from a group of skilled workers to a full-fledged profession. Since the publication of Peplau's work, interpersonal process has been universally integrated into nursing education and nursing practices throughout the USA and abroad. Some would argue that Peplau's life and work produced the greatest changes in nursing practice since Florence Nightingale.

Peplau's early childhood experience of death and illness, during the great influenza epidemic of 1918, seemed to have a profound effect on her – especially her witness of a delirious person jumping from a window near her home. After training as a nurse she went on to study interpersonal psychology and had a placement at Chestnut Lodge, where Harry Stack Sullivan was on the staff, along with Erich Fromm and Frieda Fromm-Reichmann who was her psychoanalytic supervisor. Ironically, despite its delay, her book on *Interpersonal Relations in Nursing* came out the year before Sullivan's.

She was eventually certified in psychoanalysis by the William Alanson White Institute of New York City. In the early 1950s, Peplau developed and taught the first classes for graduate psychiatric nursing students, before going on to Rutgers University where she developed and led the first graduate level programme for the preparation of clinical specialists in psychiatric nursing, all of whom specialised in either individual, group or family forms of psychotherapy. Peplau once said that the test of a good idea was whether or not it had staying power. Her original book from 1952 has been translated into nine languages and in 1989 was reissued. Peplau's ideas have, indeed, stood the test of time.

Once we asked her if she could summarise her theory in a few sentences. She sat back, drew on her cigarette, smiled and then said: 'People make themselves up, as they talk.' And so she provides a compassionate, witty, insightful link between the original theory of Sullivan and the post-modern constructivism of narrative therapy, incorporating much of Tom Szasz's thinking – especially concerning the validity of the concept of 'mental illness' in the process. Although we only knew her in the last decade of her life, she struck us as highly pragmatic, insatiably curious in intellectual affairs and, like most women, supremely practical. Having heard examples of her incisive wit and watched her 'cut to the chase' in many an intellectual wrangle, she would be our choice as ship's surgeon. For a comprehensive review of Peplau's life and work, see Callaway (2002).

---

Peplau was the first psychiatric nurse to be taken seriously by psychiatric medicine, and will probably be the last, as the discipline looks set to chart a course focused on blending itself completely into psychiatric medicine, hence losing the distinctive focus that Peplau prized. She showed that the ordinary connections which nurses made with their 'patients' could be turned into extraordinary educational journeys, with the person learning more and more about how they had come to this point in their lives, and how, with help, they might move on again.

---

### Loren Mosher: The bo'sun

Loren Mosher grew up in California, going on to obtain an MD with honours from Harvard Medical School in 1961, where he also subsequently took his psychiatric training. Like many of our crew, he has had a distinguished professional career, but it is his interest in and support for 'alternatives to hospitalisation' projects that would lead us to asking him to join the crew. He has helped establish a number of innovative programmes, including a consumer owned and operated computer company, and a residential alternative to psychiatric hospitalisation for people in crisis. He is a popular speaker at conferences, especially at user/consumer-led events. It was at one of these conferences in Birmingham, England that we first met, where he kindly gave a recorded interview from which most of these comments are drawn.

His professional training and experience is both extensive and wide ranging. He received research training at the National Institute of Mental Health (NIMH) Intramural Research Program in Bethesda, Maryland and at the Tavistock Clinic in London, where he spent time with Ronnie Laing and met others who had been involved with the Kingsley Hall 'experiment', which clearly stimulated the interests that led to his developments of the projects for which he most well known.

He opened Soteria House in San Francisco in 1971, a unique social environment which he also designed. There, young people with a diagnosis of 'schizophrenia' lived medication-free with a non-professional staff trained to listen to and understand them and provide support, safety and validation of their experience.[3] The idea was that schizophrenia could often be overcome with the help of meaningful relationships, rather than with drugs, and that such treatment would eventually lead to unquestionably healthier lives. The Soteria project's design was a random assignment, two-year follow-up study, comparing the Soteria[4] method of treatment with 'usual' general hospital psychiatric ward interventions, which relied principally on drug treatment for people newly diagnosed with schizophrenia and deemed in need of hospitalisation.

The experiment worked better than even Mosher expected. At six weeks post-admission both groups had improved significantly and comparably, despite Soteria clients having not usually received antipsychotic drugs. Two years after admission, Soteria-treated subjects were working at significantly higher occupational levels, were significantly more often living independently or with peers, and had fewer readmissions. Interestingly, clients treated at Soteria who received no neuroleptic medication over the entire two years *or* were thought to be destined to have the worst outcomes actually did the best as compared to hospital and drug-treated control subjects.

Despite over 40 publications related to the project, Mosher acknowledged that the Soteria ideal 'disappeared from the consciousness of American psychiatry'. Its message was too difficult for the field to acknowledge, assimilate and use. Most importantly it clashed with the emerging scientific, descriptive, biomedical character of American psychiatry and, in fact, called nearly every one of its tenets into question. Famously, Mosher commented that Soteria 'demedicalised, dehospitalised, deprofessionalised, and deneurolepticised what Thomas Szasz has called "psychiatry's sacred cow", schizophrenia'.

However, the influence of the Soteria project is international, making Mosher the 'prophet who is not without honour, save in his own country'. Swiss psychiatrists such as Luc Ciompi have replicated the Soteria experiment and determined that Soteria care produced favourable outcomes in about two-thirds of patients. In both Sweden and Finland, researchers have since reported good outcomes with newly identified people with 'schizophrenia', which involve family-oriented psychosocial treatment programmes using minimal or no neuroleptics (see Alanen *et al.* 1991).

Loren Mosher is our first choice as bo'sun, since he has the ideal track record for managing crew and equipment. For more details about his current work, visit www.moshersoteria.com. For an overview of the various Soteria projects see Mosher (1999).

Mosher deserves to be remembered as the person who took Laing's almost embryonic ideals about 'therapeutic households', turning them into a physical reality that could withstand rigorous scrutiny. He became even more dangerous (professionally) than Laing in that he showed that non-professional staff could crew the ship of recovery, providing that they had some decent support themselves. He is, in that sense, the ideal supervisor of our crew.

### Viktor Frankl: The cook

All our crew choices have great humanity, discovered in the main through their engagement with their life's work. Viktor Frankl discovered his humanity through his life itself, or rather as it teetered repeatedly on the cusp of life and death. Frankl survived the Holocaust, despite having been in four Nazi death camps, including Auschwitz from 1942 to 1945. His parents and other members of his family died in concentration camps. During and largely because of his suffering in the camps, Frankl developed a revolutionary approach to psychotherapy that he later called *logotherapy*. At the heart of his theory stands the belief that humanity's primary motivational force is the *search for meaning*,[5] and the work of the logotherapist focuses on helping the patient find personal meaning in life, however dismal the circumstances may be.

Frankl believed that we could discover the meaning in life in three ways: by creating a work or doing a deed; by experiencing something or encountering someone; and by the attitude we take toward unavoidable suffering. He wrote:

> The true meaning of life is to be found in the world rather than within man or his own psyche, as though it were a closed system . . . Human experience is essentially self-transcendence rather than self-actualization. Self-actualization is not a possible aim at all, for the simple reason that the more a man would strive for it, the more he would miss it . . . In other words, self-actualization cannot be attained if it is made an end in itself, but only as a side effect of self-transcendence.
>
> (Frankl 1964: 175)

Meaning, for Viktor Frankl, was experienced indirectly, by responding to the demands of the situation at hand, discovering and committing oneself to one's own unique task in life, and by allowing oneself to experience or trust in an ultimate meaning, which people may or may not call God. He offered a gripping, graphic account of his own experience in *Man's Search for Meaning*:

> We stumbled on in the darkness, over big stones and through large puddles, along the one road running through the camp. The

accompanying guards kept shouting at us and driving us with the butts of their rifles. Anyone with very sore feet supported himself on his neighbour's arm. Hardly a word was spoken; the icy wind did not encourage talk. Hiding his hand behind his upturned collar, the man marching next to me whispered suddenly: 'If our wives could see us now! I do hope they are better off in their camps and don't know what is happening to us.'

That brought thoughts of my own wife to mind. And as we stumbled on for miles, slipping on icy spots, supporting each other time and again, dragging one another on and upward, nothing was said, but we both knew: each of us was thinking of his wife. Occasionally I looked at the sky, where the stars were fading and the pink light of the morning was beginning to spread behind a dark bank of clouds. But my mind clung to my wife's image, imagining it with an uncanny acuteness. I heard her answering me, saw her smile, her frank and encouraging look. Real or not, her look then was more luminous than the sun, which was beginning to rise.

A thought transfixed me: for the first time in my life I saw the truth as it is set into song by so many poets, proclaimed as the final wisdom by so many thinkers. The truth – that love is the ultimate and the highest goal to which man can aspire. Then I grasped the meaning of the greatest secret that human poetry and human thought and belief have to impart: The salvation of man is through love and in love. I understood how a man who has nothing left in this world may still know bliss, be it only for a brief moment, in the contemplation of his beloved. In a position of utter desolation, when a man cannot express himself in positive action, when his only achievement may consist in enduring his sufferings in the right way – an honourable way – in such a position man can, through loving contemplation of the image he carries of his beloved, achieve fulfilment. For the first time in my life, I was able to understand the words, 'The angels are lost in perpetual contemplation of an infinite glory.'

. . . Had I known then that my wife was dead, I think that I still would have given myself, undisturbed by that knowledge, to the contemplation of that image, and that my mental conversation with her would have been just as vivid and just as satisfying. 'Set me like a seal upon thy heart, love is as strong as death.'

(Frankl 1964: 58–9)

Frankl often wrote about the folly of 'trying to take one's mind off a misfortune', which he called 'narcotisation'. He argued that all such diversionary tactics achieved was to escape reality.

The act of looking at something does not create that thing; neither does the act of looking away annihilate it.

(Frankl 1965: 113)

This confirms him as the most realistic member of our crew and, as his work has so often fed the souls of women and men down the past 50 years, we appoint him as our cook. For more details on Viktor Frankl's life and work visit: http://logotherapy.univie.ac.at/

Frankl could be seen as a heroic figure, but doubtless he would spurn this role. However, he is, without doubt, the most experienced member of our crew, in the human sense, with many dangerous voyages under his belt. All of these journeys seem to have provided a rehearsal space for his true vocation – providing sustenance to others.

### David Brandon: The cabin boy

Although he is no longer with us, David Brandon had that 'forever young' quality, expressed by his vigour, irreverence and often scatological outlook on life. He was a man for all seasons. Often we did not know exactly *which* man he was, but that did not prevent us calling him friend and certainly did not prevent us from valuing one another, as fellow travellers on a rather uncertain life path. In his last book, *The Tao of Survival*, he commented on his many careers – psychiatric nurse, Zen monk, field social worker, psychotherapist, administrator, teacher, researcher and, of course, writer. He cherished them all but, invariably, found his efforts wanting. To an onlooker David's life more often resembled a play, or even a film script, with David as dogged hero. His dour judgement of his own contribution to his many chosen disciplines was, however, greatly at odds with its actuality. That he remained sceptical about all 'professions' was one of his most endearing, if frustrating, characteristics. He often made us uncomfortable about feeling so comfortable.

Few, in any walk of professional life, escaped his creative wit or his scathing analysis of 'what needed to be done'. He was indiscriminate in his interests and support, finding great difficulty in understanding why, for example, we should relate to the homeless differently from people with a learning disability, or those with a presumed mental illness. Once, when he was enthusing about his work in eastern Europe, we asked how he managed the language barrier. He paused, preparing to frame the classic 'Brandon-moment', then said calmly: 'You don't need to speak the same f****** language to know what people need!' It was the calmness, rather than the expletive, that underlined the truth of his observation. Not for the first time, we felt humble in the presence of this Master of the Obvious.

Although he ended up as the UK's first Professor of Community Care, he was not the kind of man to gain gongs from Her Majesty and was for all of his life an irritating distraction on the sidelines of government policy, if not also the professional agenda of his chosen discipline, social work. Perhaps because of this marginal status, he was also a folk hero – the personification of the avenging angel, the doer of truly good deeds, the man-with-no-name who walked tall on the matinee idol screen. He often ridiculed this *posture*, as he saw it. With an uncharacteristic gentle irony, he compared himself once to the Pale Rider, portrayed by Clint Eastwood. He appeared to be acknowledging that he was, to a large extent, playing various roles. It was never clear which, if any, of them was the real Brandon.

We count our blessings that he was reincarnated in this life as both a psychiatric nurse and a social worker. David abandoned nursing early on and made the dusty, trouble-ridden plains of social work his own distinct campaign trail. Watching him at work, we knew that he was, indeed, the Pale Rider, packing a metaphorical six-gun to blast the ground from under the politically correct, the theorists, the technicians, and especially those with compassion fatigue. It was, however, often a lonely existence. Like the Pale Rider, he was the 'hired gun' who hired himself for his own very good reasons.

David's fire was first lit in his troubled childhood in Sunderland. Like all the best researchers, he knew his subject both inside and out. His own 'runaway' experience, escaping the madness and abuse of home, led to an apprenticeship in survival skills, which later he capitalised on in his work with all dispossessed people. In *The Tao of Survival* he illustrated the raw power of the lessons life had taught him. Where many social workers conjure empathy, like a clever but empty illusion, David knew the 'trick of being ordinary' like the back of his hand.

In addition to his great legacy, enshrined in a huge output of books, papers and pamphlets, we shall cherish his black humour. Once he took the stage after Ted White, a 'very decorous Englishman' who was later to become a professorial colleague, and quipped, 'The last time I saw Ted we were cell-mates!' On another occasion he challenged a member of the audience who was defending the 'modernisation' of acute psychiatric wards. 'Ah', he beamed, 'you would have wallpapered the gas chambers?' He never missed an opportunity to turn the spotlight on the double talk and denial that dominates most social and health care services, or to prick the bubbles of the pompous or indifferent. Most importantly, he never shirked the responsibility of putting himself on the line. These issues were deeply personal, not academic. David stood up to be counted, unlike most of us.

Although he rejected the 'user career' favoured by many, he was arguably the first professor with a serious psychiatric user background. He was also the most difficult man we ever met, since our every meeting left us ill at ease. He knew that change happens in the heart, not out there in some academic distance. Twenty-five years ago, in the most remarkable book of our generation, *Zen and the Art of Helping*, he wrote how he had learned to administer advice and wisdom to others, but could not apply it to his own life. We knew he was harder on himself than he ever was on the rest of us. He reminded us that we are all flawed. The dividing line between 'user' and 'provider' is thinner than the political rhetoric that first made the distinction. As we drown in a sea of political spin, cronyism and celebrity trivia, he reminded us of the virtues of conscientious objection and swimming for land. For more about David Brandon, his values and his work, see Brandon (1976, 2000a).

> Brandon is our choice as the 'voice of experience' – someone who experienced both mental distress and hospitalisation, and found his vocation as a result. Although known as a social worker, academic and Zen monk, he would prize his 'experience of madness' as the main driving force behind his practice as a helper of his fellow women and men. He was also passionately committed to 'ground floor' working, and as the youngest member of our crew, in years as well as in spirit, will make the ideal cabin boy.

### Shoma Morita: The pilot

Shoma Morita was a contemporary of Freud who represented a rare Japanese phenomenon: someone whose attitude towards life and the actual living of it heralded a revolution in thinking about therapy and 'problem solving' far beyond the shores of his home country. As Reynolds (1984) has pointed out, in his own day Morita was less concerned with the extreme propriety common among middle- and upper-class Japanese. He took patients to his home, so that he could help them further to develop their 'everyday living skills'. He encouraged them to ignore the hierarchical distinctions that commonly would have put a barrier between himself and his 'patients'. These were very bold steps in Japanese society, and especially Japanese psychiatry at the beginning of the twentieth century.

Morita modelled for us the concept of 'caring with', encouraging his patients to join him in the garden, showing them how he kneaded magazine paper to turn into toilet tissue; illustrating the virtue of recycling almost a century before it became fashionable. When a workman failed to turn up to do some work, the learned professor would drop everything, don his work clothes and do the work himself – even when this involved shovelling out the cesspool. When asked why he engaged in such menial tasks, he uttered his famous dictum, which we have taken to heart in the Tidal Model: 'I am only doing what needs to be done.'

The therapy method he developed, later called Morita psychotherapy, was influenced by the psychological principles of Zen Buddhism. Initially, it was reserved for the treatment of a type of anxiety neurosis called in Japanese, *shinkeishitsu*. However, today the method is widely used with people in psychosis, with so-called 'personality disorders' and especially with people facing death through terminal illness.

In western 'mental health' work there is an assumption that it is necessary to change or modify our feeling state before we can take action. People assume that they must overcome their fear of water before diving into a pool, or 'build up' their confidence so they might make a public presentation. Morita showed that this was unnecessary. In fact, it is our *efforts to change* our feelings that often make us feel even worse. He wisely noted:

> Trying to control the emotional self wilfully by manipulative attempts is like trying to choose a number on a thrown die or to push back the water of the Kamo River upstream. Certainly, they end up aggravating their agony and feeling unbearable pain because of their failure in manipulating the emotions.

> (Reynolds 1984)

In the west we are obsessed with labels, which purport to diagnose and describe a person's psychological functioning: depressed, obsessive, compulsive, psychotic, etc. Many of us begin to label ourselves this way, rather than explore our own experience. Morita pointed out that if we observe our experience, we find that we have a flow of awareness, which changes from moment to moment. When we become overly preoccupied with ourselves, our attention no longer flows freely, but becomes trapped by an unhealthy self-focus. The more we pay attention to our 'symptoms', the more we fall into this trap. When we are absorbed by what we are doing, we are not anxious because our attention is engaged by activity. But when we try to 'understand' or 'fix' or 'work through' feelings and issues, our self-focus is heightened and exercised. This often leads to more suffering rather than relief. Morita asked how we might be released from such self-focused attention? One of his students, Takahisa Kora commented:

> The answer lies in practicing and mastering an attitude of being in touch with the outside world. This is called a reality-oriented attitude, which means, in short, liberation from self-centeredness.

> (Kora 1995)

Morita therapy has frequently been compared to western behaviour therapy, because of its focus on 'doing' rather than feeling. However, this seems like comparing a snapshot to a painting by Picasso. Both offer an image of something, but there is a world of difference in what is actually represented in each image. Morita would likely share many of Frankl's assumptions about the independent life of feelings, and would have much in common with the compassionate pragmatism of Laing, Mosher, Sullivan and Peplau. Of course, he would be very much 'at one' with Brandon who, as a Zen monk, was a fellow traveller.

Given Morita's skill in the simple yet complex business of everyday living, we would employ him as the pilot, guiding us through the narrows and shallows into the homeland of the harbour. For more on Morita, his life and influence, visit http://www.morita-therapy.org/ and http://www.todoinstitute.org/index.html. Also read Reynolds (1984).

> So little is known of Morita in the west that it is easy to forget how influential he has been. Indeed his influence could be seen as classically quiet and respectful in a Japanese sense, were it not also – at the same time – revolutionary in its convention-breaking simplicity. Psychiatric conventions are the hardest things to break in what remains a highly superstitious world. His focus on the need to 'do what needs to be done' will hopefully become a 'bumper sticker' for the hull of our ship.

### Thomas Szasz: The lookout

Thomas Szasz wrote probably the most important book of the twentieth century – *The Myth of Mental Illness*. A bit like Joyce's *Ulysses*, it became a book everyone talked about as if they had read it, but many had not dared to read it, or at least had not troubled to read it carefully. So Tom Szasz became something of a myth in his own lifetime. His prodigious literary output would cover a fairly wide berth on board, but his 30-odd books and 600 other publications all have a similar centre of gravity: the right of people to self-determination and their concurrent responsibility for the direction of their own lives. Having arrived in the USA as a teenager, speaking no English, he became one of the finest exponents of the careful and precise use of the English language. He will make a fine lookout and will not mistake land for some mirage or sea monster.

Whether you agree or disagree with him, whether he delights or infuriates you, Szasz's work will provoke you into what has become something of a rarity – critical thought. His most trenchant criticism continues to be focused on the concept of problems of living being misrepresented as mental illness.[6] In an age when we take almost for granted the biological or biochemical basis of various forms of 'mental illness', he argues (Luft 2001): 'Show me 100 brain CAT scans, blind, that will show which patients have mental illness as reliably as 100 leg x-rays, again blind, will show which patients have fractures, and then I will believe that there is mental illness.' His contention has always been that mental 'illness' does not exist because the medical criterion for illness is the physical lesion, which in the mind, not being a material object, not being – despite recent philosophical and psychological arguments – the same 'thing' as the brain, is not possible. Instead, any 'lesion' of the mind is purely metaphorical – rather like 'heartache' or 'being soul weary' or even 'mindless'.

Szasz has often confessed to being doubtful of the concept of mental illness long before he became a psychiatrist. He accepted that people could be 'nutty' or even 'mad', but that does not mean that they are diseased, or indeed that anything at all is wrong with them. He has illustrated how the concept of mental illness evolved in Europe in the sixteenth and seventeenth centuries, but for many cultures, such as the Native Americans or the Maori, no such concept exists. They would attribute such 'states' to divine inspiration or some form of 'insight' (rather as Laing was wont to do early in his career). Only in the pages of the *Diagnostic and Statistical Manual of Mental Disorders* (*DSM-IV*) and in its huge territory of social influence would such states be classified as 'sickness' (APA 1994).

He also reminded us of the fashion-conscious nature of these concepts of 'illness'. In the USA before the Civil War, 'drapetomania' allegedly existed – the tendency for slaves to run away from their masters; and 'dysaethesia Aethiopis' – the lethargy of black slaves; and 'negritude' – the very condition of having dark skin. All were classified as diseases by many respectable American physicians. In his own time, 'masturbatory insanity' and 'homosexuality' were considered legitimate diseases, as were other sexual 'perversions' now accepted as merely part of the range of sexual preference. Infamously, at least to American eyes, the former USSR defined the desire to emigrate as a feature of 'schizophrenia'. The current popularity of ritalin prescription is based on the assumption that 'hyperactive' children (usually boys) are 'diseased', but as Szasz observes, high levels of activity have always been 'normal' for boys.

Szasz has consistently argued that the systematic classification of diseases as entities is artificial and does not advance the cause of medicine. Rather this merely gives physicians the power to pigeonhole and depersonalise patients. It also provides the means for societal and governmental oppression of certain groups of people, notably the young, the old, the poor, the politically 'undesirable' and the socially 'offensive'. Today, as we shall suggest in Chapter 15, people who have recovered from 'mental illness' and have reclaimed some of the power they lost to the psychiatric system perceive Szasz as a liberator.

Echoing Harry Stack Sullivan, Szasz has consistently reminded us that 'psychiatry does not deal with diseases, but with conflicts between people'. What we call psychiatric 'treatment' is really a personal service aimed at addressing 'unwanted' or 'undesirable' ways of behaving (thinking or feeling) if it is voluntary, and is a method of social control if administered against the person's expressed wishes. A major part of his reputation – both for good and ill – is his argument that we should feel professionally and morally obligated to respect the autonomy of each patient, rather than hastily assume that there is something 'wrong' with people. Whether or not we help people to chart the course of their own lives, or try to channel them – by whatever means, gentle or coercive – into 'fitting in' to the existing social mores, is the primary moral dilemma for all professionals, if not also for society as a whole.

Another old friend, Marius Romme, is a Dutch psychiatrist, famous for his work on the redefinition of 'auditory hallucinations' as merely 'hearing voices'. In a conversation with the English psychologist Richard Bentall, he wryly commented: 'I really like your research on hallucinations, Richard. But the trouble is, you want to *cure* hallucinations, whereas I want to *liberate* them. I think they are like homosexuals in the 1950s – in need of liberation, not cure' (Bentall 2003: 511).

Although some would argue that Szasz's influence has declined, Romme's comment illustrates the huge power of his influence. Szaszian thinking may well still be the stuff of nightmares for traditional psychiatrists, psychologists and lawmakers, but it has found a natural resting place, for the time being, in the catholic world of human liberation.

When we first met him we shared a drink at the bar as he told a story about his journey from Budapest to the USA in his late teens. We asked him, 'So, Tom, do you still feel like an Hungarian?' He smiled and said, 'Ah, good question. No, I do not feel like an Hungarian. But if you had asked me do I feel like an American, I also would have said "no". I feel like me!' Those few sentences encapsulated the man and his respect for personal identity. They also showed that he knew that wherever he was, under whatever flag he was flying, he was the captain of his own ship. For us, he will make the very finest lookout. For more on Thomas Szasz, his life and work visit http://www.szasz.com/.

> Szasz will doubtless be remembered as the philosopher of twentieth-century psychiatry, an intellectual terrorist, who demolished many a 'sacred cow' of his chosen profession. He also deserves to be remembered for his compassion, as his work is deeply imbued with this rare quality, expressed by his passion to respect personal dignity, personal choice and personal responsibility. Tom Szasz is man of great vision – both into the past and towards the horizon.

## The storm

### *Fluttering reality*

We have invoked the power of metaphor throughout this book for the simple reason that this is the way people talk about life and their experience of it. Psychiatric professionals have tried and largely succeeded in colonising people through their imposition of the clumsy, ugly language of psychiatric medicine or psychobabble. However, even these languages are also replete with metaphors. Ironically, many professionals can be unaware of the metaphorical nature of so-called scientific terms like 'neural pathways'. It is virtually impossible to communicate anything of 'the *what*' of our experience without invoking metaphor.

This is a vital starting point for our discussion of the psychic storm that often threatens to engulf, overwhelm and ultimately drown the person. The *storm* seems to be a good metaphor for the various, ill-defined disturbances that the person witnesses going on *within* themselves, or which 'go on' between themselves and other aspects of their physical or social world. We emphasise that they 'witness' this, for its meaning often depends to a large extent on perception. We believe that things are disturbing, so we attribute to them the power of 'disruption'. Whether this power is actually part of the thing itself, or merely a projection on our part, is neither here nor there. If we believe it, then we see it, and consequently we feel its effects.

The western wisdom system has led us to believe that there are things 'out there' that have an effect on us 'in here', commonly called subject–object dualism. Maybe it is an illusion. Perhaps life at all levels is more complex than the western natural sciences have led us to believe. Perhaps reality is not as stable as we often imagine. Mental 'illness', which is often viewed as a state of instability, may be no less stable than any other form of human reality. Life is chaotic – period!

*Chaos* is a fairly recent mathematical theory of the physical world, which states that small changes in initial conditions can produce chaotic and fundamentally unpredictable changes in later conditions. Chaos, along with quantum mechanics, suggests that there is a limit to our ability to know the world. In contrast to the linear models of the world that have dominated western thinking – where one thing is believed to have a knock-on effect on another thing like billiard balls – chaos attempts to describe complex *non-linear systems*. Chaos theory puts variation, change, surprise and unpredictability at the heart of the knowledge process. This is quite different from our traditional view that the world is a perfectly balanced place, from which we derive the idea that people can be 'unbalanced'. This suggests that there is a human state called 'balance' from which all 'unbalanced' (i.e. mad/ crazy/mentally ill) people deviate. If only it was that simple.

Chaos seems like an extension of systems theory, but one that pays more attention to the apparent disorder within the system. Chaotic systems are in constant flux. Chaos describes a reality that is variable and irregular, exhibiting patterns which never repeat themselves yet stay within boundaries. Chaos theory reinforces the anti-classical message of quantum theory, sharing with relativity some of its revolutionary implications. The popular caricature of chaos theory is the butterfly, which flaps its wings in Brazil and *precipitates* a chain of events that produces, ultimately, a storm in Chicago. However much we laugh at this apparent oversimplification, this image does help us gain a genuine insight into how the world 'really' works, and our part in its workings. Chaos theory may represent the conclusive weapon against the classical system and may be the finger that points at 'the truth' of our everyday experience. The American psychotherapist Milton Erickson (Haley 1968) often suggested that therapy was very like nudging some snow at the top of a mountain. The tiny effort might cause the snow to roll, becoming a ball, which then achieves its own momentum and either rolls into a crevasse or generates an avalanche that obliterates a mountain village. Maybe 'nudging' is a good way of conceptualising our efforts to help people. We merely help nudge them out of their assumption that movement is not possible. After that, they pick up their own momentum.

Weather forecasting involves a statistical analysis of past events as a way of trying to predict probable future events. However, chaos theory challenges this view of the world as simply a pile of numbers. Reducing the world to a deterministic, fully causally related system of equations simply is not possible because complexity will always overwhelm any system. Chaos – in the sense that it challenges the computability of the world – is a reversal of the classicist view that underlying laws are what count and local perturbations are trivial. In weather forecasting we cannot tell when a 'local perturbation' might explode into a storm. If we accept this proposition as true for weather, then what of *human behaviour*, far less *human experience*.

Much of the biomedical and psychological theory upon which mental health care is based assumes that *how* people *are* at any moment in time is a function of some grand, overarching theory of humanness (personality), pathology (mental illness), or both. However, it has been argued that in specific instances such assertions might be scientific delusions on a grand scale.

### Water: The mirror of our uncertainty

Reality, which we have always been encouraged to believe is a 'concrete' thing, may well be 'fluid'. Water has been a scientific enigma for centuries, at least since Leonardo's day, and has become one challenge for twentieth-century chaos theorists. In the 1930s the British physicist, Horace Lamb, told a meeting of the British Association for the Advancement of Science:

> When I die and go to Heaven there are two matters on which I hope for enlightenment. One is quantum electrodynamics, and the other is the turbulent motion of fluids. And about the former I am really rather optimistic.
>
> (Mullin 1992: 59)

Water flowing from our bathroom taps looks fairly straightforward, but presents a nightmare to scientists who try to describe its patterns, far less predict its flow (Mullin 1992). Maybe water is the perfect analogy – if not metaphor – for the 'lived experience': something that appears to have boundaries, but within which chaos reigns.

More than 60 years after Lamb, chaos theory is used to provide some answers to the enigma of 'chaotic order' of water flow. The babbling of brooks and reflections in pools intrigue poets but infuriate physicists. However, this fascination with water as the ultimate metaphor of reality has long occupied a special place in oriental thought (Reynolds 1984), where human experience is framed by the 'moon-in-the-water' phenomenon:

> The water is the subject and the moon the object. When there is no water, there is no moon-in-the-water ... But when the moon rises the water does not *wait* to receive its image, and when even the tiniest drop of water is poured out the moon does not wait to cast its reflection. For the moon does not *intend* to cast its reflection, and the water does not receive it *on purpose*. The event is caused as much by the water as by the moon, and as the water manifests the brightness of the moon, the moon manifests the clarity of the water.
>
> (Watts 1957: 72)

For David Reynolds, an American anthropologist who began to study Morita's Zen-influenced therapy almost by accident in the 1950s, water *reflects* the process of change that is fundamental to the whole universe, which includes us:

> From interstellar events to the decay of atomic particles. The reality of our experience is in constant flux, too. Feelings come and go, impulses rise and disappear, thoughts flit through our minds. Our actions ... contain the possibility for influencing the course of this change ... glimmerings of our experience of playing ball on running water.
>
> (Reynolds 1984: 77)

Therapists like Reynolds and theorists like Alan Watts have pointed out that the dualism that scientists describe – observer and object – does not appear to exist in nature. People, especially scientists, seem driven to separate themselves off from the world that they study in order to study it. In so doing, they fragment or take apart the whole nature of reality, which is our 'lived experience' of the 'whole thing'.

The western obsession with control (self-control, self-management, 'holding your tongue', keeping feelings in check, etc.) depends on exactly this kind of dualism between the knower (us) and what is known ('it'). The assumption that we can act *on* reality rather than *in* it is, to the Zen mind, another Occidental illusion (or delusion). We talk – for example of *deciding* to do this or that. Watts observed that our control over 'acts of will' seems limited.

What we cannot *stop* ourselves doing we must be doing spontaneously, so we are in a strange position of spontaneously doing what we do not want to do.[7]

(Watts 1957: 101)

In such circumstances we often '*decide* to do something about this'. If we did indeed 'decide', Watts would ask how did we *come* to decide? And more importantly, how did we decide-to-decide? And so the question goes on: ad absurdum. But there is no need to despair. As the Zen master said: 'Nothing is left to you at this moment but to have a good laugh' (Watts 1957).

This is no mere philosophical riddle, which of course it is too, but is reality in the proper sense. This is what life *is*, not what it is *like*. In the west we use all sorts of hyphenated words to describe illusions involving 'the Self': self-management; self-control, self-medication; self-actualisation; self-improvement; self-denial, ad nauseam. The hyphen itself serves as the dividing line between the *doer* and the *done*; the *action* and *acted upon*. It also illustrates the artificiality of such a dualism. Zen might therefore be construed as some kind of reflection of chaos. The chaologists may produce a mathematical formula to *explain* the turbulence of water flowing from a tap. Then again they may not. Water flows – period! Life is! People are!

So, what do we do? Well, we could begin by simply accepting that if we are obliged, by circumstance or choice, to get into the water, then we shall get wet. How wet, of course, depends on the circumstances. The deeper into the water we go, the more we would benefit from knowing how to swim, or how to access some kind of support vehicle. However, ultimately, we must accept that water will always have the upper hand, so to speak, and will test out individual and collective ingenuity. Perhaps the secret to living with chaos involves a combination of pragmatism and creativity, which the Oriental might just have called 'being realistic'.

## The voyage

We have borrowed so liberally from chaos theory that the chaos theorists are probably furious at our impertinence. However, it seems obvious: human experience is characterised by incessant change and unpredictability. Even the traditional assumptions concerning personality *traits* and *states*, no longer holds water. People described as 'manic depressive' (or in the popular classification bipolar) have been studied carefully in an effort to find patterns in their apparent 'cyclic variation between positive and negative moods'. However, even the most carefully conducted studies (e.g. Gottschalk *et al.* 1995) show that patients' moods do not follow a regular rhythm; they are chaotic. This fluidity provides us with the basis of the core metaphor of the Tidal Model:

Life is a journey undertaken on an ocean of experience. All human development, including the experience of illness and health, involves discoveries made on the journey across that ocean of experience. At critical points in the life journey the person experiences storms or even piracy (crisis). At other times the ship may begin to take in water and the person may face the prospect of drowning or shipwreck (breakdown). The person may need to be guided to a safe haven to undertake repairs, or to recover from the trauma (rehabilitation). Once the ship is made intact or the person has regained the necessary sea-legs, the ship may set sail again, aiming to put the person back on the life course (recovery).

Traditional psychiatric models assume that there is a state of 'normality' from which 'mentally ill' people deviate. The Tidal Model holds few assumptions about the proper course of a person's life. Instead, the focus is on the kind of support that people might need to rescue them from crisis, or to help put them back on the life course (development). The Tidal Model assumes that people chart their own life course. Who are we to say that it is the wrong course?

The Tidal Model recognises that the life experiences associated with mental ill-health are invariably described in metaphorical terms. People do not so much live a life as undertake a voyage. It is worth repeating: People who experience life crises are (metaphorically) in deep water and risk drowning, or feel as if they have been thrown onto the rocks. Those who have experienced trauma (such as injury or abuse), or more enduring life problems, often report loss of 'sense of self', akin to the trauma associated with piracy. Such people need a sophisticated form of life-saving (psychiatric rescue) followed, at an appropriate interval, by the kind of development work necessary to engender true recovery. This may take the form of crisis intervention in the community or the 'safe haven' of a crisis stabilisation unit, or inpatient setting. Once the rescue is complete (psychiatric nursing) the emphasis switches to the kind of help needed to get the person 'back on course', returning to a meaningful life in the community (mental health nursing).

At one level none of this is real, at least in any objective sense. The experience of depth, drowning, loss, rescue, safe haven and recovery are all deeply personal. Only the person *knows* such experiences because (s)he constructs them all. However, life is known only through the living of it – whatever we *make* of the experience; and we can only have the experience by *immersing* ourselves in life. Those who watch us from the shore might have very interesting tales to tell as to what it looked like from their perspective, but need we really spell out the obvious?

## The captain's log

Various writers have argued that rather than being 'out there' reality was 'constructed', arguably, 'in here', within the person who was talking about 'reality' (for example, Von Foerster 1984; Von Glaserfeld 1984; Watzlawick

1984; Maturana and Varela 1987). How people performed this construction depended on the 'lenses' through which they viewed and made distinctions about themselves and the world (Walter and Peller 1996). These 'world views' were picked up by 'solution-focused' therapists who assumed that since patients had 'constructed' their problems, they could construct their own solutions. The 'patient's' language could be employed to construct cognitive solutions, which could be enacted in the person's day-to-day life.

Structural thinking is the basis of the accepted scientific view of the world: something 'out there' can be measured and studied, with a view to generating predictive theories about events 'in' *that* world. Structuralist psychotherapists, in particular *psychodynamic* and *behaviour therapists*, aim to know the human world of the patient, uncovering it by detailed observation, analysis and interpretation, within a specific frame of reference, which is their guiding theory. Traditionally, psychotherapists have looked for the truth beneath the surface structure of 'what the patient says', exploring the subtext and reading between the lines of his narrative.

The post-structuralist position that embodies narrative (White and Epston 1990) and solution-focused approaches (De Shazer 1994), acknowledges that it is useful (if not actually vital) to take the physical world 'apart' when, for instance, looking for a fault in a car engine. Human problems such as low self-esteem or depression are, however, qualitatively different. In Watzlawick's view, it is not the case that people 'are' or 'are not' *depressed*. Rather the truth of the person's situation is negotiated through dialogue; meaning is invented rather than discovered (Watzlawick 1984).

Arguably, the key theorist of this therapeutic outlook is Steve de Shazer (1991: 45), who argued that 'meaning is here open to view since it lies between people rather than hidden away inside an individual'.[8] In his view, if there is not enough information in what the person says to establish what a resolution of their problem would involve, the therapist should ask more questions about this future state and listen more carefully: 'What will be different when you are no longer depressed?' rather than 'How did you become depressed?' or 'What depresses you?'

This view of the *co-creation* of *reality* is not only incompatible with the structuralist position, but in Harland's (1987) view is also 'radically anti-scientific'. Hawkes *et al.* (1998) recognised that the solution-focused approach could appear to be psychologically 'agnostic' since, unlike other therapies, it does not hold to any psychological theory about personality development (or ideology). Indeed, the solution-focused therapist is uninterested in causation, but assumes that the construction of the solution need have no relationship with the 'cause' of the problem. This philosophy is manifestly influenced by some of Wittgenstein's views of language and the 'language games' that human living entails (Wittgenstein 1958). It also shares a remarkable affinity with eastern philosophies such as Taoism. Alan Watts (1961) described Taoism as a 'way of life' that should be seen more as a psychotherapy than a religion. Taoism acknowledges that stability in life is an illusion and a function of memory, rather than of reality. Life (Tao) 'flows' through people, producing incessant change of which people are (in general) unaware. Solution-focused therapy may simply draw patients' attention to this flow of change, helping them steer in one direction rather than another (Barker 1996).

These philosophical assumptions have a major implication for the working relationship between the helper (therapist) and the person (patient), and have been hugely influential in redirecting the delivery of mainstream psychiatric services (Vaughn *et al.* 1995). In traditional forms of therapy, the therapist observes, interviews and gives the patient information and feedback, often making interpretations concerning the patient's story. In narrative and solution-oriented work, the patient's story *is* reality, rather than being seen as representing 'reality'. In that critical sense the person is the captain of the ship and the 'crew' (therapists and other helpers) merely help to support the navigation of the journey, which ultimately 'belongs' to the captain.

As a result, the person and the various helpers are involved in a process of live and highly mutual meaning making. The language of conversation, narrative, reflections and text replaces the traditional therapeutic language of observation, interview, interpretation, and so on. The way that the therapist seeks to *understand* the person by listening (only) to what is said embodies the narrative, solution-focused, therapist–patient relationship. It is also illustrated by the kind of 'genuinely curious' questions that the therapist asks, and also does not ask; what the therapist says and does, as well as avoids saying and doing.

The story that emerges, word by word, adds to the existing story of the person's life and in some cases involves a serious editing of some parts of the original story. When the person appears to be moving to a new position in relation to some 'problem' or appears to be adopting a different perspective, they might appropriately be described as re-authoring the story of their lives. However, in the flow of reality, which is always defined by time itself, this is really a 'new' story – not a revision of an old one. Enlightenment, for Morita, was like 'moving a teacup from here to there'. Perhaps people experience some ordinary enlightenment when their story reveals that 'once I was like that, now I am like this'.

## Flying the flag of common decency

The Tidal Model acknowledges that the life problems which overtake and threaten to drown people described as 'suffering from mental illness' can be understood, on at least one level, as spiritual crises. They threaten the complete identity of the person and who the person believes her or himself to be (Hummelvoll and da Silva 1994; Morris 1996; Thomas 1997). Frankl's experiences in the Nazi death camps helped people to realise that spirituality was not something restricted to the world of religion, far less to monasteries, sitting meditation or the latest New Age fad. Whatever we decide to call mental, emotional or psychological disturbances, they involve of necessity a disturbance of the various meanings attached by the person to the experience of being human and being alive. In that sense they are spiritual crises, as the original meaning of psychiatry and psychology implied.[9] In a very important sense, Frankl's work helped to breathe life back into an ailing psychotherapy. Certainly, his work provides much of the wind in our sails.[10]

The Tidal Model acknowledges that the kind of care that distressed people may at times need appears quite ordinary (Taylor 1994), but given the context of care and the often limited resources available, such care can represent acts of extraordinary courage and compassion. As we noted at the beginning of this chapter, psychiatry has largely relocated itself to the laboratory, flying under a flag of convenience known locally as neuroscience. So, what flag are we flying from our masthead? In the working-class community of our childhood, very strict moral and ethical codes operated that, given the relatively limited education of our parents, must have been passed down through the cultural system, rather than inherited from the philosophers of the classroom. The phrase 'common decency' was frequently used to identify people and their actions that were valued; not least because of the inherently galvanising effect of such action on the community in general and its members in particular. We suspect that 'common decency' was something *experienced* as a whole thing, rather than as any sum of its estimable parts. Certainly, our parents, who valued this so much, were never able to describe its constituent parts, or to give anything like a concrete example of its manifestation.[11]

The idea that we might 'know' that something is important and valuable, yet not be able to collapse it into smaller units or examples, holds a great attraction for us. As systems theory illustrated, it suggests that the whole is indeed greater than the sum of its parts. As with any attempt to explain a joke, this merely kills the thing we at first valued. So, 'commony decency' is something we can appreciate for what it *is* as an experience. People can come to *know* it, and might even be able to *develop* their awareness of it. However, it is not something that can be collapsed into constituent parts and taught in modular form.

We raise the flag of common decency to the very top of our masthead. Long may we look up at it and feel its importance swelling within us, without having to justify its colours.

# Chapter 14

# Origins and Developments

## In the shallows and in the deep

And the one throwing the lifebelt,
Even he needs help at times,
Stranded on the beach,
Terrified of the waves.
(Brian Patten)[1]

## Introduction

In this chapter we reflect on the history of the Tidal Model, which is less than ten years old: a mere footnote in the history of psychiatry; a blip in the history of human consciousness. We hope that in framing the Tidal Model we have embraced some of the key human values that first inspired those who wanted to be part of the genesis of a compassionate form of help for those in mental distress. We hope also that we have learned something, perhaps of a different order of value, from the people with whom we have worked; the people who have used, or been required to use, psychiatric and mental health services.

In this penultimate chapter, we reflect on the origins of the model and on various dimensions of its development over its short history. Given the model's emphasis on the 'necessity of change', indeed the 'inevitability of change', we want to give particular emphasis to how the model has evolved over its short lifetime. This book has been written largely in our voices, although we hope that due recognition has been paid to the voices of those who inspired us, those who challenged us and those who brought us to our present point of understanding. In the spirit of empathy, first proclaimed poetically by our bard, Robert Burns, who entreated us to 'see oursels as ithers see us'[2] we have included the voices of some people whose views we hold in the highest respect, and whom we hope will provide a different yet complementary perspective on the Tidal Model.[3]

## Background to the development of the model

### The rising tide

The Tidal Model has its origins in our clinical work in psychotherapy and counselling, stretching back over 25 years. In the early part of our careers we found considerable value, at least for us, in various psychodynamic, humanistic, cognitive behavioural and family models of therapeutic intervention (Barker 1999). That gave way over time to an appreciation of the value of a more pragmatic approach to helping people, especially one focused on the person's emergent narrative (Barker and Kerr 2001); appreciating the therapeutic power of metaphor (Barker 2001b); and how both we and the people in our care might be on a similar journey towards becoming 'wounded healers' (Barker *et al.* 1998b). People like Irene Whitehill, who contributed to the Foreword, helped specifically in developing our appreciation that this might represent a form of 'caring with' people rather than, as traditional therapy has professed, an objective 'caring for' or 'caring about' people.

### The Newcastle origins

However, the formal origins of the model lie in work conducted at the University of Newcastle, England where, along with clinical colleagues, an attempt was made to map a realistic yet pragmatic meta-theory of clinical practice in psychiatric nursing (Barker 1997a). This led to an international study of the 'need for psychiatric nursing' that sought to establish the specific human needs which people in care, their family members or other professionals believed were met by the delivery of psychiatric nursing (Barker *et al.* 1999b).

With considerable support from academic colleagues like Dr Chris Stevenson and clinical colleagues who helped pilot early examples of the various assessment and care planning strategies, the Tidal Model was first introduced into practice within two acute psychiatric wards in the city of Newcastle in 1998 (Barker 1998a), in North Tyneside in 1999, and was formally adopted by the Mental Health Programme, responsible for the whole service for Newcastle and North Tyneside, in the spring of 2000, when the model was 'rolled out' across nine acute psychiatric wards and one 24-hour care facility in the community.

### Support and growth

The original invitation to develop an alternative model of mental health care came from the Multidisciplinary Programme Group, who believed that nursing in acute admission wards needed a more specific focus. The significance of the management group's role cannot be overstated, as it provided support, through visionary leadership, and also the necessary resources to allow in-service education for the staff involved. In that sense, the Newcastle project in its original form was a fine illustration of the kind of 'top-down–bottom-up' management necessary for any programme development at the care face.

Within two years, the Newcastle service had extended use of the model to medium secure (forensic) settings, and had built significant bridges with community support services. Over the last five years, the model has developed from a discrete focus on psychiatric nursing practice in acute settings, to a more flexible mental health recovery and reclamation model, for any setting, relevant to any discipline, with a discrete emphasis on empowering forms of engagement (Barker 2001b), the importance of the lived experience (Barker 2000a), with an appreciation of the potential for healing that lies within the re-authoring of the narrative (Barker 2002). As we have noted repeatedly, the model continues to assert the central importance of 'nursing' and is promulgated in the main by nurses, within the context of nursing care. However, increasingly, projects based around the model are featuring a more discrete interdisciplinary approach, which we would welcome.

## International developments

### Going with the flow

From its early beginnings in Newcastle and North Tyneside, the Tidal Model began to attract interest from local services in the North of England. But as reports of the model began to be published, interest was shown from all over the UK at first, then Ireland and further afield.[4] A loose network of Tidal Model implementation and evaluation projects was established in 2000, providing support to professionals interested in learning about the model and evaluating it within their services.

By the summer of 2003, there were around 50 Tidal Model projects in different clinical practice setting in different countries – England, Scotland, Wales, Eire, Australia, New Zealand, Japan, Canada. All these projects were encouraged to adapt the original philosophy and practice principles to suit the specific demands of their situation, rather than attempt to imitate slavishly the project which had begun in Newcastle. All members of the network were also encouraged to explore ways of developing meaningful evaluations of the model in practice. Many chose to use the approach first adopted to evaluate the Newcastle project (which is summarised below), but others have developed alternative evaluative processes, aimed at addressing local or national agendas for research and development.

Here, we provide an insider's view of the implementation of the model in different countries, courtesy of some of the people who have been instrumental in leading implementation projects, or stimulating interest in the Tidal Model and its relevance to recovery in general.

## England

### Reassuring echoes

*Tom Keen* is one of England's foremost psychiatric nurses, with an enviable depth of experience in a wide range of clinical and educational settings. Despite having spent the past 15 years in top-level education, he remains a practitioner at heart. The concern to 'make a difference' remains at the forefront of his concerns and is, of course, one of principal aims of the model. Tom Keen was instrumental in bringing the Tidal Model to the South West of England and led the attempts to explore the necessarily fluid links between education and practice. Tom wrote:

> At first I was dismayed by Professor Barker's determination to develop what seemed to be a new psychiatric nursing model, as most nursing models seemed to me profoundly uninteresting; tortuously academic; clumsily simplistic; or bearing little resemblance to the nature of people's real-life social and psychological difficulties. Surely, this – problems of living – was the central concern of mental health nursing, at least as I understood it. The last thing we needed was yet another so-called model, which could potentially reinforce any nursing tendency towards medical reification, and do nothing to remedy the increasing incompatibility of various partners in the mental health field – especially the subjugation of users' own views.
>
> When it finally emerged from its long gestation, the Tidal Model neatly subverted all my anticipated cynical objections. In the jargon-ridden terms, beloved of the Establishment, the Tidal Model is deeply collaborative; person-centred, solution-focused, narrative-based, pragmatic and systemic. The Tidal Model offers a framework for investigating problems and aspirations from the person's own viewpoint. In so doing, it takes proper account of people's individuality and relationships. It enables staff of all disciplines to work courteously and respectfully within people's own time-frames, using their own language and preferred outcomes. It does not impose diagnoses or other professional problem-formulations although, as the Tidal Model is therapeutically non-prescriptive, it doesn't hinder such methods, if preferred by users.
>
> The Tidal Model institutionalises or, if you prefer, operationalises a culture of responsiveness to people's problems of living, rather than one of imposition – whether of diagnosis, prescription, behaviour-control or programme of care. The Tidal Model explicitly places cooperation with the person at the heart of its structure, and gives the highest priority to the person's own perspectives upon their life-so-far, and the person's aspirations for the future.

Perhaps most importantly, the Tidal Model endorses ordinary decencies as being at the heart of personal mental health care. It respects people's own account of their story. It requires engagement and sharing of ideas, rather than enforced observation schedules and stylised care plans. The Tidal Model encourages people's recognition of the dangers and hazards evident within their own lives, and enables ownership of their unique risk management process (the 'Personal Security Plan'). It insists that people have their own copy of questions used in all interview schedules and expects that people will carry their own original care-plan, which they can update as often as necessary, not only at some regimented distant time suitable for nursing audit, rather than within an individual 'pace of change'.

On reflection, the Tidal Model is *not* yet another psychiatric nursing model. It is an interactive structure designed to preserve people's independence and dignity, whilst ensuring that the ordinary decencies that should characterise care will not easily be displaced by brutishness or casual disregard. I hope it will become a forerunner of many more courteously effective frameworks for collaborative mental health care.

### Caring – the heart of nursing

However, nursing, as we have pointed out in previous chapters, is a confusing and highly confused affair. Invariably, it is almost impossible to establish what nursing 'is', such is the conflict between different professional theories of nursing and – in this era where professionalism itself is greatly in doubt – the conflict between lay and professional understandings of the 'need for nursing'. We have taken a conservative line in this book by trying to conserve the traditional understandings of nursing as a social construct. Little of professional nursing practice, especially the practice of 'mental health nursing', is focused on 'growth and development' – as the concept of 'nourishment' first implied – being driven towards an increasing focus on delivering, or supporting 'treatments', which may ultimately be disempowering, damaging and delimiting.[5]

However, although some members of the new generation of mental health nurses in England have welcomed the 'extension' of their roles into prescribing and psychological therapies, others have struggled to maintain and develop the emphasis on *caring*, assuming that with the proper infrastructure care could realise its own therapeutic potency.

Angela Simpson is one such believer in the value of nursing per se. Now a lecturer at the University of York with responsibilities for diploma, graduate and postgraduate education, at heart Angela remains a practitioner deeply connected to the living reality of mental health care. She continues to be drawn through her research to the exploration of the intriguingly complex, yet compassionately simple business of how we might care for our fellow women and men. Angela developed and led one of the first Nursing Development Units in mental health care in the UK.[6] In so doing she learned much about the politics of health care. It is to her credit that she remains committed to the ideals that stimulated the genesis of her own visionary unit in Harrogate, England. Angela wrote:

> The Tidal Model encourages nurses to re-engage with nursing, in its truest sense; providing a supportive framework to develop nursing practice in practice that is both holistic and person focused. The Tidal Model requires nurses to become actively involved in a practice development process, which challenges them to think and act beyond the traditional or routine approaches to practice that are, almost, ingrained within them. In choosing to develop nursing practice, through the Tidal Model, nurses are doing much more than improving the quality of the care experience of the person in distress (although this is a laudable goal in its own right). Of equal significance, will be the sense of increased confidence in their ability to influence clinical practice, which nurses will begin to experience.
>
> The Tidal Model supports and guides the development of psychiatric nursing. Nurses who work within the model to develop their practice will discover within themselves the capacity to develop nursing as a therapeutic practice in its own right. This is highly significant, as it will allow mental health nurses, and nursing itself, to 'find its feet' as an equal member of the multi-professional team. In so doing, nurses will re-engage with the heart of psychiatric nursing practice, *person centred caring*, and by so doing, create the freedom to practise psychiatric nursing on its own terms – in its own right. So, actioning the Tidal Model in practice inevitably involves nurses in a development process that harnesses the potential for growth and empowerment for the person in care and psychiatric nursing alike.

## Eire

### Revisiting the roots of nursing

Ireland is one of the homes of story telling. The Irish are undoubtedly the finest lyrical speakers and writers of the English language anywhere in the world. We only wish that we had the capacity to appreciate their lyrical prowess in the use of the Irish language.

Perhaps because of our 20-year professional association with Ireland, aided by our own Irish ancestry, the Tidal Model was first introduced to Dublin in 2001, when Jimmy Lynch and his colleagues at the Mater Hospital introduced the model to the acute care setting of St Aloysius ward. Given that he is a member of the new generation of mental health nurses in Ireland (qualified within the past decade), it is encouraging that Lynch both knows and understands the history of his chosen profession and remains attracted to the traditional notion of nursing as a 'nurturing' practice. That said, he also appreciates the importance of research and theory for the continued development of his profession, within a multiprofessional milieu. Jimmy Lynch wrote:

> Mental health nursing has had an uneasy relationship with nursing theories and models. This may well reflect nurses' lack of confidence in the value of nursing itself, or the enduring supremacy of medical, psychological and social theories of mental distress, and the models of practice that have been developed from such theories. The Tidal Model was developed by nurses who believe in the value of nursing as an enduring social construct. It was developed for practice by a nurse (Phil Barker) actively involved in practice, using practice-based research findings, and is currently being evaluated by practice-based researchers in several countries.
>
> This research focuses on the roles and functions of mental health nursing, the interrelationship between community and in-patient care (Barker's concept of the seamless service) and the empowerment of people with more disabling forms of mental illness. The fact that the model was born out of this research was what attracted me to the model in the first place.
>
> Hildegard Peplau said that nursing has its deepest roots in nuture. Historically, mental health nursing practices were primarily nurturing ones – helping people to live – while the psychiatrists went about their business of figuring out what were the diseases of mental illness. Attempts to derive viable nursing practices from the theories of prescriptive psychiatry were largely unsuccessful. Throughout its history, mental health nursing has been modified in response to changing circumstances. Innovations in practice arise from the findings of nursing research, from changes within health care systems or from demands in society. The Tidal Model is part of this innovation and represents a critical shift in emphasis for mental health nursing practice. Phil Barker believes that many nurses are casting around, looking for methods and models of practice in other fields that somehow might fill the perceived vacuum in their nursing lives. Many nurses are encouraged to believe the need to develop 'new' skills or learn 'new' therapeutic models in order to become effective in mental health care. I believe that The Tidal Model challenges this assumption. It offers a philosophy that strikes a chord in the hearts of today's practitioners. It strengthens the relationship between practice, theory and research and it facilitates the role that nurses play in the future of our discipline. Now that daybreak has finally dawned on this new millennium mental health nurses will face many challenges. I believe that the Tidal Model will help them face these challenges. We await with optimism the realisation of its legacy.

## Leading from the front

Ireland also provided the first project to explore the introduction and development of the Tidal Model in community mental health care. Nurses from Cork city, in the south of Ireland, established a Tidal Model project in a day hospital in the city. This catered mainly but not exclusively for people in the tertiary care context, located within the Developmental Care setting of the care continuum. Their colleagues went on to establish other projects in community mental health projects attached to primary care, focused more on the Immediate Care end of the spectrum. Nurses within at least one of the projects have already completed evaluations of the Tidal Model in practice and presented their findings to national conferences. By the summer of 2003 there were more than ten Tidal Model projects in various community and hospital settings in the county of Cork.

All of these projects were led and supervised by Ann Coughlan, who works as a Clinical Practice Co-ordinator, linking university nurse education of nurses at University College Cork, with various clinical placements in practice settings. Ann Coughlan has illustrated one of the emergent practice principles concerning implementation of the Tidal Model: committed leadership is essential, *on the ground*, if implementation is to be successful.

Practitioners have long since grown tired of various experts, think-tanks or committees telling them that they should be working in a different way; delivering a different kind of service. Such expert advisers rarely, if ever, know the clinical realities of practice, and never follow through on their advice by actually joining with the team in exploring how change might be facilitated. In an era of 'champions' for various health and social care projects, we would attribute Ann Coughlan's remarkable success to 'leadership from within'. Almost like a managerial illustration of the concept of 'caring with', she has joined with her colleagues in negotiating and actively supporting the process of change, which the introduction of the Tidal Model requires. We asked Ann to offer a brief commentary on the work undertaken in Cork and, in the best Irish creative tradition, she framed her thoughts within the Tidal acronym (see Figure 14.1).

## Wales

### The Celtic fringe

Wales is another country with a strong oral tradition in story telling. Ian Beech is a mental health nurse, therapist and lecturer at the University of Glamorgan, with a strong clinical interest in people in depression and psychosis. He helped develop the first educational programme for practitioners, and has continued to provide supervision to his clinical colleagues, who are implementing the model in several different sites in South Wales. Ian Beech noted:

**T**
The Tidal Model

THE TIDAL MODEL was introduced in the first pilot site in the Cork Mental Health Services in 2000 at Ravenscourt Day Hospital. Since then the nursing staff in nine sites in Cork have introduced the Tidal Model. Historically psychiatric nursing has had a very poor relationship with nursing models. This radical new approach to the practice of psychiatric nursing helps define how psychiatric nurses might work with users and their families.

**I**
Innovative

This *innovative* model has challenged how we, as psychiatric nurses, work with people with mental health problems. The model recognises that the individual's experience of problems and needs ebbs and flows, and suggests how we professionals can work more effectively with people experiencing these problems.

**D**
Development

Through the introduction of the Tidal Model psychiatric nursing practice has changed. Clinical staff are *redeveloping* the proper focus of psychiatric nursing, realising the importance of having their own framework to develop practice.

**A**
Assessment

The attempt to understand the individual's world is explored at the *Holistic Assessment*, which provides a means to explore and help the individual start telling their story and to develop what needs to be done now to address their problems with living.

**L**
Language

Using the individual's *own words* places the value of personal experience at the core of the Holistic Assessment and Personal Security Plan. The individual's story is written in the person's voice and not translated into objective *language* used by the nurse historically.

**M**
Motivation

The *motivation* of the clinical staff to embrace the Tidal Model needs to be highlighted, alongside the work of our academic colleagues who are incorporating the theory and philosophy of the model in the undergraduate diploma/degree programmes. This represents further narrowing of the theory–practice gap.

**O**
Opportunity

Old ideas/old nursing models in use can lead to challenging exchanges with clinical staff when change is being discussed. However, the Tidal Model encompasses old and new ideas, bringing both together to address crisis in people's lives, which the model sees as *opportunity*. We have been fortunate in the Cork Mental Health Services to have had the *opportunity* to work so closely with Phil and Poppy on the introduction of this model.

**D**
Doing

The model in practice emphasises and focuses upon *doing* what needs to be done as opposed to what might be wanted. Small steps are emphasised: the steps that the person needs to take to move away from the circumstances which brought the person into the 'care setting'.

**E**
Empowerment

The development of a therapeutic relationship through discrete methods of active *empowerment* is one of the underlying philosophies of the model in practice. Psychiatric nursing is effective when the person is encouraged to grow and develop. When the results of the Holistic Assessment are shared in the person's own words this is giving the person back their own voice, which is a very *empowering* action.

**L**
Long-term view

Further expansion and use of the Tidal Model in clinical settings will take place in the Cork Mental Health Services. We need to continue evaluating how the model has changed nursing practice and the professional partnership with the multidisciplinary team. Users' views of the use of the Tidal Model also need to be explored further. We need to spread the philosophy of care and the therapeutic assumptions used in the Tidal Model – locally, nationally and internationally.

*Figure 14.1* The Cork perspective on the Tidal Model

The people of Wales lay claim to the wisdom and aesthetic heritage of their Celtic forebears in establishing their new identity. In a similar way, the Tidal Model provides a link back to the wisdom and aesthetics of an earlier age of nursing while encouraging nurses to move forwards in establishing a new identity for psychiatric and mental health nursing.

Ian's principal colleague is Lynne Roberts, a Consultant Nurse in Mental Health from St Tydfil's Hospital, Merthyr Tydfil. Lynne has championed the introduction of the model within acute settings, which represents an area of major concern in the broader Welsh context. Lynne Roberts said:

Improving the quality of care in acute mental health units has been identified as a priority in Wales and has been welcomed by all. The Welsh culture has had a tendency to rely heavily upon hospital admissions. In the absence of assertive outreach and intensive home support teams hospitalisation has become the only option available to people in crisis. This has meant that the focus of inpatient service provision has been on dealing with people in crisis with a wide variety of complex needs. This has resulted in the provision of 'custodial care' on wards that were often locked, with nurses posted as 'door watchers' to prevent patients leaving. The nursing role had become 'bogged down' in the bureaucracy of risk assessments and paperwork, to the detriment of basic communication with patients. Many nurses felt that they were being increasingly drawn away from personal contact with patients, which was proving to be having a detrimental effect on overall job satisfaction. Patients, for their part, were finding a tremendous lack of meaningful contact, which included not knowing who their primary nurse was; no knowledge or involvement in care planning, and feeling bored with the mundane ward activities.

Nursing staff had begun to lose their skills and confidence in working collaboratively with patients, particularly with those who had become despondent or disagreed with the care and treatment offered. Nurses were often heard to say, 'How can you negotiate care with someone who does not see themselves as ill or does not want to be here?' This was probably part of the loss of confidence concerning openness, negotiation and honesty, which is developed from regular personal contact and communication with patients.

The introduction of the Tidal Model has begun to address the fundamental components of providing a good quality inpatient care, including creating a meaningful and therapeutic environment. For many, this involves 'going back to basics', developing their skills in the promotion of collaborative working. It has allowed staff to revisit their aspirations and strengthen their links with the original reasons for choosing to work in the field of mental health. The personal contact and curiosity about people's experiences have been brought back into the forefront. Changes to date have been fairly radical and have ranged from nurses being amazed by the new (and highly relevant) information gained from initial meetings to some patients being a little reluctant to accept responsibility for identification of their needs whilst in hospital.

We have been involved now with the Tidal Model project for six months. Prior to implementation a baseline quality evaluation of the inpatient environment was undertaken. This included patient and staff satisfaction measures. A recent mid-point audit has demonstrated considerable changes in practice and an increased rate of satisfaction by patients and staff alike. A follow-up study is planned for January 2004 to formally measure such changes and review the quality of care offered within the unit.

## Canada

### A passion for nursing

The Royal Ottawa Hospital is the largest provider of specialised mental health services for people with serious and complex mental health problems in Eastern Ontario, Canada. It is a teaching hospital affiliated with the University of Ottawa and provides a number of different clinical programmes across the care continuum. Here, Nancy Brookes and Margaret Tansey, along with Lisa Murata and other colleagues, implemented the Tidal Model in 2002. Nancy and Margaret put their project into its national context, reinforcing their belief in the value of nursing:

In Canada, about ten years ago, the national psychiatric and mental health nursing community chose to create and participate in a specialty certification program. Psychiatric and mental health nursing was described as a specialised area of nursing, which has as its focus the promotion of mental health, the prevention of mental illness, and the care of clients experiencing mental health problems and mental disorders. Benner's (1984) domains of nursing practice framed the process. While no one theory is prescribed, it is expected that nurses will use a theoretical framework/nursing model to guide their practice. We support our nurses to gain this important credential. The Tidal Model, with its emphasis on collaboration and partnerships, empowerment, interdisciplinary teamwork and narrative interventions, celebrating narrative knowledge and stories, is our choice.

National trends to evidence-based practice – and what is better evidence than the person's own perception/words! – and best practice guidelines are expressed and supported through the Tidal Model. Indeed, the Registered Nurses Association of Ontario (RNAO) has developed Best

Practice Guidelines for Client-Centred Care (www.rnao.org). Even the language of the Tidal Model is echoed in these guidelines. For example, Recommendation One clearly shares Tidal language and values:

- Nurses embrace as foundational to Client-Centered Care the following values and beliefs:
- Respect; human dignity; clients are experts for their own lives; clients as leaders; clients' goals coordinate care of the health care team; continuity and consistency of care and caregivers; timeliness; responsiveness and universal access to care.

At the Royal Ottawa Hospital, we had just articulated a vision for nursing to become an internationally recognised centre of excellence for psychiatric and mental health nursing, which has at its core committed, person-centred professional practice and scholarship when Professor Barker's paper on the Tidal Model was published in *Perspectives in Psychiatric Care*. Reading the article was an ah-ha experience for us. It was a gift to find our beliefs and values echoed in the Tidal Model. Not only did it address the need for nursing and the proper focus of nursing, but it also came complete with a documentation system. What a blessing!

We joined the international Tidal community – becoming the first North American site – within weeks of our acquaintance with the model. Using the multimedia education program, we introduced the model to three of our programs: mood and anxiety, forensic, and substance use and concurrent disorders. A research project evaluating the implementation of the model using the criteria developed by Professor Barker's Newcastle group is in progress.

The concept of engagement resonates with us. We have incorporated this across our facility in our work on creating healthy, healing environments and also in our observation policy. Security assessments and plans are now an integral part of our hospital-wide constant observation policy. One outcome is that the number of hours for Constant Observation has significantly decreased.

Our passion is psychiatric and mental health nursing. The Tidal Model has fanned the fires of our passion, or perhaps has affirmed it. Certainly, it provided us with language to speak our practice.

## New Zealand

Rangipapa Regional Forensic Unit in Porirua, New Zealand, was the first unit in New Zealand and the first forensic unit in the world to implement the model. The project is led by Ngaire Cook, a Clinical Nurse Specialist who introduced the model in 2000 and who has led several evaluations of the Tidal Model in practice since then.

Here, we present a brief summary of the recent study[7] of the model conducted by Ngaire Cook, Brian Phillips, a Research Nurse at Victoria University, and Diane Sadler, Nurse Consultant for Capital Coast District Mental Health Services:

> The Tidal Model is a research-based nursing model currently being used as the nursing model at Rangipapa Regional Forensic Unit. The assessment and care planning focuses upon the narrative of the patients so that their experience of distress can be addressed in the nurse's responses.
>
> The current research project focused on the lived experience of four forensic psychiatric inpatients that have received nursing care using the Tidal Model, as well as that of four Registered Nurses. Semi-structured interviews were used to obtain reflective description of the nursing care experience from the different perspectives of patients and nurses. Analysis drew upon hermeneutic phenomenology. Themes were identified from the interview transcripts in the context of receiving or providing nursing care. The analysis identified the following five themes:
>
> - *Relationships*: The participants reported that their experience provided a much more adult-to-adult relationship and feels right. They had an increased a sense of self and of connectedness to each other. This provided further opportunities for personal interaction and motivation to make a contribution.
> - *Levelling*: Levelling is viewed positively and as beneficial by patients. It was a notion that arose from both participant groups experiencing a shift in power and relationship to one that aimed at 'getting well'.
> - *Working together*: The participants' responses gave rise to the notions of working together and co-creating the type of support needed. This created a sense of control and freedom for the patients. For the nurses, it helped make the process more open.
> - *Hope*: Patients said that being able to communicate to all staff in their own words using the Tidal Model gave them hope. The nurses reported their nursing was making a difference so also felt hopeful. Hope was a view of the future that created optimism and expectation of positive outcomes and a reason to keep on living.
> - *Human face*: Participants saw the model as coming from a humanistic framework; they felt as though they mattered. They reported that forensic psychiatry has a human face to it. The nurse–patient relationships were based on a human-to-human encounter.

These themes reflected the meaning attached to the events of receiving and providing care. The participants' reactions and integration of the Tidal Model were approaching a process of analysis and synthesis of their lived experiences within a forensic psychiatric context.

The outcomes of this study suggest that the implementation of the Tidal Model has resulted in positive experiences for nurses and patients, as well as identifiable beneficial outcomes. This is consistent with United Kingdom research on the Tidal Model. Based on these outcomes, a wider implementation of the Tidal Model is recommended along with an appropriate evaluation.

## Australia

### Camped by the billabong

Tom Ryan is a New Zealand psychiatric nurse who now leads the nursing services in Townsville, Queensland. Tom is leading the introduction of the Tidal Model within his services, but clearly believes that the Model might help address a wider agenda than simply the redevelopment of nursing care:

> Australia is a land of stories. Often such stories are the stories of water – of billabongs and of the sea, and of the creatures of myth and spirit that inhabit them. For Australians are dwellers in a dry land and thus have the deepest respect for water, its seasons, its meanings and its absolute centrality in life. Australia's unofficial but best-recognised anthem is the story of a homeless man who chooses a watery grave rather than face the justice of the ruling classes for his theft of food. Among the other stories in the multicultural complexity of the national psyche are those of the convicts shipped from Britain, the vast majority dispossessed and oppressed in their turn by an inequitable justice system, and wave upon wave of immigrants with their own stories, often suffering their own experiences of oppression and repression and seeking in Australia the famous 'fair go'. With some regrettable lapses, Australia has been a compassionate and welcoming refuge for many.
>
> The reverberations of more than 40,000 years of uninterrupted weaving of deeper tales are just beginning to be heard clearly again as aboriginal culture rallies from the impact of colonisation and its inherent suppression of language and of the people's stories. These stories of the indigenous people of this place have unbroken links to the dawn of man's language and they hold an awesome promise of healing.
>
> Despite the distancing of the 'system' from the real pain of those it serves, which has become evident in both our approach to psychiatry and immigration, there is ample evidence of a thirst to be heard and of the compassion necessary to create a space for the necessary stories to be told. The Tidal Model will take hold in Australia because of this thirst and because there is inherent in the national character a respect for narrative and a recognition of its healing power.
>
> There is, however, much to do and some urgency, particularly as the awful impact of colonisation on Australia's indigenous people is

beginning to be recognised. The centrality of the human story in the Tidal Model and its recognition of the importance of attending to meaning rather than symptom, will fit well with the new Australian culture of healing that must be co-created, and which will benefit all in distress.

The Townsville mental health services in Queensland were briefly famous over ten years ago for a major inquiry that became known as the '10B' inquiry after the designation of its psychiatric ward. That people were traumatised in 10B is hardly in doubt, but then our mainstream psychiatric systems have been traumatising people for years, despite what are often the best intentions of the people working within them. There is evidence to suggest that things got out of hand in 10B, but whether it was notably worse or not in terms of oppression and failing to listen I do not know, as I was not here then and stories vary, as they are wont to do.

Inquiries do, however, have a way of focusing attention and resources. The response to the events of the inquiry was increased respect for consumer and carer voices, and the active importation of expertise and enlightenment – factors that have shaped the evolution of the service since that time. Ironically then, the events surrounding 10B might be said to have created fertile ground for the Tidal Model in Townsville.

The issues here are similar, however, to the issues faced in most western psychiatric systems that gave rise to the approach we call the Tidal Model. Mental health workers have felt the distancing from patients and the spiritual bankruptcy of an overly deterministic dependency upon pharmacology. Nurses in particular, like nurses elsewhere, have felt the lack of an adequate model to address what it is they really need to do to meet the needs of the distressed people they serve.

With the active cooperation of the mental health service, overall health service executive and the Queensland Nurses' Union we are on the threshold of nurse-led implementation of the Tidal Model. The next year or so will tell the tale, but we have every reason to be optimistic and to continue to do what has brought us this far – trust the process!

## The consumer focus

We referred in previous chapters, to the important role played by people who either have used mental health services or are currently using them in the original shaping and continued development of the Tidal Model. We were fortunate that our friends, Irene Whitehill and Sally Clay, offered short forewords to the book. These might suggest not only their own appreciation of our emphasis on value making, but perhaps also the hopes of others who have known the psychiatric system.

## The journey of rediscovery

Laurie Davidson is a Practice Development Manager for the Devon Partnership, a mental health service in the South West of England. In a short paper, written in the spring of 2002, he reflected on the enthusiastic response of some of his colleagues to the Tidal Model at a conference held in Devon, and explored the simplicity of the model's value base, and how this might be a powerful echo of the voices of many users and consumers of mental health services:

> In a conference in South Devon in the late 80s, service users were asked who had been most helpful in their distress. A group who were mentioned frequently were the cleaners on the wards because they listened and spoke the same language. Professionals scored very low on that particular straw poll.
>
> Somewhere along the line, these simple truths have remained obscured in inpatient settings by the belief that, 'this is all very well, but this doesn't apply to people with psychosis or more serious illnesses'. The idea that normal rules don't apply has led to appalling abuses over the years. What the Tidal Model is starting to show is that the same rules do apply and that with treating people with respect and by listening, there is a reduction in aggression (presumably due to a reduction in frustration at not being heard or taken seriously), an increase in satisfaction and people get better quicker. The attitude changes from 'doing to' to 'doing with'; the service user takes control of their care plan and hope is encouraged rather than crushed.
>
> The similarities between the Tidal Model and Recovery ideas are obvious, probably because they both came out of listening to people who are 'experts by experience' rather than 'experts by attribution'. The tragedy is that the Tidal Model is currently used in in-patient settings only (though there are early experiments in the community) and only with nurses. By adopting a traditional nursing approach of labelling ideas as a 'model', the illusion is created that this is a static, well-formulated approach and this is 'owned' by nurses. There is no reason at all why this should be the case and the people who have developed the approach would be the first to say that. It is a dynamic development, which should be multi-disciplinary in focus. OTs, for example would say that they have been using a Tidal or recovery model for years. Social workers certainly would subscribe to the person-centered philosophy and the principles behind the approach.
>
> Advocates of recovery have rightly resisted it being called a 'model' because they know that as soon as they do, it will be dragged off, packaged, professionalised and lined up on the dusty shelf with all the other fads and fancies. The core values, ideas and beliefs are about listening,

respect, giving time, staying with the individual's own construction of the world, taking positive risks, building trusting relationships, not interpreting, not being experts in ways which disempower, sharing knowledge in ways which can be understood, looking at people's 'spiritual' needs, encouraging self-management and self-determination, etc. These have not changed over the years; they just continually have to be rediscovered.

### The human revolution

Laurie Davidson captured the Zeitgeist of that Tidal conference, if not of the short-lived history of the Tidal Model itself. His concern that the model might be tied too narrowly to the uniform of nursing was almost prophetic. As we have noted previously, although the model began as a 'nursing model', it has increasingly been supported and embraced by other disciplines. Perhaps, as we have argued repeatedly throughout, all professionals – not just nurses – have a capacity for caring. Maybe all those who appreciate the Tidal Model are simply those who appreciate the value base and the value generation associated with the model, whether they be nurses or psychiatrists, social workers or consumer-advocates.

For us, this is the important revolution – the return (full circle) to the appreciation of the power of caring, by all disciplines, and all who would seek to support professional caring, or provide viable alternatives to it. We are aware that it is no longer fashionable to speak of the need for *revolution*. Even the notion of 'scientific revolutions' has been a source of distressing contention for almost four decades.[8] However, by returning to embrace the values of humanism,[9] we may begin to appreciate our careless loss, and how *value making* represents the great challenge in mental health care in the twenty-first century.

Leaving the value base aside, the Tidal metaphor itself rings bells for many people who have known madness, or psychiatric treatment, or both. Ed Manos is a distinguished consumer-advocate in New Jersey, and has had a lengthy experience of mental health care. Ed Manos wrote:

> Tidal is an apt title for the model, since many of us have felt like a tidal wave has swept over us at least once in our lives! But then again there are some nice tidal pools of serenity as well. This Model has helped me re-explore those tidal pools; the places that have allowed me to cope with this crazy world. Phil and Poppy's accumulated knowledge, life experience and compassion for their fellow man, have contributed to a wonderful source of education and hope not just for Consumers/Survivors/Users, but anyone wishing to learn so much about life, past, present and future.

Many of our colleagues have remarked on the insidious trend towards processed, impersonal and in some cases dehumanising forms of care. By emphasising a return to traditional humanistic values, some have indirectly developed an appreciation of the spiritual dimension of care – whether for the cared for person or the helper. One such person was Cathy Wiles, a Mental Health Chaplain at Springfield Hospital in London: Cathy Wiles said:

> The Tidal Model seeks to take the humanity of the person-in-care seriously. The uniqueness of individuals and their experience is recognised and by discussing resolutions and identifying resources – including spiritual supports – the Model acknowledges the capacity for health. This is an approach that wants to reveal the person behind the 'patient'. As a Chaplain I find this both welcoming and refreshing.

## Cultural considerations

As we discussed in Chapter 6, who we are is in part a personal construction, but one that is framed by family, society and perhaps most of all by culture. We believe that culture, in terms of the values, attitudes and codes of conduct, is a significant force within all societies, but is possibly most significant within societies that either maintain or fear the loss of links with their cultural past. It is also particularly important for migrants or refugees who find themselves adrift in an alien culture; or perhaps one that actively disparages the cultural values and practices, which are embedded within the person's psyche.

Tom Ryan wrote earlier of the devastation of the culture of the indigeneous people of Australia, and here we offer two short two short commentaries on the people of Aotearoa (New Zealand) and Japan, and how the Tidal Model might help to restore some of kind of cultural balance to their lives.

### Under a long white cloud

Jacquie Kidd is a New Zealand psychiatric nurse and lecturer with a special interest in the restoration of cultural dignity to all people, but especially to the indigenous peoples of the Antipodes and Pacific Islands. Jacquie Kidd wrote:

> The islands of Aotearoa (New Zealand) are shared by people from all over the world. Our population is composed of the indigenous Maori, and tauiwi (those who came after), some of whom choose to maintain the cultural identity of their homeland, and some of whom take on the identity of the New Zealander, also known as Pakeha, or Kiwi. Through almost 200 years of tauiwi settlement, and colonisation by methods both malicious and benevolent, cultural realities for Maori and Pakeha have become rich and varied.

Mental health services in Aotearoa[10] have historically been developed in line with those in England, which has not served this unique population well.

The introduction of the Tidal Model has allowed mental health practitioners in Aotearoa the choice of a way of working that embraces cultural difference. The metaphor of tidal water is fitting in this country of islands, where spirituality and water are closely linked; the Maori word for spirituality is *wairua*, or 'two waters'.

The emphasis the Tidal Model places on human connections values the range of *whanau* (family) found in this place, where *whanau* may be a single parent and child unit, or a vast interconnecting web of people who trace their descent from a single ancestor.

The centering of the person in distress values the uniqueness of that person's story, allowing their vision of wellness to guide the process of care, and inviting a personal interpretation of the meaning of each manifestation of distress. Thus in the Tidal Model cultural diversity is expected and welcomed, rather than viewed as a departure from the norm.

The Tidal Model offers a safe, peaceful, regardful way for mental health practitioners in Aotearoa to be with our people in their distress.

> He aha te mea nui i te Ao?
> He tangata, he tangata, he tangata.
>
> What is the most important thing in the world?
> It is people, it is people, it is people.

### East meets west meets east

In 2001, Dr Tsuyoshi Akayama, Director of Psychiatric Services at the Kanto Medical Center, NTT East, in Tokyo, visited us in Newcastle as part of a study tour focused on psychiatric care in acute settings in England. Although Dr Akayama and his team had not heard of the Tidal Model before their visit, they became very interested in the practice described by ward staff and took home with them the available training videos and manuals developed for Newcastle. Dr Akayama had many contacts in England and the USA as well as at home in Japan, and so was very conversant with much 'western' psychiatric and psychological thinking.

He was particularly amused to discover our interest in Japanese psychotherapy, in particular the work of Shoma Morita. He particularly noted the irony in the fact that he had travelled all the way from Japan to Newcastle to rediscover the value of Japanese thinking on mental health. Perhaps this represented an oriental rewriting of the old expression about 'taking coals to Newcastle'. Commenting on the cultural context of psychiatric care in Japan, Tsuyoshi and his colleagues[11] wrote:

Traditionally Japanese culture was patriarchal. The father was supposed to have the authority. Actually the relationship between the mother and the children was close and the mother was the key person in forming the consensus among the family.

With the development of democracy, the notion has changed. The father has lost the authority. Now the parents have to help develop the healthy assertion of the children. However, unfortunately, in many cases the parents fail to do so, and the children do not learn how to express themselves. They do not learn how to deal with the stress of the social relationships and to assert themselves. They may withdraw and exert violence at home as an expression of their frustration and helplessness.

This has a relevance to mental health care in Japan and the Tidal Model.

In Japanese mental health care, the prevailing model is still too patriarchal in that the psychiatrists often assume that they should know best, and decree what is right for the patients. In actuality it is the nurses who have the close relationship with the patients and support to form the consensus regarding the treatment.

However, in general, the Japanese nurses, and the psychiatrists as well, do not know how to help develop the healthy assertion of the patients. This can lead to unnecessary and unhealthy dependency, withdrawal or acting out.

The Tidal Model helps the patients to be aware of and accept themselves as they are and it helps them to aim at changing at the same time. This is an interesting therapeutic contradiction. This therapeutic contradiction coincides with much Chinese and Japanese philosophy.

The patriarchal model is fading away in the Japanese mental health care. Now it is legally required to respect the patient's right and to provide appropriate explanation to obtain consent.

Many Japanese psychiatrists are still not fully aware of this change. They do not understand the necessity and the value of healthy assertion, and do not appreciate what the nurses can contribute in this task.

The Tidal Model is ahead of Japanese mental health care. We are hoping that the Japanese mental health care will catch up with the Tidal Model soon. This will be good for the patients and the whole staff as well.

## Interdisciplinary care

As we noted at the beginning of this chapter, the Tidal Model has moved from being exclusively a nursing model to being a mental health recovery model, embraced mainly by nurses, but which values and often demands the support of other disciplines. Such is the complexity of most mental health care today that few settings can function without sophisticated interdisciplinary collaboration. Here, we offer two short commentaries on the importance of interdisciplinary appreciation.

As we have noted, Tsuyoshi Akayama and his colleagues introduced the Tidal Model into their ward in Tokyo in 2002. Indeed, Dr Akayama was the first psychiatrist from outside the UK to express an interest in the Tidal Model. His interest was aptly illustrated by his translation of all the training materials from English to Japanese, to provide a basis for the education of nurses and psychiatrists within his hospital. Dr Akayama has, in his own words, taken a 'back seat' following the implementation of the model, but remains committed to supporting its implementation, through the medium of nursing care. Dr Akayama and his colleagues[12] made the following observation on the importance of interdisciplinary working from a Japanese perspective:

> In Japan the psychiatric nurses work in adverse circumstances. Firstly, the nurses receive only 3 years of general education. The psychiatric nurses enter into practice without any specialised training in mental health. (There exists still a sub-registered nurse qualification, which requires only 2 years of general education.)
>
> Secondly, the Japanese government considers that psychiatric treatment should consists of harbouring chronic patients for a long time, without much therapeutic input. The nurse assignment is 1 to 3 beds in psychiatry as opposed to 1 to 2.5 in other departments. (In Newcastle the assignment rate was 1 nurse to 1 bed in the ward we visited.)
>
> Thirdly, there is little differentiation of the patients. In our ward, you will see schizophrenia, mood disorder, personality disorder, epilepsy, alcoholism, dementia, organic disorder, and other forms of psychiatric pathology. In addition, there are a few patients with serious physical illness including incurable cancers.
>
> Q:   Is the Tidal Model helpful under such an adverse circumstance?
> A:   Yes, and tremendously. It is almost unbelievable how smoothly the nurses of our ward have absorbed the philosophy of the Tidal Model. These are nurses who have never received a formal training of psychotherapy or even psychiatric nursing. Although we have been adjusting the model according to the clinical situation of our ward, the core philosophy of the Tidal Model remains the same.

The nurses find that the Tidal Model provides an effective framework for them to have an effective interaction with the patients. The Tidal Model helps them in the professional discussion with the other staff too, since other staff now understand better how the nurses plan and interact with the patients. All are in agreement that with the Tidal Model, the psychotherapeutic support offered by the nurses has been enhanced greatly. Consequently, the nurses' identity is better established.

The nurses feel that they need to increase their skills in questioning, discussion and interpretation, so that they can frame better care plans with the patients. We believe this illustrates progressiveness as well as professional awareness.

Is the Tidal Model helpful in Japan? Yes and tremendously.

Because the Tidal Model does not explicitly endorse the use of psychiatric diagnosis, or indeed any psychiatric or psychological language, some have formed the incorrect impression that the model is 'anti-psychiatric'. We see little value in being opposed to things, except abuse, injustice, intolerance and any process which dehumanises people. We are more concerned with identifying what we are 'for': which is the promotion of the person's voice, and the wider engagement of the person. We aim to help the person 'be aware of and accept themselves as they are', as Dr Akayama said, through the process that he appropriately called 'healthy assertion'. If the use of psychiatric and legal jargon and concepts aids and abets this process, and the person consents to its usage, then we would be quite comfortable with this arrangement, at least for this particular person. Alternatively, the natural language, metaphors and concepts employed by the person might well prove more than sufficient.

Other psychiatrists appear to appreciate this pragmatism, recognising the potential for the development of complementary relationships between nursing and medicine. Dr Jean-Claude Bisserbe is Professor of Psychiatry at the University of Ottawa, and a colleague of Nancy Brookes and Margaret Tansey. Professor Bisserbe commented:

> The Tidal Model is an excellent approach. It parallels and enriches physicians' clinical approaches with its assessment of the patient's personal clinical picture. In our setting, it supports the move to a research-based program. Nurses have a closeness in their relationships with patients, and their involvement needs a framework with goals and boundaries as offered by the Model. The Tidal Model promotes nurses' self-confidence, fosters interaction, and increases inter-disciplinary team work. The Personal Security Assessment and Plan, especially for suicide is excellent, tactful, and thorough. Nurses who practice within the Tidal Model don't need anything more, it is enough!

## Evaluation

We have noted how members of the international Tidal Model network are involved, in different ways, in evaluations of the model in practice. It is important to acknowledge that, at least in our experience, research into the clinical effectiveness of health care is complicated and the often too-confident investigative processes of the natural sciences rarely apply to human situations. Indeed, evaluation should be treated cautiously, exploring (for example) what might be the most applicable design; the most interesting outcome measures; the most important people; who might offer the most interesting responses.

When the first Tidal Model evaluation was conducted at the University of Newcastle (see Stevenson *et al.* 2002), we were interested in answering three questions:

1    What measures might suggest '*outcome effects*' of the Model in action?
2    What difference does the implementation of the Tidal Model make to the *process* of delivering care?
3    What effect does the delivery of the Tidal Model have on the person's experience of being cared for?

In an increasingly 'evidence-based' and 'outcome-oriented' health care culture, it is important to maintain a focus on developing an understanding of 'what happens' within the practice and experience of the model; as well as what appears to happen 'as a function' of professionals working in this way. Consequently, we are disinclined to be too prescriptive with regard to what more specific questions might be asked in an effort to develop any evaluation of the Model 'in action'. However, the following might represent the basic framework for any evaluation, from the perspective of organisational outcome, professional experience and (most importantly) user/consumer experience.

### Organisational outcome

An evaluation of the implementation of the Tidal Model in any mental health care setting might consider addressing the following topic areas.

#### Resource expenditure

Given that the introduction of any new model of care requires the dedication of time to planning meetings, formal training and other administrative issues, the evaluation should consider *how much time* needs to be devoted to:

- preparation of staff in the use of the Model
- clinical supervision of individual team members
- overall project management.

#### Destination and status

Monitoring what 'happens' to people following a period of care might suggest positive or negative outcomes. Consequently, descriptions of 'where' people go next – home, more intensive care, rehabilitation unit, etc.

*Length of stay*

How long people need to remain in care may be an indicator of the effectiveness of the service. This also is an important economic indicator.

*Admission to assessment interval*

When people are in acute distress, they are often unwilling or unable to engage in dialogue concerning their problems and/or needs. Consequently, the beginning of the assessment process is an important marker for the commencement of the attempt to frame collaborative care.

*Engagement levels*

The differing levels of engagement provide an indication of the perceived vulnerability of the person. Monitoring the length of time a person needs to be supported on different levels of engagement provides an indication of changes in vulnerability status and, by implication, improvement or deterioration.

*Legal status*

Changes in the person's legal status also provide a useful indicator of perceived vulnerability.

*Harm*

Measures of the frequency and perceived severity of all episodes of harm to self, suicide attempts, or harm to others provide further measures of the person's vulnerability and improvement/deterioration.

*Direct quotes*

Given the model's emphasis on empowerment of the person's voice, discrete measures of the number of verbatim quotes (perhaps even number of words) included in the various assessment and care planning records provides a useful index of the extent to which the person's story is forming the basis of the care plan.

*Complaints*

Most clinical situations encourage the expression of complaints as a way of channelling feedback on failing within the service. Consequently, a measure of complaint rates will provide a global index of dissatisfaction.

### The professional

Changes in practice represent a source of potential stress for professional team members. Unless the professional has actively sought the new model of care, this may be seen as an imposition – a professional burden. Consequently, any professional evaluation should examine the extent to which the implementation of the model has:

- enhanced the professional's own practice
- enhanced the practice of the team
- encouraged greater team cohesion or solidarity
- changed the individual team member's view of her/his practice
- changed the professional's view of the people in care
- encouraged job satisfaction
- affected the team member's professional identity
- affected the morale of the team.

Also any evaluation must compare the professional's experience of the Tidal Model, with experience of other models of nursing or mental health care. To what extent is the Tidal Model different? In what way is it different? What does this mean for the individual's and the team's professional practice?

### The user/consumer

The experience of the person in receipt of care is obviously the most vital measure of 'success/failure' of any model of care. The following questions might help to frame an overview of the nature of the person's experience and to what extent specific dimensions of the Tidal Model were experienced. Any such evaluation should be conducted at a reasonable interval following discharge from care. Where people's views are studied during a period of care (as in the Rangipapa study noted earlier) special care must be taken to ensure that the person has an opportunity to express views openly and perhaps anonymously. Given that we are attempting to gain an appreciation of the person's experience, this evaluation is weighted towards the collection of qualititative data. To what extent did the people in care think that:

- they were involved actively in a collaborative approach to designing their own care *from the outset*?
- they were involved in developing and revising their own care during the whole period of care?
- their story, or narrative, was given full attention (for example, by verbatim recording of their own words) by professional staff?
- adequate time was given to the assessment and care planning process?
- they understood the functions of the various assessments?

- the resultant care was focused on their actual needs/wants and wishes?
- the whole interdisciplinary team was involved in supporting and developing their care plan?
- the process of Individual Care was relevant to their needs in the beginning and across time?
- the groupwork was relevant to their needs across time?
- they were involved in preparations for discharge/transfer (Transitional Care)?
- the programme addressed the origins or background to their problems of living (Developmental Care)?
- this period of care differed from other experiences of mental health care (if appropriate)?

## Keeping practitioners afloat

In this chapter we have provided a brief tour of the development of the Tidal Model over its short history and how it is perceived around the world. We have also suggested how the model might fit in with emergent mental health policy in different countries, and also the need to develop creative forms of evaluation, to judge its relative usefulness both for people in care and the professional teams that serve them. Finally, we would like to offer some thoughts on the need for supervision.

We have noted in previous chapters that the professional team member is often required to act like an 'emotional life-saver', delivering some kind of 'psychiatric rescue'. This is clearly a risky occupation, as the life-saver is almost as much at risk as the person whom (s)he intends to save. In mental health care, this perceived threat has often led to the development of highly distant forms of care. As we noted previously, often professional staff are very reluctant to 'get into the water' with the person, far less 'swim out' to where the potential drowning action might be taking place. We can understand this. Anyone who would rashly dive into potentially dangerous waters without adequate forethought risks the accusation of foolhardiness. They also risk generating even more of a panic than first prevailed.

People who are involved in the delivery of the Tidal Model – as with all other models of mental health care – need the support of a supervisor; someone with whom they can discuss their experience of delivery care; someone who might help them develop their awareness of what they might be doing 'right'; and what things about their work or themselves they might need to change. Stated simply, we believe that supervision has two main aims: to protect people in care from professionals and to protect professionals from themselves (see Barker 1998b). Maintaining the Tidal metaphor, many professionals become 'hooked' by the person's distress. The professional, in experiencing something of the person's distress generates great anxiety, which in turn drives the professional to try to eliminate the distress within the person, which started the ripple that risks turning into a tidal wave. Despite his/her helping intentions, the professional risks trying (subconsciously) to deal with her/his own issues, rather than those of the person.

Clinical supervision is needed to ensure that the person is getting the kind of help that (s)he really needs at any point in time (rather than the care that the professional feels obliged to deliver to protect her/himself). However, only the sainted among us can be totally selfless in dedicating even a portion of our waking days to ministering unto the needs of others. Consequently, the other vital function of supervision is to provide emotional (and perhaps physical) support to the professional, so that the dangerous waters of emotional burn-out may be avoided, and the professional can feel valued, even when manifestly struggling to stay afloat.

In principle, the organisation of supervision is simple. Professionals need a dedicated time within which they can share with a supervisor – either alone, or collectively with colleagues – thoughts and feeling about the whole process of caring. This time may provide the necessary means of 'staying afloat'. This support must be offered first, so that professionals can begin to feel safe in the threatening waters of their working lives.

Supervision also involves dedicating time to a consideration of 'what' is being offered in the name of care. Again, either individually or in a group, the professional has an opportunity to review an instance or example of her/his work, revisiting perhaps as a clinical memory the situation, painting in the scene physically, interpersonally and emotionally. Now the professional can begin to ask, with the supervisor's support, questions of her/himself in relation to the person in care. The professional can begin to wonder *why* (s)he was *how* (s)he was. Why did (s)he say *what* she said? Why did she do *this* rather than anything else? Through such a re-examination of her/his own 'lived experience', the professional can begin to understand better the motivations behind certain actions; and can begin to be more knowledgeable about the whole complex business of trying to offer person-centred care.

We have been at pains to point out the simplicity of the Tidal Model. However, we appreciate that this is rather like saying that swimming is simple; even an infant will float if left unattended. Indeed, this is the nub of the issue – we are not infants. Our education – both formal in terms of training, and natural in terms of our social conditioning – has robbed us of our natural propensity to 'float'. If we were genuinely naive, the experience of madness would not terrify us, or at least would not put us on our guard. We would simply approach this (carefully) with the natural curiosity we reserve for other unusual things or events. However, the world and its various 'educations' has made us timid, suspicious, cautious and most of all fearful of that, which we believe represents the 'unknown'. We have been at similar pains, throughout this book, to point out that madness is *not* the unknown but is, indeed, recognisable to all of us. Therein, of course, as Shakespeare would have said, lies the rub. That is the difficulty. If we accept that madness is an ordinary, commonplace 'thing', this implies that we know it personally.

One of the things that the astute supervisor will do is to help the professional to appreciate to what extent (s)he is like the person whom (s)he is caring for. We are all more simply human than otherwise, as Sullivan famously remarked. In a very important sense, the professional's relationship with the supervisor mirrors, exactly, the professional's relationship with the person in care. The supervisor's role is that of a curious enquirer. The supervisor knows very little of what is happening in the professional's inner world. The naive enquiries, posted as curious questions by the supervisor, differ little from the questions that the professional has asked of the person in care. The supervisory process will reveal aspects of the professional's lived experience of which (s)he has previously been unaware. The Tidal Model's emphasis on the nurturing of awareness within the person in care is mirrored in the professional–supervisor relationship. By becoming more aware of what (s)he is doing in the name of care, the professional can become more aware of possible subconscious motivations; and consequently can become more aware of the threat (s)he might pose both to her/himself as well as the person in care.

# Chapter 15

# The voyage from recovery to reclamation

To discover new lands, one must be willing to lose sight of the shore for a very long time.

(André Gide)

When we began our own Tidal voyage almost ten years ago, recovery was rarely discussed in mainstream mental health care, and even less understood. In 2003, as we sat down to write this book, 'recovery' seemed to be on everyone's lips, if only for the purpose of paying lip service. It has become the flavour of the month, the most popular buzzword, the phrase that might guarantee us entry to the most celebrated mental health circles, and which definitely must be mentioned in the next conference presentation, the next departmental memo, and the next invitation extended to the local user/consumer groups.

Recovery is rapidly being assimilated into the mainstream (Barker and Buchanan-Barker 2003a), where it risks being sanitised and turned into a 'thing', which professionals 'do' or 'facilitate' and which, ultimately, will be measurable and included in governmental statistics. By then, the 'dream of recovery' envisioned by the likes of Pat Deegan or Ron Coleman, Dan Fisher or Judi Chamberlin, Sally Clay or Irene Whitehill will likely have turned into the processed nightmare of much of what passes for 'human services' in the twenty-first century.

Given that 'recovery' suggests an end point, which in itself may be no more than illusion, increasingly we have emphasised *reclamation*: the hard work necessary to try to turn something that was 'lost' into a constructive force for good in the world.

Across the estuary from our home in Scotland lies an airfield that was once under the sea. Over many years the land that had once been part of the mainland, but which had been submerged by the sea, was 'reclaimed'. The whole process took over 20 years, but now a long flat strip that was once under water serves as a landing strip for the local airport. In a sense, the land that once was submerged is now stronger than ever; a testament to all that time spent out of sight, beyond use, lost to the known world.

If people whose lives have been overwhelmed and drowned by mental distress need help, they need to be helped to reclaim their lives, and with it their identities *as persons*. They need help to drain the distress from their lives, dry out their sodden and waterlogged personas, and begin to feel their potential strength rising from within their reclaimed selfhood.

All too often, the personhood and the stories of such people are overlooked, only to be replaced by simplistic forms of classification, and even simpler and often absurd forms of inappropriate 'intervention'. Pat Deegan wrote:

> So much of what we were suffering from was overlooked. The context of our lives was ignored. The professionals who worked with us had studied the science of physical objects, but not human science. No one asked for our stories. Instead they thought our biographies as schizophrenics had already been written nearly a century before by Kraeplin and Blueler.
>
> (Personal Communication, 1997)

Pat's words sum up beautifully why we have emphasised *story* throughout this book. Who we are is story – no more and no less. There is no psychology – only stories that are written about us by others and stories that we write or talk about or think about ourselves. The stories others write and talk about us may be interesting – they may even be powerful, they may even be restrictive – but they are only ever the truth as the authors see it. The *personal* truth of our lives is embedded in *our* stories, about *ourselves*. Even when others think that we are lying to ourselves, we are telling the truth. As the song says: 'They can't take that away from me.'

Ownership of our lives lies at the heart of the Tidal Model. Although the Tidal Model has gained much from research and earlier theories concerning mental health and psychotherapy, it remains essentially a values-based model of practice. The Tidal Model is concerned to answer only one question: How do we help people to *reclaim* ownership of their lives? What else is there to do? What else could possibly be of any genuine help to people as persons?

Rae Unzicker, one of the great voices of the survivor movement and of self-advocacy in the USA, died of cancer in 2002, aged 52.[1] This tireless opponent of force and coercion consistently said: 'We are all fighting for the same things: for personal choice, autonomy, dignity and respect.' She wrote powerfully and eloquently:

> To be a mental patient is to be stigmatised, ostracised, socialised, patronised, psychiatrised.
> To be a mental patient is to be a statistic.
> To be a mental patient is to wear a label, and that label never goes away, a label that says little about what you are and even less about who you are.
> And so you become a no-thing, in a no-world, and you are not.

Rae's was an egalitarian voice: not the jaundiced, petty, hurting voice of those of the dispossessed; as if all who have avoided mental health services had, by default, been leading a half-life. Rae knew the issue was about power, and how power can corrupt, and how we all need to play our part in dismantling the perverse power tactics that exploit our all too-human weaknesses.

Raj Patel noted:

> A fertilizer bomb that kills hundreds in Oklahoma. Fuel-laden civil jets kill 4000 in New York. A sanctions policy kills one and a half million in Iraq. A trade policy immiserates whole continents. You can make a bomb out of anything. The ones on paper hurt the most.[2]

Clearly, the potential harm that can be inflicted by ECT, psychoactive drug cocktails and the enforced torpor of hospital admissions, seclusion rooms with broken windows, not to mention staff with hard hearts, is considerable. However, these are merely the mechanical extension of the psychiatric fable, written on paper, of the process of human becoming; a fable that may be worthy of study as a piece of folklore, but which has no place in twenty-first-century health and social care. If anything has devalued us as human beings, it is to be found in the story of how we handed over the copyright of our human story to an assortment of laboratory scientists, sociologists and entrepreneurial psychologists and psychiatrists – all of whom had their eyes fixed on the next big research grant, the next prize, the next promotion. In the process, they failed to notice the distressed fellow traveller who stood tall in their towering shadow.

Although rarely associated with the survivor movement, Tom Szasz recently praised the movement as the most encouraging development in his 60 years associated with psychiatry:

> The most encouraging development is essentially the uprising of the slaves, the increasing protestation by ex-mental patients, many of whom call themselves victims. Through all kinds of groups that have a voice now, which they didn't have before. We should hear from the slaves. Psychiatry has always been described from the point of view of the psychiatrists; now the oppressed, the victim, the patient also has a voice. This, I think, is a very positive development.
>
> (Szasz 2002: 150)

This must rank as one of the greatest plaudits afforded to the survivor movement, given that it is conferred by the psychiatric 'antichrist' himself. More notably, it signals appreciation that a genuine alternative opposition (however small) has been mobilised to challenge the proposition that, culturally, we should conceive of ourselves primarily as biochemical mechanisms.

This not only dehumanises but also spiritually diminishes humankind. It goes without saying that it also reflects an escapist attitude towards the real-world problems of abuse, poverty, stress, prejudice and discrimination, which are the psychosocial correlates or precipitants of what medicine and (ergo) society view as mental *illness*.

For people experiencing problems of living, the Tidal Model offers a simple process through which they might begin to examine and explore their immediate experience; from which they might begin to chart a way forward, given that the tide is right, and given that they have the right kind of crew. Even if the tide is against them, and even if the crew are found to be lacking, the Tidal Model will still help the person to realise the full potentiality of their distress. The person will at least know that (s)he is on a journey of reclamation.

For the professional, the Tidal Model offers similarly the potential of many things. Our experience of leading Tidal Model workshops, and in advising on practice-based projects in different parts of the world, tells us that some professionals will find in the Tidal Model an echo of their original vocation. It will sing to them in the heartfelt voice that first drew them to the mental health field, as the ocean sings into our ear from the giant conch. What we hear is something of ourselves.

The Tidal Model is, however, not for the fainthearted and we hope would be kept away from the foolhardy. It is part of the heroic tradition of human inquiry, capitalising on our search for goodness, as we tread the path into the forest as Frankl did on that fateful day. Leaving aside the tiresome statistics, the dry academic treatises, the inscrutable experimental studies, what is mental health care really about? We would hope it is no more complex than one person or a group of people trying to be of human help to another woman or man. Herein lies the quiet heroism of compassion, of collegiality, of common decency.

History, comic books, the cinema and sport have collaborated in the creation of one of the great illusions – the construction of the hero and more recently the Superhero. The living myths of the hero range from John Wayne acting heroically from the safety of the movie set, through Clark Kent transforming himself heroically into Superman, from within a two-dimensional phone-box, to various, obscenely overpaid 'superstars' performing heroically for a few minutes, once a week, on some sports field. However, the real heroes walk among us – expressing the simple human desire to distinguish themselves through noble action, through everyday acts of common decency. That they do not know that they are heroes is unimportant. Their heroic action is not a performance, it is not designed for effect, but is done as an end in itself. However, it does have heroic impact. The hero[3] and heroic action:

- has noble and grand intention – to help people to reclaim their lives, to recover their human identities and to continue with the greatest of all human projects – the development of one's own unique life story.

- embraces the principle of consent, striving to help others do what needs to be done, providing this does not infringe the rights of others.
- brings out the best in people – both that of the person who is helped and the hero him or herself.
- is invariably quiet and private, motivated by the desire to do the right thing, rather than to 'be seen' to be doing the right thing.
- is dogged and determined, relentless in pursuit of accomplishment.
- overcomes all odds. As Hannibal famously remarked, If I cannot find a way, I shall make one!
- can succeed in failure. Heroism is more about doing than its results.
- need not be perfect. Indeed many of our heroes, featured in this book, have been flawed characters. This has not detracted from their heroic standing. Indeed, it casts them resolutely on our side – the frail and mortal – not among the gods of fiction.

We shall not embarrass our friends and colleagues by according them heroic status, but many of them have already been mentioned, some several times over, in this book. We hope they will continue with the 'quiet revolution' of mental health care; changing the game plan; reframing the language; coining new metaphors; becoming more and more resourceful; burning more brightly, as their passion for common decency touches new hearts.

And so the revolution will turn full circle. We shall have circumnavigated the globe of our human vocation and, having rested, we can set out again, in search of new lands, less afraid to lose sight of the shore again.

# Chapter 16

# The compass

## The ten commitments

No pessimist ever discovered the secret of the stars, or sailed to an uncharted land, or opened a new doorway for the human spirit.

(Helen Keller)

The Tidal Model draws on a wide range of theoretical and philosophical influences, from both the recent and the distant past. We have tried to acknowledge the many influences on our work in the preceding chapters. All too often, we run the risk of assuming that we have discovered something 'anew' when it is no more than an echo of a much older understanding.

However, as the Tidal Model has grown, through the work of its various practitioners, in different countries, the key features of the model, as a lived experience of helping, have become clearer. Notably, we understand better how both the professional and the person in care need to make a *commitment* to change. Rarely is this easy. However, this commitment is what binds them together. To conclude the book, we offer the following *Ten Commitments*, which distil the essence of the practice of the Tidal Model. These commitments represent the final arbiter as to whether or not anyone is working within the philosophy of the Tidal Model. If the model that we have outlined in the preceding chapters represents the *map* of recovery and reclamation, then the Ten Commitments represent the *compass*. These values guide us when the sky is dark, the tide is high and we are afraid.

1  *Value the voice*: the person's *story* is the beginning and endpoint of the whole helping encounter. The person's story embraces not only the account of the person's distress, but also the hope for its resolution. This is the voice of experience. We need to guard it well, as the voice begins to help the person to make her or himself anew.
2  *Respect the language*: the person has developed a unique way of expressing the life story, of representing to others that which the person alone can know. The language of the story, complete with its unusual grammar and personal metaphors, is the ideal medium for lighting the way.

3 *Develop genuine curiosity*: the person is writing a life story but this does not mean that the story of the person's life is an 'open book'. We need to develop ways of expressing genuine interest in the story – as written, and as it continues to be written – so that we can better understand the storyteller.

4 *Become the apprentice*: the person is the world expert on the life story. We can begin to learn something of the power of that story, but only if we apply ourselves diligently and respectfully to the task by becoming the apprentice.

5 *Reveal personal wisdom*: the person has developed a powerful storehouse of wisdom in the writing of the life story. One of the key tasks for the helper is to assist in revealing that wisdom, which will be used to sustain the person and to guide the journey of reclamation and recovery.

6 *Be transparent*: both the person and the professional embody the opportunity to become a team. If this relationship is to prosper both must be willing to let the other into their confidence. The professional helper is in a privileged position and should model this confidence building by being transparent at all times, helping the person understand *what* is being done and *why*.

7 *Use the available toolkit*: the person's story contains numerous examples of 'what has worked' or 'what might work' for this person. These represent the main tools that need to be used to unlock or build the story of recovery.

8 *Craft the step beyond*: the helper and the person work together to construct an appreciation of what needs to be done 'now'. The *first* step is the crucial step, revealing the power of change and pointing towards the ultimate goal of recovery.

9 *Give the gift of time*: there is nothing more valuable than the time the helper and the person spend together. Time is the midwife of change. There is no value in asking 'How much time do we have?' We have all the time there is. The question is surely 'How do we use this time?'

10 *Know that change is constant*: the Tidal Model assumes that change is inevitable, for change is constant. This is the common story for all people. The task of the professional helper is to develop *awareness* of how that change is happening, and how that knowledge might be used to steer the person out of danger and distress back on to the course of reclamation and recovery.

A wet sheet and a flowing sea
A wind that follows fast
And fills the white and rustling sail
And bends the gallant mast.
    (Alan Cunningham, 1784–1842)

# Epilogue

The challenge of change belongs to both the person who is the professional, and the person in care. One cannot change without the other – both face differing challenges for change. We have learned that much already. We hope to learn it again, and again and again.

Father Anthony de Mello, a Jesuit priest in India, mapped the journey of change, which first begins in our hearts and then in our minds:

> Put this program into action, a thousand times:
>
> - identify the negative feelings in you;
> - understand that they are in you, not in the world, not in external reality;
> - do not see them as an essential part of 'I'; these things come and go;
> - understand that when you change, everything changes. (1988)

He also noted that change is a very pragmatic business:

> Better to put on slippers, than to try to clear every rock from the face of the earth.

The sparkling and currently fashionable worlds of neuroscience and genetics hold much promise for the furtherance of our understanding of some of the complex mechanics of being human. They promise to reveal more of the *basis* of specific states of human being. However, they will never reveal the true mystery of what 'being human' means, since this extends far beyond our gene pool and our biological make-up, encompassing our personal histories, our culture and myriad social and interpersonal influences. As we have noted throughout this book, being human is essentially a story: one which continues to be written as we breathe, as we think and as we consider writing the next page of our own biography. The author is life herself.

Our challenge is to remind ourselves of our human *value* and our cosmic *insignificance*. We cannot control and contain the forces that act upon and often through us. However, we can decide what we need to 'do' next. In that simple act of 'step taking' lies our human freedom, and also the promise of human wisdom.

# The Holistic Assessment

Name:

Assessing Nurse:

Date:                    Time:

Others Present:

Summary:

Primary Nurse/Keyworker:

Signature:                    Date:

**The Holistic Assessment**

Complete Assessment as soon as possible after entry to service

1. Explain purpose of assessment.

2. Encourage active participation.

3. Record person's name/ assessing nurse/ keyworker.

4. Record date and time.

5. Record names of others present – e.g. advocate, student, friend.

6. Record brief summary of circumstances of entry to service.

7. Inform person of Primary Nurse/Keyworker and record details.

How this all began:

How this affected me:

How I felt in the beginning:

How things have changed over time:

The effect on my relationships:

**The Holistic Assessment**

**Entry to the service:** 'What has brought you here?'

1. **Problem origins:** 'so when did you first notice ... or become of aware of ...?'

2. **Past problem function:** 'and how did that affect you at first?' etc.

3. **Past emotions:** '... and how did you feel about that at the time?' etc.

4. **Historical development:** '... and in what way has that changed over time?' etc.

5. **Relationships:** 'and how has that affected your relationship with people?' etc.

How do I feel now?

What do I think this means?

What does all of this say about me, as a person?

What needs to happen now/what do I want or wish would happen now?

What do I expect the nurse to do for me?

**The Holistic Assessment**

Ask permission to continue

**6. Current emotions:** '... and how do you feel about that now?'

**7. Holistic content:** '... and what does all of that mean for you?'

**8. Holistic context:** '... and what does that say about you as a person?'

**9. Needs, wants, wishes:** '... and what would you hope would be done about that?'

**10. Expectations:** '... and what do you think we can do for you here in this service?'

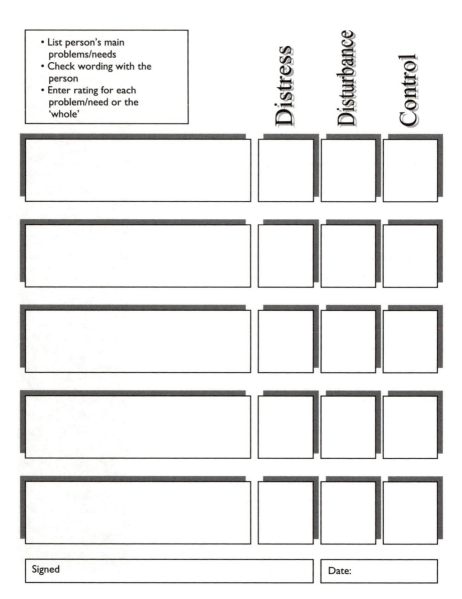

- List person's main problems/needs
- Check wording with the person
- Enter rating for each problem/need or the 'whole'

Distress

Disturbance

Control

Signed

Date:

**People who are important:**

**Things that are important:**

**Ideas or beliefs about life that are important:**

## The Holistic Assessment

**Personal resources**

Ask person to describe personal assets or resources that might help in resolution of the problem or need.

**1. Who** is important in your life – family, friends, groups, others? **Why** are they important?

**2. What** is important in your life – money, home, possessions etc. **Why** are these important?

**3.** What are your **beliefs** about life in general – faith, personal philosophy, values?

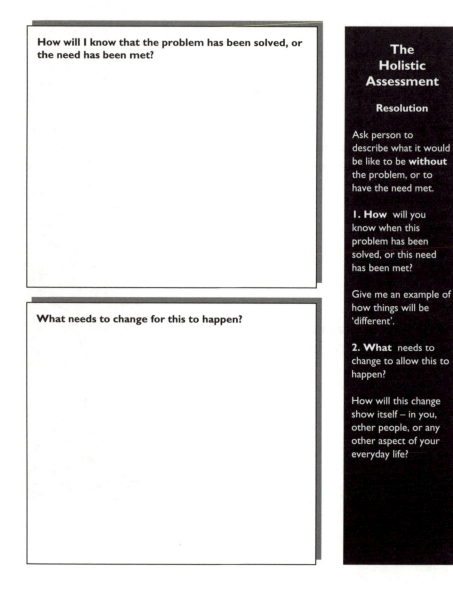

**How will I know that the problem has been solved, or the need has been met?**

**What needs to change for this to happen?**

**The Holistic Assessment**

**Resolution**

Ask person to describe what it would be like to be **without** the problem, or to have the need met.

**I. How** will you know when this problem has been solved, or this need has been met?

Give me an example of how things will be 'different'.

**2. What** needs to change to allow this to happen?

How will this change show itself – in you, other people, or any other aspect of your everyday life?

# Rating scale

---

## Evaluation of the problem or need

- To what extent does this *distress* you?
- To what extent does this *interfere* with your life?
- To what extent can you *control* it?

### Distress

| None | 2 | 4 | 6 | 8 | 10 |
|------|---|---|---|---|-----|
| 1 | 3 | 5 | 7 | 9 | Extreme |

### Disturbance

| None | 2 | 4 | 6 | 8 | 10 |
|------|---|---|---|---|-----|
| 1 | 3 | 5 | 7 | 9 | Extreme |

### Control

| None | 2 | 4 | 6 | 8 | 10 |
|------|---|---|---|---|-----|
| 1 | 3 | 5 | 7 | 9 | Complete |

# Notes

**The poetics of experience**

1 This poem is reprinted with permission from the book *Landscapes of the Mind*, published by Borderland Voices, an arts workshop which provides a creative space for people interested in self-expression and the promotion of mental health (www.borderlandvoices.org.uk).

**1 Tales of shipwrecks and castaways**

1 The notion of the *Self* is almost wholly a western construction. As we shall note later, our friends and colleagues from Japan, or from the indigenous peoples of Australia and Aotearoa (New Zealand), have no *natural* appreciation of the Self. Instead, *who* they are is defined by family or community relationships. Perhaps that was also, once, the rule in the west, and we have merely become fascinated by the illusion of individual identity.
2 As Roy Porter (1991) noted, the term *madness*, although objected to by modern psychiatry on the grounds of its unscientific nature, is the most appropriate term to describe the wide range of human experiences of distress, disturbance, passion and exhilaration. As Porter noted, 'no synonym or euphemism is half so evocative'.
3 We recognise that most of the people who will read this book, will be working within western societies, and perhaps will be framed by very powerful western conceptions of Self and Others.
4 Details of contemporary developments in the implementation of the Tidal Model can be found at: www.tidal-model.co.uk

**5 A map of the territory**

1 In the same way that film actors go 'on location', the actors in the therapeutic drama (whether patient, family member, friend or professional) need different locations to realistically engage with the emergent script of the person's life. Of course, the person who plays the 'patient' is the lead actor, all others taking supporting roles.

**7 The assessment of suicide risk**

1 The 15 factors in the NGASR were originally developed by John Cutcliffe at the University of Sheffield, England in 1998. These were further operationalised by

Phil Barker at the University of Newcastle in a series of developmental studies of the use of the global assessment in clinical practice (1998–2000).

2 The items on the Focused Suicide Risk Interview draw on many sources, but especially the work of Morgan (1993).

3 Transparency is vital across all three domains of the Tidal Model. Traditionally, professionals adopt a paternalistic role in relation to suicidal people, which may create difficulties when collaboration and self-care are expected of the person in the future.

4 The levels of engagement used in the Tidal Model are based on extensive consultation in the UK with professionals involved in the care of suicidal people.

## 8 Bridging

1 Nursing is the health and social care discipline that provides most by far of the supportive, direct care of people with mental health problems. This does not ignore the important contributions made by other disciplines, but acknowledges that nursing operates at the 'care face'. Consequently, nursing and nurses are referred to most often here.

2 Nursing derives from the Old French and Latin meaning 'to nourish'. The forester 'nurses' a young tree by selecting the best condition for its growth – soil, irrigation and shelter. Once the sapling begins to grow, the forester tries to maintain these 'ideal conditions' for growth, removing anything that might hinder growth or damage the tree, and ensuring the sapling's access to the necessary nourishment of soil, light and water. In the same way, the nurse tries to ensure that the environment – both physical and social – provides the best conditions for the person to 'grow through' the experience of mental distress.

3 The term 'engagement' has slowly begun to creep into the bureaucratic language of mental health care in the UK. The process of *engagement* within the Tidal Model was first defined in the original training materials (Barker 1998a).

4 It is acknowledged that within many mental health services, discrete policies may exist, which guide the care of people deemed to be at risk of harm to self or others. In most instances these policies exist to meet the requirements of mental health law or government legislation. The guidance here regarding levels of engagement should be seen to *complement* rather than override such local policies.

5 In many countries, unqualified 'support staff' or students, are often deployed to conduct 'observations' on people at risk. In some parts of the UK and the USA, security guards (and university students, with no background in health or social care) have been employed to complement the staff team, for the purpose of doing 'observation'. Aside from the fact that such 'observation' becomes little more than empty 'containment' or 'custody', the use of low-ranking staff or strangers sends a powerfully mixed message to the person-in-care. The message appears to say: 'You need our closest attention but you do not need the attention of our best staff.' For people who are already experiencing the fragile insecurity of the Self in crisis, this may only add further damage.

6 We are aware that often the person in care does not share the view of the professional team. However, we are also aware that in most countries the professional team has a 'duty of care', which requires team members to offer the kind of support that will ensure the physical and emotional security of the person. This does not mean, however, that the team does not acknowledge, or attempt to take cognisance of, the views of the person in care.

7 By asking the person to think about what someone would be *doing*, a powerful invitation is given to *remember* or *imagine* an *experience* of helpfulness. This is

very different from simply talking about what may or may not be helpful, which may remain grounded at the level of 'mere words'. By invoking the person's powers of recall or imagination, the nurse is helping the person to tap into some of her/his most powerful resources. The recall or imagination of a 'goal' is the first step to its realisation.

8  If the person is at 'very high risk' then the assessment might be repeated within a few hours or later that day. If the person represented any significant level of risk (1, 2 or 3) the assessment would be repeated the following day. If the person represented 'no risk' then the nurse would make a judgement as to when it would be appropriate to repeat the assessment.

9  Asking permission is not simply 'good manners', but illustrates the nurse's awareness that the Monitoring Assessment belongs to the person, not to the team. This request, therefore, conveys a powerful message about *ownership*.

10  The person is *helping* the nurse rather than vice versa, since the completion of the assessment is a professional responsibility. The person would (likely) not choose to do this of her/his own volition. Acknowledging the person's support of the professional process of care is another important aspect of the development of the collaborative 'caring with' relationship.

11  When the Tidal Model was first launched in practice, some professionals criticised the language of the 'security' plan, suggesting that this might be interpreted as an indication of 'policing' of the person in care. Over time, however, as people began to talk about 'my Personal Security Plan', it became clear that this was the most appropriate title for this care plan, acknowledging the importance – for the person – of the feeling of personal security.

12  Although such arrangements usually pertain only to 'clinical' settings, where people are supported in their own homes the therapeutic team has a similar responsibility for noticing and addressing any obvious risk factors in the person's environment.

13  We recognise that in special circumstances (e.g. where the person has some major cognitive deficit or major learning disability) this rule will not apply. However, our experience tells us that even people who are experiencing very severe forms of mental distress can (and do) identify the conditions that might nurture their sense of emotional security. The key requirement is a functioning cognitive system. Despite the myths that abound regarding the distorted thinking of people (e.g. in psychosis), most such people are able to think very clearly, albeit in very unusual ways.

14  When exploring the person's resources the nurse might ask: 'Have you ever been able to control your temper?' (To which the answer could be 'no'). In using a presuppositional question, the nurse would ask: 'Tell me about the last time you controlled your temper, even in a small way.' (The assumption – or supposition – is that the person *has* done this, at some time, in the past. This makes it less likely that (s)he will close down the conversation by saying 'no'.)

This is not a 'trick question' as if the person has never had the experience (s)he is unlikely to invent it. By emphasising the 'existence' of things, presuppositional questions make it more likely that the person will search for them in their memory.

## 9 The World Domain

1  We hope that we appreciate this concern with categorisation and classification. In most parts of the western world it is impossible to gain any formal support if, first, a diagnosis has not been made. However, given the often fickle nature of diagnosis, and the evidence of its various social, political ideological and gender-related

influences, we need to be wary of expecting too much from the classificatory process.

2 Although we are not supporters of this bureaucratic process, we understand why this is necessary in a bureaucracy such as contemporary health and social care.

3 Given that the person is likely to feel very vulnerable, (s)he should have the opportunity to be supported by a friend, family member or advocate, in this important – and potentially demanding – interview. We appreciate, from our professional experience, that such support is rarely provided. Hopefully, professional attitudes towards 'making the person comfortable' will change in the future.

4 The nurse needs to support the person, rather than simply acquiesce. Usually, by offering more options, the person has a chance to make fresh choices, and so the collaborative conversation has a chance to continue at least a little further.

5 The aim here is to help the person stand back from the problem – or a part of the problem – and view it through the lens of the rating scale. When the scale is printed on card or laminated, the person can hold the card with the analogue scales for distress, disruption and control. People often report feeling *as if* some distance has been established between themselves and the problem.

6 The linear scale usually is helpful, allowing people to locate their experience somewhere along the line. If the person finds this in any way difficult, the nurse should employ other graphic approaches – e.g. drawing a simple 'mountain' on a scrap of paper, with 'none' at the bottom and 'extreme' at the top.

7 *Respect* for the person and the person's story should be the thread that runs through the whole process.


## 10  The Others Domain

1 It is noteworthy that Freud's final major work was called '*Civilisation and its Discontents*'. He noted in his conclusion that 'Men have gained control over the forces of nature to such an extent that with their help they would have no difficulty in exterminating one another to the last man. They know this, and hence comes a large part of their current unrest, their unhappiness and their mood of anxiety'. Seventy years later, the 'discontents' have multiplied and with it, our capacity for unrest, unhappiness and anxiety (Freud, in Gay 1995).

2 We apologise for the exclusive use of UK terminology

3 We are aware, from our own extensive professional experience, that the revision of such professional meetings can be extremely difficult. Although psychiatrists no longer *tour* psychiatric wards with a retinue of junior staff in tow, in many acute hospital ward (at least in the UK) review meetings are often still referred to as the 'ward round'. This may well be a sign of the resistance to change endemic among many professionals. Similarly, where people (patients) are allowed access to such meetings, this can often take the form of an inquisition or a psychic 'undressing' before a room largely full of strangers – medical and nursing students and various members of the interdisciplinary team, few of whom make any direct input to the care of the person.

4 Many such review meetings carry vestiges of the worst inquisitorial aspects of the medical 'ward round', where the 'patient' is the object of objective medical examination, and often the most disturbing aspects of past or present life circumstances are opened up to inquiry.

### 11  The lantern on the stern

1  This is not to say that there is no knowledge base. However, this knowledge is social or theoretical, representing descriptions of people, or populations and how they function *in general*. The person is in need of a more particular form of knowledge – one that relates, specifically, to the person and the life the person is leading.

2  Of course some will argue that many people in mental health services are not there out of choice but have been 'committed' there under the law, and in no way are customers. Given that we are opposed to compulsory psychiatry on principle, we would agree. However, the Tidal Model principle still applies. How can the person become aware of what (s)he needs to do or become to negotiate release from legal detention so that (s)he might take the next step on the recovery journey?

3  This appears to represent a more radical, pragmatic focus than prevails in most traditional mental health services. Typically, the aim is to 'treat the symptoms of the illness' or to 'improve the person's affective/cognitive or behavioural functioning'. By focusing on the 'what' of necessary change, we shall discover the method (how) this might be realised.

4  A Chinese scholar once told us that an alternative translation from the Chinese was: 'the journey of a thousand miles begins under your very feet'. This seems very apposite, noting that the person is already on the recovery path, the only decision to be made involves which way to turn to take that critical first step.

5  Of course some people are unable, or unwilling (for whatever reason), to participate in any dialogue about their need for care and what this might entail. In such circumstances a team member will arrange general supportive care until the person is willing or able to participate. This will include making discrete attempts to reopen discussions, which hopefully will eventually be interpreted by the person as an expression of genuine interest.

6  Acknowledging the name of the nurse may be even more significant than at first it appears. People often find it difficult to concentrate on 'information' and find processes like the 'orientation to care' awkward and confusing. By confirming the name of the person who has guided her/him through the whole process, the person puts down at least one, metaphorical, anchor in the collaborative care plan. This represents a signal of the person's success in beginning the process of recovery.

7  The medical concept of the 'episode' of illness suggests a block of experience akin to an instalment of a soap opera or chapter in a book.

8  We hope that this is *realistically* optimistic.

9  This does not prevent professional staff (and sometimes family members) from complaining that the person 'does nothing all day'. No mean feat, given what we said earlier about meditation!

10  We are aware that many professionals are reluctant to enter into these sorts of conversations on the grounds that they would be 'buying into the delusion'. We take the view that we could never prove that someone was not the Son of God, or from Mars, or that they did not have special powers of which we were unaware. All we could do is prove that we didn't believe them, which doesn't seem like a good starting point for developing a collaborative relationship.

11  For us, 'normal' is a phase on the spin cycle of a washing machine; probably the best place for it.

12  Given the focus of the Holistic Assessment, we are fully aware of the irony in this observation. In general, people like to tell their story – from the beginning. However, when they are in deep waters people tend to want to be rescued – not someone yelling psychotherapeutic platitudes from the shore.

13 Even when people are in 24-hour care, the person spends most of that time alone (often all except the odd hour of two of social contact or therapy).

## 12  All hands to the pumps

1 Over the past 20 years the focus of groupwork has changed. Where once all patients would be expected to join and participate in psychodynamic groups, now this is largely reserved for people who are 'less disturbed' or have 'special needs'. People with more complex needs, especially the person deemed to be psychotic, will invariably be referred to various diversional groups that 'make things with paper', or discuss the contents of the daily newspaper. These activities are important, but one cannot help but think that the group leaders are processing the clientele, rather than using the group as a means of developing understanding.
2 Originally, these groups were called Recovery Groups.
3 People who have reading problems often take a card and then ask someone else to read it on their behalf – a powerful sign that members are bonding together.
4 If two facilitators lead the group, this provides an opportunity for them to comment to one another, starting a conversation about how individual members are moving forward, which might serve as a model for the individual participants to make similar constructive comments.
5 We are aware, from supervising colleagues' work that some professionals experience difficulty with this kind of self-disclosing, positively reinforcing and curiously inquiring style of facilitation. Some become embarrassed and tongue tied, others feel awkward and self-conscious. Many think that it is 'unprofessional' to reveal anything of themselves to 'patients'. We believe that the assumptions about change that underpin the Tidal Model are universal. If facilitators can acknowledge this fact, then this might help the people in care accept the model, and might also help in the destigmatisation process.
6 Notice, that the facilitators 'show' Jack the 10 (the worst) but do not invite him to 'go there'.

## 13  Making waves

1 Indeed, Sally Clay was helped directly by Ed Podvoll and went on to become a Windhorse worker.
2 It should not surprise the reader that our crew is predominantly male in gender. However, we hope to show that gender is largely irrelevant. The heart is not driven by biological sex but by something far more sensitive.
3 Note the echoes of Laing and Sullivan and how these attributes heralded Podvoll's work.
4 The Greek for 'salvation' or 'deliverance'.
5 In Christian theology *logos* is the Word of God. In the original Greek, as Frankl used it, this meant 'the word' or 'reason' itself (as if spoken by God). Hence, *logotherapy* became the process by which people 'search for reason or meaning' in their lives.
6 As we noted earlier, he has promoted and developed Sullivan's use of this term as an alternative to psychopathology or mental illness.
7 All of this, of course, infuriates the western psychologist. (The average western psychiatrist has long since given up even thinking about this.)
8 The reader will note the echo of Sullivan's interpersonal relations theory.
9 Psyche was the Greek personification of the soul, or spirit, sometimes represented as a butterfly.

10 It is also worth remembering that psyche can mean the 'breath' and 'life' itself.
11 Tom Keen picks up this thread of 'decency' in Chapter 14.


## 14 Origins and developments

1 Reprinted by permission of HarperCollins Publishing Ltd. © Brian Patten, *Grave Gossip* 1979.
2 Robert Burns wrote:

> O wad some Pow'r the giftie gie us
> To see ourels as ithers see us!
> It wad frae mony a blunder free us,
> And foolish notion. (1786)

In effect, (and less poetically) if we could have the benefit of seeing ourselves from the perspective of others, perhaps we might be saved from making such a fool of ourselves, or saved from holding on to foolish ideas.
3 We have not included the voices of our critics, since readers will encounter those voices soon enough. The Tidal Model is still an 'infant' and, arguably, deserves careful handling.
4 Readers interested in obtaining details of the range of countries and services involved currently in Tidal Model implementation projects, should visit the website: www.tidal-model.co.uk where they can also correspond with the authors.
5 The drive, originally in the USA, but latterly witnessed in the UK, Australia and New Zealand, towards mental health nurses conferring psychiatric medical diagnoses and prescribing medication, is one important example. Even if these 'services' were actively sought by the user/consumer, we would question whether such 'extension of the nurse's role' would be at the expense of the continued development of the traditional understanding of *care*.
6 Cedar Ward in Harrogate was one of the first group of Nursing Development Units sponsored by the Kings Fund in London.
7 The full report is entitled 'Evaluation of a Nursing Model: The Tidal Model in the context of a Regional Forensic Psychiatric Unit' and is available from Ngaire Cook (Ngaire.cook@ccdhb.org.nz).
8 T.S. Kuhn *The Structure of Scientific Revolutions*, Chicago, University of Chicago Press, 1996, first published 1962.
9 Although *humanism* is frequently confused with some of the wilder excesses of 'humanistic psychology or psychotherapy', this is an outlook or way of thinking about life that owes few allegiances, least of all to the Johnny-come-latelys of West Coast American culture or New Age philosophy. Humanism attaches prime importance to human rather than divine or supernatural matters. It is not a unified theory but probably originated during the Renaissance, when there was a cultural opposition to the theological bias of medieval scholasticism. In keeping with much ancient Greek and Roman thought, humanism stresses the potential value and inherent goodness of people, our common human needs, and believes in the value of rational ways of finding solutions to human problems.
10 Literally, 'the land of the long white cloud'.
11 This piece was written by Tsuyoshi Akiyama, Junko Sonehara, Shie Kaihara, Ayumi Fujiwara, and Miho Maeda
12 This piece was written by Tsuyoshi Akiyama, Junko Sonehara, Shie Kaihara, Ayumi Fujiwara, and Miho Maeda

## 15  The voyage from recovery to reclamation

1  http://www.narpa.org/rae.unzicker.celebration.htm
2  http://www.zmag.org/patelbombs.htm
3  We acknowledge the remarkable philosophical guidance of John F Groom, in outlining his list of heroic attributes. J.F. Groom *Living Sanely in an Insane World: Philosophy for Real People*. New York, Attitude Media, 2002.

# References

Aaronovitch, D. (2003) 'Why suicide? Only one person knows', *The Guardian* 22 July: 5.

Alanen, Y., Lehtinen, K. and Aaltonen, J. (1991) 'Need-adapted treatment of new schizophrenic patients: Experiences and results of the Turku Project', *Acta Psychiatrica Scandanavica* 83: 363–72.

Alberg, C., Hatfield, B. and Huxley, P. (1996) *Learning Materials on Mental Health Risk Assessment*, Manchester: Manchester University and the Department of Health.

Altschul, A.T. (1972) *Nurse–Patient Interaction: A Study of Interactive Patterns on an Acute Psychiatric Ward*, Edinburgh: Churchill Livingstone.

Alvarez, A. (1970) *The Savage God: A Study of Suicide*, New York: Random House.

Alves, D. and Cleveland, P. (1999) *The Maori and the Crown: An Indigenous People's Struggle for Self-determination*, Auckland: Greenwood.

American Psychiatric Association (1994) *Diagnostic and Statistical Manual-IV*, New York: American Psychiatric Publishing.

Ames, R.T. (1994) *Self as Person in Asian Theory and Practice*, New York: State University of New York Press.

Bandura, A. (1977) *Social Learning Theory*, Englewood Cliffs, NJ: Prentice Hall.

Barker, P. (1982) *Behaviour Therapy Nursing*, London: Croom-Helm.

—— (1996) 'Chaos and the way of Zen: Psychiatric nursing and the "uncertainty principle" ', *Journal of Psychiatric and Mental Health Nursing* 3: 235–43.

—— (1997a) 'Toward a meta theory of psychiatric nursing', *Mental Health Practice* 1(4): 18–21.

—— (1997b) *Assessment in Psychiatric and Mental Health Nursing: Towards the Whole Person*, Cheltenham: Stanley Thornes.

—— (1998a) 'It's time to turn the tide', *Nursing Times* 18(94): 70–72.

—— (1998b) 'Psychiatric nursing', in A.C. Butterworth, J. Faugier and P. Burnard (eds) *Clinical Supervision and Mentorship in Nursing*, Cheltenham: Stanley Thornes.

—— (1998c) 'The future of the theory of interpersonal relations. A personal reflection on Peplau's legacy', *Journal of Psychiatric and Mental Health Nursing* 5(3): 213–20.

—— (1999) *The Talking Cures: A Guide to the Psychotherapies for Health Care Professionals*, London: NT Books.

—— (2000a) 'The Tidal Model: The lived experience in person-centred mental health care', *Nursing Philosophy* 2(3): 213–23.

—— (2000b) 'Reflections on the caring as a virtue ethic within an evidence-based culture', *International Journal of Nursing Studies* 37: 329–36.

—— (2000c) 'The virtue of caring', *International Journal of Nursing Studies* 37: 329–36.

—— (2000d) 'Working with the metaphor of life and death', *Journal of Medical Ethics: Medical Humanities* 26: 97–102.

—— (2001a) 'The Tidal Model: Developing an empowering, person-centred approach to recovery within psychiatric and mental health nursing', *Journal of Psychiatric and Mental Health Nursing* 8(3): 233–40.

—— (2001b) 'Working with the metaphor of life and death', in D. Kirklin and R. Richardson (eds) *Medical Humanities: A Practical Introduction*, London: Royal College of Physicians.

—— (2001c) 'The Tidal Model: A radical approach to person-centred care', *Perspectives in Psychiatric Care* 37(3): 79–87.

—— (2002) 'The Tidal Model: The healing potential of metaphor within the patient's narrative', *Journal of Psychosocial Nursing and Mental Health Services* 40(7): 42–50.

—— and Buchanan-Barker, P. (2001) 'Apologising for our colonial past', *Openmind* 112: 10.

—— and Buchanan-Barker, P. (2003a) 'Death by assimilation', *Asylum* 13(3) 10–13.

—— (2003b) *Breakthrough: Spirituality and Mental Health*, London: Whurr.

—— and Buchanan-Barker, P. (2003c) *Spirituality and Mental Health: Breakthrough*, London: Whurr.

—— and Cutcliffe, J. (1999) 'Clinical risk: A need for engagement not observation', *Mental Health Care* 2(8): 8–12.

—— and Kerr, B. (2001) *The Process of Psychotherapy: A Journey of Discovery*, Oxford: Butterworth-Heinemann.

—— and Whitehill, I. (1997) 'The craft of care: Towards collaborative caring in psychiatric nursing', in S. Tilley (ed.) *The Mental Health Nurse: Views of Practice and Education*, Oxford: Blackwell.

—— Campbell, P. and Davidson, B. (1999a) *From the Ashes of Experience: Reflection on Madness, Recovery and Growth*, London: Whurr.

—— Jackson, S. and Stevenson, C. (1999b) 'The need for psychiatric nursing: Towards a multidimensional theory of caring', *Nursing Inquiry* 6: 103–11.

—— (1999c) 'What are psychiatric nurses needed for? Developing a theory of essential nursing practice', *Journal of Psychiatric and Mental Health Nursing* 6: 273–82.

—— Keady, J., Croom, S., Stevenson, C., Adams, T. and Reynolds, B. (1998a) 'The concept of serious mental illness: Modern myths and grim realities', *Journal of Psychiatric and Mental Health Nursing* 5(4): 247–54.

—— Leamy M. and Stevenson C. (1999d) *Nurses Empowerment of People with Enduring Forms of Mental Illness*. Report to the Northern and Yorkshire Regional Research Committee, Newcastle.

—— Manos, E., Novak, V. and Reynolds, B. (1998b) 'The wounded healer and the myth of mental well-being: Ethical issues concerning the mental health status of psychiatric nurses', in P. Barker and B. Davidson (eds) *Psychiatric Nursing: Ethical Strife*, London: Arnold.

—— Reynolds, W. and Ward, T. (1995) 'The proper focus of nursing: A critique of the caring ideology', *International Journal of Nursing Studies* 32(4): 386–97.

Baron-Cohen, S. (2003) *The Essential Difference: Men, Women and the Extreme Male Brain*, London: Allen Lane Science.

Barraclough, B., Bunch, J., Nelson, P. and Sainsbury, P. (1974) 'A hundred cases of suicide: Clinical aspects', *British Journal of Psychiatry* 125: 355–73.

Beck, A.T., Kovacs, M. and Weissman, M. (1989) 'Assessment of suicidal intention: The scale for suicidal ideation', *Journal of Consulting and Clinical Psychology* 47: 343–52.

—— Weissman, M., Lester, D. and Trexler, L. (1974) 'The measurement of pessimism: The hopelessness scale', *Journal of Consulting and Clinical Psychology* 42: 861–5.

Beck, U. (1992) *Risk Society: Towards a New Modernity*, London: Sage.

Benner, P. (1984) *From Novice to Expert: Excellence and Power in Clinical Nursing Practice*, California: Addison-Wesley Incorporated.

Bentall, R.P. (2003) *Madness Explained: Psychosis and Human Nature*, London: Allen Lane

Berger, P. and Luckmann, T. (1967) *The Social Construction of Reality*, Harmondsworth: Penguin.

Borgmann, A. (1993) *Crossing the Postmodern Divide*, Chicago: Chicago University Press.

Bosing, W. (2001) *Hieronymus Bosch: Between Heaven and Hell*, Cologne: Midpoint Press.

Bradshaw, A. (1994) *Lighting the Lamp*, London: Scutari Press.

—— (1996) 'Lighting the lamp: The covenant as an encompassing framework for the spiritual dimension of nursing care', in F.-S. Fanner (ed.) *Exploring the Spiritual Dimension of Care*, Salisbury: Quay Hooks.

Brandon, D. (1976) *Zen in the Art of Helping*, London: Routledge and Kegan Paul.

—— (2000a) *The Tao of Survival*, London: Viking.

—— (2000b) *Tao of Survival: Spirituality in Social Care and Counselling*, Birmingham: Venture Press.

Briggs, P.F. (1974) 'Specialing in psychiatry: Therapeutic or custodial?', *Nursing Outlook* 22: 632–5.

Brill, A.A. (1947) 'Introduction', in S. Freud *Leonardo Da Vinci: A Study in Psychosexuality* (trans. A.A. Brill), New York: Random House.

Browne, V. (2001) 'No defence of the dirt at St Kevin's', *Irish Times* 24 January.

Browning, D. (2003) 'Internists of the mind or physicians of the soul: Does psychiatry need a public philosophy?', *Australian and New Zealand Journal of Psychiatry* 37(2): 131–7.

Buchanan-Barker, P. and Barker, P. (2002) 'Lunatic language', *Openmind* 115: 23.

Bulham, H.A. (1985) *Frantz Fanon and the Psychology of Oppression*, New York: Plenum Press.

Burston, D. (1996) *The Wing of Madness: The Life and Work of R D Laing*, London: Harvard University Press

—— (2000) *The Crucible of Experience: R D Laing and the Crisis of Psychotherapy*, London: Harvard University Press.

Busteed, E.L. and Johnstone, C. (1983) 'The development of suicide precautions for an in-patient psychiatric unit', *Journal of Psychosocial Nursing and Mental Health Services* 21: 15–19.

Callaway, B.J. (2002) *Hildegard Peplau: Psychiatric Nurse of the Century*, New York: Springer.

Campbell, J. (1972) *Myths to Live By*, New York: Viking Press.

Campbell, P. (1996) 'The history of the user movement in the United Kingdom', in T. Heller *et al.* (eds) *Mental Health Matters: A Reader*, London: Macmillan/Open University.

Cargile, J. (1969) 'The Sorites paradox', *British Journal for the Philosophy of Science* 20: 193–202.

Charlton, J., Kelly, S., Dunnell, K., Evans, B. and Jenkins, R. (1992) 'Trends in suicide deaths in England and Wales', *Population Trends* 69: 6–10.

Clay, S. (1999) 'Madness and reality', in P. Barker, P. Campbell and B. Davidson (eds) *From the Ashes of Experience: Reflection on Madness, Recovery and Growth*, London: Whurr.

Clay, S. (2004) 'Discipline', in P. Barker and P. Buchanan-Barker *Spirituality and Mental Health: Breakthrough*, London: Whurr.

Conrad, P. (1992) *Deviance and Medicalization: From Badness to Sickness*, Philadelphia: Temple University Press.

Cooper, D.E. (1986) *Metaphor*, Oxford: Blackwell.

Cowen, E.L. (1982). 'Help is where you find it: Four informal helping groups', *American Psychologist*, 37: 385–95.

Crick, F. (1994) *The Astonishing Hypothesis: The Scientific Search for the Soul*, New York: Charles Scribner and Sons.

Cutcliffe, J. (2003) 'The assessment of suicide and self harm', in P. Barker (ed.) *Psychiatric and Mental Health Nursing: The Craft of Caring*, London: Arnold.

—— and Barker, P. (2002) 'Care of the suicidal client and the case for engagement and inspiring hope or "observations" ', *Journal of Psychiatric and Mental Health Nursing* 9: 611–21.

Daniels, A.K. (1970) 'The social construction of psychiatric diagnosis', in H. Drezel (ed.) *Recent Sociology No 2*, New York: Macmillan.

Dawson, P.J. (1994) 'Contra biology: A polemic', *Journal of Advances in Nursing* 20: 1094–1103.

—— (1997) 'A reply to Kevin Gournay's "Schizophrenia: A review of the contemporary literature and implications for mental health nursing theory, practice and education" ', *Journal of Psychiatric and Mental Health Nursing* 4: 1–7.

Deiter, C. and Otway, L. (2001) *Sharing Our Stories on Promoting Health and Community Healing: An Aboriginal Women's Health Project*, Winnipeg: Praire Women's Health Centre of Excellence.

De Mello, A. (1988) *One Minute Wisdom*, New York: Doubleday.

Dennet, D. (1992) 'The self as the center of narrative gravity', in F. Kessel, P. Cole and D. Johnson (eds) *Self and Consciousness: Multiple Perspectives*, Hillsdale, NJ: Lawrence Erlbaum Associates, Inc.

De Shazer, S. (1991) *Putting Differences to Work*, New York: Norton.

—— (1994) *Words Were Originally Magic*, New York: Norton.

Doi, T. (1986) *The Anatomy of Self: The Individual and Society*, Tokyo: Kodansha.

Dossey, L. (1991) *Meaning and Medicine*, New York: Bantam.

Duffy, D. (1995) 'Out of the shadows: A study of the special observation of suicidal patients', *Journal of Advanced Nursing* 21: 944–50.

Dumont, M.P. (1984) 'The non-specificity of mental illness', *American Journal of Orthopsychiatry* 54: 326–34.

Dyson, I. (1997) 'An ethic of caring: Conceptual and practical issues', *Nursing Inquiry* 4(31): 196–201.

Eddins, B.B. and Riley-Eddins, E.A. (1997) 'Watson's theory of human caring: The twentieth century and beyond', *Journal of Multicultural Nursing and Health* 3(3): 30–35.

Eisenberg, N. (1986) *Altruistic Emotion, Cognition and Behavior*, Hillsdale, NJ: Lawrence Erlbaum Associates, Inc.

Evans, F.B. (1996) *Harry Stack Sullivan: Interpersonal Theory and Psychotherapy*, London: Routledge.

Farber, S. (1987) 'Transcending medicalism', *Journal of Mind and Behaviour* 8(1): 105–32.

Fawcett, J., Scheftner, W., Clark, D., Hedeker, D., Gibbons, R. and Coryell, W. (1987) 'Clinical predictors of suicide in patients with major affective disorders: A controlled prospective study', *American Journal of Psychiatry* 144(1): 35–40.

Ferster, C.B. and Skinner, B.F. (1957) *Schedules of Reinforcement*, New York: Appleton-Century Crofts.

Fletcher, R.F. (1999) 'The process of constant observation: Perspectives of staff and suicidal patients', *Journal of Psychiatric and Mental Health Nursing* 6(1): 9–14.

Fogel, A., Melson, G.F. and Mistry, J. (1986) 'Conceptualising the determinants of nurturance: A reassessment of sex differences', in A. Fogel and G.F. Melson (eds) *Origins of Nurturance: Developmental, Biological and Cultural Perspectives on Caregiving*, Hillsdale, NJ: Lawrence Erlbaum Associates, Inc.

Fortuna, J. (2000) 'Therapeutic households', in P. Barker and C. Stevenson *The Construction of Power and Authority in Psychiatry*, Oxford: Butterworth Heinemann.

Fox, N. (1993) *Postmodernism, Sociology and Health*, Buckingham: Open University Press.

Frankl, V.E. (1959) *The Doctor and the Soul: From Psychotherapy to Logotherapy*, New York: Alfred Knopf.

—— (1964) *Man's Search for Meaning*, Harmondsworth: Penguin.

—— (1965) *The Doctor and the Soul: From Psychotherapy to Logotherapy*, Harmondsworth: Penguin.

—— (1973) *The Doctor and the Soul: From Psychotherapy to Logotherapy*, Harmondsworth: Penguin.

Freud, S. (1947) *Leonardo Da Vinci: A Study in Psychosexuality* (trans. A.A. Brill), New York: Random House.

Freud, S. In P. Gay (1995) *The Freud Reader*, London: Vintage.

Fromm, E. (1956) *The Sane Society*, London: Routledge and Kegan Paul.

Gasser, M. (1961) *Self-Portraits from the Fifteenth Century to the Present Day*, London: Weidenfeld and Nicolson.

Gaut, D.A. (1993) 'Caring: A vision of wholeness for nursing', *Journal of Holistic Nursing* 2: 164–71.

Gleick, J. (1987) *Chaos*, New York: Viking.

Goffman, E. (1986) *Stigma: Notes on the Management of Spoiled Identity*, New York: Simon and Schuster.

Gottschalk, A., Bauer, M.S. and Whybrow, P.C. (1995) 'Evidence of chaotic mood variation in bipolar disorder', *Archives of General Psychiatry* 52: 947–59.

Greenhalgh, J., Vanhanen, L. and Kyngas, H. (1998) 'Nurse caring behaviours', *Journal of Advanced Nursing* 27(5): 927–32.

Grob, G.N. (1983) *Mental Illness and American Society*, Princeton, NJ: Princeton University Press.

Gunnell, D. and Frankel, S. (1994) 'Prevention of suicide: Aspirations and evidence', *British Medical Journal* 308: 1227–33.

Hagen, S. (1995) *How Can the World be the Way it is: An Inquiry for the New Millennium into Science, Philosophy and Perception*, Wheaton, IL: Quest.

Haley, J. (1968) *Uncommon Therapy: The Therapeutic Techniques of Milton Erickson*, New York: Grune and Stratton.

—— (1979) *Problem-Solving Therapy: New Strategies for Effective Family Therapy*, San Francisco: Jossey-Bass.

Hall, B.A. (1996) 'The psychiatric model: A critical analysis', *Advances in Nursing Science* 18(3): 16–26.

Hall, R.C., Platt, D.E. and Hall, R.C. (1999) 'Suicide risk assessment: A review of risk factors for suicide in 100 patients who made severe suicide attempts', *Psychosomatics* 40: 18–27.

Hanson, K. (1986) *The Self Imagined: Philosophical Reflections on the Social Characters of Psyche*, London: Routledge and Kegan Paul.

Harkavy-Friedman, J.M. and Nelson, E.A. (1997) 'Assessment and intervention for the suicidal patient with schizophrenia', *Psychiatric Quarterly* 68(4): 361–75.

Harland, R. (1987) *Superstructuralism: The Philosophy of Structuralism and Post-Structuralism*, London: Methuen.

Hawkes, D., Marsh, T.I. and Wilgosh, R. (1998) *Solution-focused Therapy: A Handbook for Health Care Professionals*, Oxford: Butterworth Heinemann.

Hawthorne, S. and Klein, R. (eds) (1999) *Cyberfeminism: Connectivity, Critique and creativity*, Melbourne: Spinifex.

Hawton, K. (1994) 'Causes and opportunities for prevention', in R. Jenkins, S. Griffiths, I. Wylie *et al.* (eds) *The Prevention of Suicide*, London: HMSO, pp.34–45.

Henderson, V. (1969) *The Basic Principles of Nursing Care*. Geneva: International Coucil for Nurses.

Hubble, M.A., Duncan, B.L. and Miller, S. (1999) *The Heart and Soul of Change: What Works in Therapy*, Washington, DC: American Psychological Association.

Hughes, T. (1994) *Winter Pollen*, London: Faber and Faber.

Hume, D. (1992) *Essays on Suicide and the Immortality of the Soul* (Orig. 1757), Bristol: Thoemmes Press.

Hummelvoll, J.K. and da Silva, A.B. (1994) 'A holistic–existential model for psychiatric nursing', *Perspectives in Psychiatric Care* 30: 7–14.

Jackson, D.D. (1968) *Communication, Family and Marriage*, Palo Alto, CA: Science and Behaviour Books.

Jackson, S. and Stevenson, C. (1998) 'The gift of time from the friendly professional', *Nursing Standard* 12(51): 31–3.

James, O. (1988) *Britain on the Couch*, London: Random House.

Keen, T. (1999) 'Schizophrenia: Orthodoxy and heresies. A review of alternative possibilities', *Journal of Psychiatric and Mental Health Nursing* 6: 415–24.

Khalkhali, S.M.R., Rahbar, M., Farde Masood, R. and Jamadi, A. (2001) 'Survey of life events prior to suicide attempt', *Journal of the Medical Faculty Guilan University of Medical Science* 10: 39–40.

Kirk, S.A. and Kutchins, H. (1992) *The Selling of the DSM: The Rhetoric of Science in Psychiatry*, New York: Aldine de Gruyter.

—— (1997) *Making us Crazy: The Psychiatric Bible and the Creation of Mental Disorders*, New York: Free Press.

Kismayer, L.J. (1994) 'Improvisation and authority in illness meaning', *Culture, Medicine and Psychiatry* 18: 183–209.

Kora, T. (1995) *How to Live Well: The Secrets of Using Neurosis*, New York: State University of New York.

Laing, R.D. (1967) *The Politics of Experience*, New York: Ballantine.

Lehtonen, J. (1994) 'From dualism to psychobiological interaction: A comment on the study of Tienari and his co-workers', *British Journal of Psychiatry* 164(suppl. 23): 27–8.

Leibrich, J. (1999) *A Gift of Stories*, Dunedin: University of Otago Press.

Leifer, R. (1990) 'The medical model as the ideology of the therapeutic state', *Journal of Mind and Behaviour* 11(3–4): 247–58.

Luft, E. (2001) 'Thomas Szaz: Philosopher, psychiatrist, Libertarian', Upstate Medical University Medical Alumni Association, www.upstate.ed.

Lynch, T. (2001) *Beyond Prozac: Healing Mental Suffering without Drugs*, Dublin: Marino.

MacIntyre, A. (1981) *After Virtue*, Notre Dame: Notre Dame University Press.

Masaryk, T.G. (1970/1881) *Suicide and the Meaning of Civilisation*, London, University of Chicago Press.

Maturana, H. and Varela, F. (1987) *The Tree of Knowledge*, Boston: New Science Library.

Modrow, J. (1995) *How to become a Schizophrenic: The Case against Biological Psychiatry*, Everett, WA: Apollyon Press.

Morgan, H.G. (1993) *Suicide Prevention: The Assessment and Management of Suicide Risk – A Guide for Healthcare Professionals and Managers*, London: National Health Service Advisory Service.

Morris, L.E. (1996) 'A spiritual well-being model: Use with older women who experience depression', *Issues in Mental Health Nursing* 17: 439–55.

Mosher, L. (1999) 'Soteria and other alternatives to acute psychiatric hospitalization', *Journal of Nervous and Mental Disease* 187: 142–9.

Motto, J.A., Heilbron, D.C. and Juster, R.P. (1985) 'Development of a clinical instrument to estimate suicide risk', *American Journal of Psychiatry* 142(6): 680–86.

Mullin, T. (1992) 'Turbulent time for fluids', in N. Hall (ed.) *The New Scientist Guide to Chaos*, Harmondsworth: Penguin.

Musker, M. and Byrne, M. (1997) 'Applying empowerment in mental health practice', *Nursing Standard* 11: 45–7.

Nagel, T. (1974) 'What is it like to be a bat?', *Philosophical Review* 83(4): 435–50.

Nahas, V. (1997), 'Muslim patients' perception of caring', *Professional Nurse* (Singapore) 24(2): 20–23.

Newnes, C., Holmes, G. and Dunn, C. (1999) *This is Madness: A Critical Look at Psychiatry and the Future of Mental Health Services*, Ross-on-Wye: PCCS Books.

—— (2000) *This is Madness Too: A Further Look at Psychiatry and the Future of Mental Health Services*, Ross-on-Wye: PCCS Books.

O'Connor, R. and Sheehy, N. (2000) *Understanding Suicidal Behaviour*, Leicester: British Psychological Society.

Paterson, J. and Zderad, L. (1976) *Humanistic Nursing*, New York: Wiley.

Peck, M.L. (1992) 'The future of nursing in a technological age: Computers, robots and TLC', *Journal of Holistic Nursing* 10(2): 183–91.

Peplau, H.E. (1952) *Interpersonal Relations in Nursing*, New York: Putnam.

Platz, G. (2003) 'Spirituality, madness and the man who lost a thousand masks', in P. Barker and P. Buchanan-Barker (eds) *Breakthrough: Spirituality and Mental Health*, London: Whurr.

Podvoll, E.M. (1990) *The Seduction of Madness: A Compassionate Approach to Recovery at Home*, London: Century.

Porter, R. (1991) *The Faber Book of Madness*, London: Faber.

Powell, A. (2001) 'Beyond space and time: The unbounded psyche', in D. Lorimer (ed.) *Thinking Beyond the Brain: A Wider Science of Consciousness*, Edinburgh: Floris.

Powell, J., Geddes, J. and Hawton, K. (2000) 'Suicide in psychiatric hospital in-patients', *British Journal of Psychiatry* 176(3): 266–72.

Pylkkanen, K. (1997) 'The Finnish National Schizophrenia Project', in C. Mace and F. Margison (eds) *Psychotherapy of Psychosis*, London: Gaskell.

Read, J. and Reynolds, J. (1996) *Speaking our Minds: An Anthology*, Buckingham: The Open University Press.

Reynolds, D. (1984) *Playing Ball on Running Water*, London: Sheldon Press.

Richards, B. (1989) *Crises of the Self: Further Essays on Psychoanalysis and Politics*, London: Free Association Books.

Robitscher, J.B. (1980) *The Powers of Psychiatry*, Boston: Houghton/Mifflin.

Romme, M., Hoing, A., Noorthoorn, E. and Escher, A. (1992) 'Coping with hearing voices: An emancipatory approach', *British Journal of Psychiatry* 161: 99–103.

Ryan, T. (1999) *Managing Crisis and Risk in Mental Health Nursing*, Cheltenham: Stanley Thornes.

Ryle, G. (1949) *The Concept of Mind*, London: Hutchinson.

Samuels, C. (2000) *Colonisation, American Indian Boarding Schools and Long-term Physical and Mental Health*, Michigan: Centre for Research on Culture and Health, University of Michigan.

Sartorius, N., Jablensky, A., Regier, D.A., Burke, J.D. and Hirschfeld, R.M.A. (eds) (1990) *Sources and Traditions of Classification in Psychiatry*, Toronto: Hogrefe.

Schrag, P. (1978) *Mind Control*, New York: Pantheon.

Scull, A. (1979) *Museums of Madness*, New York: St Martin's Press.

Smail, D. (1988) *Taking Care: An Alternative to Therapy*, London: Dent.

Smith, J. (1981) 'Self and experience in Maori culture', in P. Heelas and A. Lock (eds) *Indigenous Psychologies*, New York: Academic Press.

Sourial, S. (1997) 'An analysis of caring', *Journal of Advanced Nursing*, 6(6): 1189–92.

Spiro, M. (1993) 'Is the western conception of the self "peculiar" within the context of world cultures?', *Ethos* 21: 107–53.

Stern, D. (1985) *The Interpersonal World of the Infant*, New York: Basic Books.

Stevenson, C., Barker, P. and Fletcher, E. (2002) 'Judgement days: Developing an evaluation for an innovative nursing model', *Journal of Psychiatric & Mental Health Nursing* 9(3): 271–6.

Sullivan, H.S. (1953) *The Interpersonal Therapy of Psychiatry*, New York: WW Norton and Co.

Szasz, T.S. (1961) *The Myth of Mental Illness: Foundations of a New Theory of Personal Conduct*, New York: Harper and Row.

—— (1974) *Ideology and Insanity: Essays on the Psychiatric Dehumanization of Man*, Harmondsworth: Penguin.

—— (1994) *Cruel Compassion: Psychiatric Control of Society's Unwanted*, New York: Wiley.

—— (1996) *The Meaning of Mind: Language, Morality and Neuroscience*, Westport, CT: Praeger.

—— (1999) *Fatal Freedom: The Ethics and Politics of Suicide*, Westport, CT: Praeger.

—— (2000) 'Curing the therapeutic state: Thomas Szasz on the medicalisation of American life. Interviewed by Jacob Sullum', *Reason* July: 27–34.

—— (2002) *Liberation by Oppression: A Comparative Study of Slavery and Psychiatry*, London: Transaction Publishers.

Taylor, B.J. (1994) *Being Human: Ordinariness in Nursing*, Melbourne: Churchill Livingstone.

Thomas, P. (1997) *The Dialectics of Schizophrenia*, London: Free Association Books.

Tienari, P., Wynne, L., Moring, J., Lahti, I., Naarala, M., Sorri, A., Wahlberg, K., Saarento, O., Seitman, M., Kaleva, M. and Lasky K. (1994) 'The Finnish adoptive study of schizophrenia: Implications for family research', *British Journal of Psychiatry* 164 (suppl. 23): 20–26.

Travelbee, J. (1971) *Interpersonal Aspects of Nursing*, 2nd edn, Philadelphia: Saunders.

Turner, A.R. (1995) *Inventing Leonardo: The Anatomy of a Legend*, London, Papermac.

Vaughn, K., Webster, D., Orahood, S. and Young, B. (1995) 'Brief inpatient psychiatric treatment: Finding solutions', *Issues in Mental Health Nursing* 16(6): 519–31.

Von Foerster, H. (1984) 'On constructing reality', in P. Watzlawick (ed.) *The Invented Reality*, New York: Norton.

Von Glaserfeld, E. (1984) 'An introduction to radical constructivism', in P. Wazlawick (ed.) *The Invented Reality*, New York: Norton.

Walker, L. and Barker, P. (1998) 'The required role of the CPN: Uniformity or flexibility?', *Clinical Effectiveness in Nursing* 2: 21–9.

Walter, J.L. and Peller, J.E. (1996) 'Rethinking our assumptions', in S.D. Miller, M.A. Hobble and B.L. Duncan (eds) *Handbook of Solution-Focused Brief Therapy* (pp. 9–26), San Francisco: Jossey-Bass.

Watts, A. (1957) *The Way of Zen*, London: Thames and Hudson.

—— (1961) *Psychotherapy East and West*, New York: Pantheon Books.

Watzlawick, P. (1984) *The Invented Reality: How Do We Know What We Believe We Know? Contributions to Constructivism*, New York: Norton.

Weisharr, M.E. and Beck, A.T. (1992) 'Hopelessness and suicide', *International Review of Psychiatry* 4: 177–84.

White, M. and Epston, D. (1990) *Narrative Means to Therapeutic Ends*, New York: Norton.

Wittgenstein, L. (1958) *Philosophical Investigation*, London: Macmillan.

Yalom, I.D. (1968) *Theory and Practice of Group Psychotherapy*, New York: Basic Books.

—— (1975) *The Practice of Group Psychotherapy*, New York: Basic Books.

Yang, C. Lu M. (1998) 'The effects of human caring education on nurses: A human caring knowledge, attitude and behaviour study', *Nursing Research* (China) 6(3): 206–18.

Young, M.A., Fogg, L.F., Schefter, W.A. and Fawcett, J.A. (1994) 'Interactions of risk factors in predicting suicide', *American Journal of Psychiatry* 151(3): 434–5.

Zeldin, T. (2000) *Conversation: How Talk Can Change Our Lives*, Mahwah, NJ: Paulist Press.

# Index

Page numbers in **bold** type represent figures/diagrams